The Persian Gulf and the West

Written under the auspices of the
Center for International Affairs, Harvard University

Written under the auspices of the
Center for International Affairs, Harvard University

The Persian Gulf and the West

THE DILEMMAS OF SECURITY

Charles A. Kupchan
Department of Politics
Princeton University

Boston
ALLEN & UNWIN
London   Sydney   Wellington

Allen & Unwin, Inc.
8 Winchester Place, Winchester, MA 01890, USA.

The U.S. Company of
Unwin Hyman Ltd,

P.O. Box 18, Park Lane, Hemel Hempstead, Herts HP2 4TE, UK
40 Museum Street, London WC1A 1LU, UK
37/39 Queen Elizabeth Street, London SE1 2QB, UK

Allen & Unwin Australia Pty Ltd,
8 Napier Street, North Sydney, NSW 2060, Australia

Allen & Unwin (New Zealand) Ltd,
in association with the Port Nicholson Press Ltd
Private Bag, Wellington, New Zealand

Library of Congress Cataloging-in-Publication Data

Kupchan, Charles.
   The Persian Gulf and the West

   Bibliography: p.
   1. Persian Gulf Region—National security.   2. United
States.   Central Command.   3. North Atlantic Treaty
Organization.   4. United States—Military policy.
5. Europe—Military policy.   I. Title.
UA853.P47K87   1987   355'.0330536   87-1233
ISBN 0–04–497057–9
ISBN 0–04–497058–7(pbk.)

British Library Cataloguing in Publication Data
Kupchan, Charles A.
   The Persian Gulf and the West : the
   dilemmas of security.
   1. World politics—1945–   2. Persian
   Gulf region—Foreign relations
   I. Title
   327'.09171'3   DS326

ISBN 0–04–497057–9
ISBN 0–04–497058–7(pbk.)

To Cliff

CONTENTS

PREFACE

During the postwar era, the most vociferous and divisive debates about national security within the Western community have focused upon the Third World—the "periphery"—not upon Europe. Though far more attention and resources have been devoted to European security, the debate about Europe has taken place within fairly narrow margins. Within both individual states and the NATO alliance, there has been a steady consensus about the overriding importance of deterring Soviet aggression against Western territory. There have indeed been wide differences of opinion about how best to erect a credible deterrent and what military strategy to adopt should deterrence fail. Yet, this debate has essentially focused upon identifying the most appropriate means to achieve recognized and generally accepted ends.

The debate over security in the periphery has been much wider in scope; it has addressed both ends and means. The crux of the problem is that it has proved to be very difficult to identify what geographic areas in the periphery are worth fighting for. In what cases and under what circumstances are vital Western interests at stake? Some areas of the periphery are of intrinsic value because of the raw materials that they contain or because of their strategic importance. Other areas are of extrinsic value; they become important because of the global nature of the Cold War and the perceived need to maintain the credibility of the West's defense commitments. Calculations of the costs and benefits of intervention also turn on the nature of the apparent threat. A Soviet or Soviet-backed invasion of a pro-Western state is likely to have far greater implications and elicit a sharper Western response than indigenous regional conflict which challenges the status quo. The central dilemma of regional security for the Western community has been to identify how to characterize and how to respond to the wide range of interests and threats that have emerged in different regions of the periphery.

This book focuses upon one particular area of the periphery—the Persian Gulf—as a means of delving into the postwar debate about regional security. The Persian Gulf serves as a rich case study for such an investigation because of the variable, yet consistently prominent position that it has occupied in Western conceptions of global security. The Persian Gulf has been of steadily increasing intrinsic importance since 1945 because of growing Western dependence on its oil reserves. It has also emerged as a focal point of U.S.-Soviet competition for regional political influence; Western interests have been defined in terms of maintaining global commitments and credibility. Despite the consistent presence of East–West tensions, the threats to these interests have by no means come only from the Soviets. Regional anti-Western and anticolonial sentiment, endemic conflict among local states and the relationship between the Gulf and the Arab–Israeli dispute have repeatedly threatened to throw the region into turmoil.

The need for a thorough reassessment of the West's political and military position in the Gulf was clearly illustrated by the events of 1979–1980. The Iranian revolution led to the loss of America's principal strategic ally in the region—the Shah—and contributed to the eventual outbreak of the Iran–Iraq war. The Soviet invasion of Afghanistan raised the spectre of a direct Soviet move into the Persian Gulf. These events led to a radical alteration in the assumptions upon which Western security policy toward the region was based.

The political turmoil surrounding the Reagan administration's sale of weaponry to Iran and the Iraqi attack on the USS Stark have more recently revealed continuing inadequacies in U.S. policy toward the Gulf. The Iran–Contra affair suggests three important lessons. First, it illuminated the futility of relying on arms sales to achieve specific political goals. Second, it suggested that U.S. decision-makers were operating under illusory, if not naive, assumptions about intraregional political dynamics. Third, the sale of weapons to Iran and its relationship to U.S. funding of the Contras in Nicaragua pointed to the profound impact of the decision-making process on policy. The constraints placed upon the White House by congressional oversight and interagency checks and balances were circumvented by the furtive behavior and autonomy of officials in the National Security Council. The attack on the USS Stark raised serious questions about the role of U.S. forces in the Persian Gulf region and illuminated the need for a reassessment of military operations and planning. As the following pages will confirm, these lessons are not new. In fact, they are reflective of recurring shortcomings in U.S. policy which are linked to a fundamental and deep-rooted flaw in the American approach to regional security.

The goal of this book is to examine these shortcomings by undertaking a systematic study of how the Western community—and, in particular, the United States—has defined and dealt with its security interests in the Persian Gulf. I have not attempted to present an exhaustive review of the literature on the region nor to chronicle in a detailed manner the evolution of various military strategies for the area. Rather, I have sought to cast the formulation of security policy in a broader analytic, comparative, and historical light. In doing so, I have treated the Persian Gulf as a distinct and unique geographic area and have set out to understand the nature of the security problem—in both conceptual and operational terms—that it presents to the West. In approaching these issues, I have asked how decision-makers have conceived of "security" in the Persian Gulf and how that conception has changed over time. The book thus addresses policy-relevant issues as well as more theoretical questions about the determinants of policy and the study of regional security. Its breadth will, I hope, make the text accessible and of interest to both specialists in security affairs and curious but uninitiated laymen.

Three general questions will be used to examine both the substance of policy and the process of policy formulation and these questions will appear, both in explicit and implicit form, throughout the study. First, assuming the existence of a coherent policy at a given point in time, what does that policy consist of? Here, I will be concerned with the ends identified by policymakers and the means designated to achieve those ends. Second, what are the sources of and the motivations behind the given policy? Factors to be considered and ranked as to importance include the perceptual framework of decision-makers, relative economic and military capabilities, alliance politics, bureaucratic dynamics, and domestic pluralism. Third, what are the key shortcomings of policy? I will be concerned not only with identifying enduring problems but also with determining their sources. Have weaknesses in Western security policy resulted from the imprudent identification of ends, the application of inappropriate or insufficient means to those ends, or the manipulation of policy by self-interested bureaucracies?

When applied in a systematic and comparative manner to the postwar period, these questions will contribute to the study of foreign policymaking in the United States and in NATO and shed new light on how the West should deal with the dilemmas of regional security in the Persian Gulf.

ACKNOWLEDGMENTS

I would like to express my deep gratitude to all those who gave of their time and thought in the completion of this book. While the following list is hopefully complete, I apologize to those individuals whom I may have failed to mention.

In its formative stages as a dissertation at Oxford University, the following members of the Social Studies and History Faculties provided helpful instruction and comments: Hedley Bull, Michael Howard, Wilfrid Knapp, Iain Mclean, and Adam Roberts. Sir Michael Howard and Sir Anthony Parsons also offered useful criticism as my examiners. Fellow students Grant Parsons and John Cable provided good sounding boards for new ideas and offered comments on early drafts.

I owe a debt of gratitude to the staff at several of Oxford's libraries: the Bodleian, the Codrington, Rhodes House, and the Social Studies Library. The staff at the Radcliffe Camera were particularly courteous and helpful, despite the fact that my requested volumes were always cluttering their reserve shelves. The International Institute for Strategic Studies proved to be an invaluable oasis for research and discussion in London, both because of its library and because of the knowledgeable and stimulating research community that it attracts. The staff in the Clippings Library of the Royal Institute for International Affairs were also quite helpful.

I must thank the Keasbey Memorial Foundation for sending me to Oxford in the first place and providing financial support throughout. The U.K. Overseas Research Council and the Cyril Foster Fund also provided financial assistance.

The manuscript was revised during my tenure as a fellow at the Center for International Affairs, Harvard University. I owe an initial debt of gratitude to Samuel Huntington for bringing me to the Center and for building a national security program that offered an excellent environment in which to work. While rewriting, I received valuable comments on my work from the following individuals: Robert Art, Michael Brown, Anne-Marie Burley, Stephen Flanagan, Andrew Goldberg, Lori Gronich, Fen Hampson, Martin Indyk, Clifford Kupchan, Jim Miller, Edward Rhodes, Nadav Safran, Gregory Treverton, and Stephen Van Evera. Financial support during my tenure at the CFIA was provided by the Olin Foundation, the Scaife Foundation, the Ford Foundation, and the North Atlantic Treaty Organization.

I would also like to thank the staff of the CFIA for their assistance in the preparation of the manuscript. The time and skills of Elizabeth Cox, Bonnie Diamond, Hope Harrison, Lisa Lightman and Janice Rand are much appreciated.

I would also like to express my gratitude to the editorial and production team at Allen & Unwin. It was a pleasure to work with John Michel, Lisa Freeman-Miller, and Russ Till. Lee Bearson contributed his artistic talents to the cover design.

Finally, special thanks are due to my family. My parents, through example and no small amount of nudging, urged me toward scholarship since day one; it seems to have worked. Richard Sonis provided the support and friendship crucial to recovering from the effects of long hours spent in front of a computer screen. And my brother, to whom this book is dedicated, has carried me along through the many crucial moments of doubt. Furthermore, he slaved through an early and painful draft and listened to me drone on about the Persian Gulf until even I was bored.

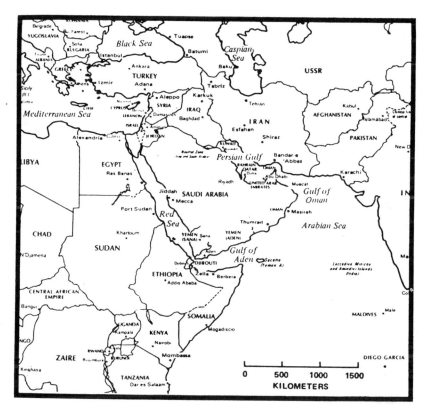

Map 1. Southwest Asia. [Reproduced from U.S. Congress, Senate, Armed Services Committee, *Department of Defense Authorization for Appropriations for Fiscal Year 1983*, Part 1 (Washington, DC: GPO, 1982), 291.]

Map 2. Iran. [Reproduced from Joshua Epstein, *Strategy and Force Planning: The Case of the Persian Gulf* (Washington, DC: Brookings Institution, 1987), 46.]

Chapter One

INTRODUCTION

International military conflict in the postwar era has been confined largely to the Middle East, East Asia, Latin America, and Africa—all regions outside the areas covered by the two major blocs. Although indigenous rivalries have stimulated many of these conflicts, the United States and the Soviet Union have been implicitly and, in some cases, explicitly involved. The erosion of European colonialism after World War II was a fundamental cause of political change in the Third World. European empires did not erode at once, but the psychological, physical, and financial damage of the war irrevocably diminished the willingness and ability of the imperial powers to continue exerting their military and economic power around the globe. The end of colonialism led old and new states in the Third World to struggle for economic and political independence. Yet the search for autonomy and nonalignment has been hindered by the global scope of superpower competition.

Events in the Middle East fit neatly into this general pattern. After the war, the French and the British reassessed their commitments in the region and gradually withdrew. This process was paralleled by a steady escalation in the intensity of American–Soviet competition for regional allies and strategic access. Yet the security problems that the United States has faced in the Middle East, and in the Persian Gulf in particular, differ in several important respects from those faced in other areas of the periphery.[1]

1. The terms "Southwest Asia" and the "Middle East," with some qualification, will be used interchangeably in this work. The former term emerged in an attempt to define a single strategic theater for the region; Southwest Asia includes the horn of Africa, the Gulf states, the Arab states bordering on the Mediterranean from Egypt east, and Israel. The Middle East does not include Ethiopia and Somalia. The "Persian Gulf" refers to those states on the Arabian peninsula and those with a coastline on the Gulf itself. The term "periphery" refers to any area not located within or between the territory covered by the two major blocs.

The Gulf's physical assets—its oil reserves and its geographic location—give it special strategic importance. The dependence of the Western economy on Persian Gulf oil creates a direct and vital strategic interest in the area.[2] This is in addition to other indirect interests—such as maintaining prestige, honoring commitments, and bolstering noncommunist regimes—that have previously led to U.S. involvement in conflicts in the Third World. Western dependence on Gulf oil naturally elicits Soviet interest, simply by virtue of the fact that a resource vital to the West's economic strength lies not far from Soviet borders.[3]

In geographic terms, the Soviets perceive the area as a southern tier that presents both opportunities and dangers. They have historically coveted the Gulf territories as a potential access route to a port on the Indian Ocean. As demonstrated by their invasion of Afghanistan in 1979, the Soviets have also become increasingly concerned with the political orientation of states in the region.[4] Since the 1940s, the West has viewed the Gulf area as a northern tier, a group of rim states serving to contain Soviet expansionism. Implementing containment in Southwest Asia potentially involves contending with Soviet forces, not only with Soviet ideology or Soviet surrogates. The United States thus faces a particularly acute strategic problem: The Soviets can send up to 30 divisions across their border into an area that is a great distance from a reservoir of U.S. military power. As described in a Department of Defense statement: "The true locus of U.S. power—which can, if necessary be brought to bear in the [Gulf] region—lies at some distance principally at Guam and Subic Bay."[5]

The vast oil reserves in the Gulf distinguish the region from other areas of the periphery in a political as well as strategic sense. A potential Soviet attempt to seize the oil fields has been a secondary and distant threat. Managing the West's relationship with the Arab Gulf states, the actors that are ultimately responsible for determining both the amount and the price of Persian Gulf oil made available to the industrialized world, has presented a more immediate problem. The United States has had to balance the complexities of regional politics with the larger strategic problems posed by the Soviets. This task has been complicated by the numerous sources of instability within the Middle East: territorial dis-

2. At the time of this writing in 1987, a glut on the world oil market has filled stockpiles and reduced prices. It would be a dangerous illusion to assume, however, that this situation will continue indefinitely and that the West is no longer vulnerable to an oil shortage or the economic shock of a drastic rise in prices.

3. I do not mean to suggest that the Soviets see an attack on the oil fields as an attractive means of damaging or strangling the Western economy. Indeed, one would assume that the importance of Western interests in the Gulf would induce Soviet restraint. The Soviets have, however, voiced concern about recent American attempts to increase U.S. military capability in the region.

4. For a historical view of Soviet perspectives see Milan Hauner, "Seizing the Third Parallel: Geopolitics and the Soviet Advance into Central Asia," *Orbis* (Spring 1985).

5. Congressional Research Service, *United States Foreign Policy Objectives and Overseas Military Installations* (Washington: GPO, 1979), p. 118.

putes; regional rivalries; Arab–Persian, Sunni–Shiite, and secular–fundamentalist tensions; and the Arab–Israeli conflict. Similarly disruptive and volatile divisions certainly existed in other peripheral areas where the United States has become involved. But because the United States needs Arab cooperation both to secure access to a concrete resource and to contain the Soviets, intraregional politics have been of particular importance to the attainment of America's overall strategic objectives.

The Middle East has also presented a unique strategic problem within the context of the postwar international system because of its *collective* economic importance to the Western world. Since the formation of NATO, the allies have frequently consulted on the military operations of its members outside the geographic areas defined by the North Atlantic Treaty. NATO communiques have periodically referred to the importance to Western security of events occurring outside the European theater.[6] Yet only within the context of policy toward the Middle East has the Western alliance—not just individual allies—attempted to forge a coherent collective approach. Since the first oil crisis in 1973, alliance members have sought to coordinate their policies toward Southwest Asia on a broad range of issues. The problem of cooperation within the framework of the alliance raises important questions about the nature of Western interests in areas outside Europe. These questions focus not only on how and to what extent the allies have succeeded in forging a common security policy toward the Gulf, but also on how events in Southwest Asia have shaped relations within the alliance.

These factors point to one preeminent difference between the strategic value of the Persian Gulf and that of other areas of the Third World. Though part of the periphery in geographic terms, the Persian Gulf, in strategic terms, is by no means peripheral. The contribution of the 1973 Arab oil embargo and related oil price rises to current problems in the international economy—high rates of unemployment and inflation and large deficits and foreign debt—gives some indication of the potential effects of a cutoff of Persian Gulf oil on the industrialized and developing world. Because of the vital interests at stake and because of the Gulf's geostrategic location, local conflicts in Southwest Asia are more likely than those in other regions to involve either or both of the superpowers. This increases the chances that a war initially confined to the Middle East would escalate to a broader East–West confrontation. Events in Southwest

6. See, for example, the final communique of a meeting of Heads of State and Government, Paris, December 1957. Paragraph 1 reads: "Our alliance cannot therefore be concerned only with the North Atlantic area or only with military defense. It must also organize its political and economic strength on the principle of interdependence, and must take account of developments outside its own area." Cited in North Atlantic Assembly, Political Committee, "Interim Report of the Sub-Committee on Out-of-Area Challenges to the Alliance" (Brussels, November, 1984), p. 26. Similar statements can be found in the North Atlantic Council final communiques of April 1959 (pars. 4 and 6), December 1963 (par. 5), and May 1976 (par. 2).

Asia have, and will likely continue, to pose clear threats to the structure and the stability of the postwar international system. These considerations illustrate the need for a reassessment of the security problems that the West faces in the Persian Gulf.

Strategic Dilemmas

The principal goal of this work is to examine the unique strategic dilemmas that the Persian Gulf poses to the West by undertaking a detailed study of U.S. security policy toward Southwest Asia from both an historical and an analytic perspective. Despite the existence of numerous works on specific conflicts in the Middle East, no attempt has been made to deal with Gulf security on a more conceptual level. This study posits that the United States has faced three central strategic dilemmas in the Persian Gulf: strategy versus capability, globalism versus regionalism, and unilateralism versus collectivism. The analysis attempts to step back from the details of the policy debate itself and examine those intellectual, perceptual, and organizational factors that underlie policy. The work will therefore have implications both for the study of regional security problems more generally and for the formulation of security policy and military strategy toward Southwest Asia.

The first strategic dilemma focuses on the restrictions placed upon strategy by limited military capability. The tension between strategy and capability emerges when looking at either of the two general military missions that the United States must confront in Southwest Asia: containing the Soviet Union and responding to intraregional conflict.

In terms of implementing containment, because the British remained in the Gulf through the 1960s and because the United States viewed a Soviet move into the region as very unlikely during the first three postwar decades, limited U.S. capability was not perceived as a constraint on America's Middle East strategy until the late 1970s. Military aid, periodic deployment of naval vessels to "show the flag," and the surgical insertion of troops in Lebanon in 1958 appeared sufficient to counter the threat posed by Soviet proxies and communist ideology. The Soviet invasion of Afghanistan in 1979, however, focused American attention on the direct military threat posed by the Soviets. The United States responded with the Carter Doctrine, spelling out a clear commitment to defend the Gulf from external intervention.

In strategic terms, this new military commitment required the extension of a credible American deterrent to Southwest Asia. The two options available to fulfill this mission—erecting either a nuclear or a conventional deterrent—both faced serious shortcomings. The nuclear option lacked credibility (would the United States risk nuclear war to defend Iran?), while a conventional strategy confronted severe limitations in terms of projecting sufficient troops and fire-power to the region. By 1980, U.S. perceptions of the Soviet threat had shifted radically, leading to the assumption of a new and more demanding military mission in the Gulf. These changes made necessary both a reassessment of America's regional strategic priorities and a rethinking of the relationship be-tween strategy and capability in the Gulf itself.

On the intraregional level, the question of capability focused more on the efficacy, rather than the amount, of military power that the United States could bring to bear in the region. Potential missions emerged from many sources: the Arab–Israeli conflict, the Gulf War, the instability of friendly regimes, and the vulnerability of oil facilities and tankers in the Persian Gulf. Yet it was unclear under what conditions the United States should intervene in the Middle East. In what circumstances would the use of force be appropriate? Would U.S. involvement in the Gulf War stimulate Soviet intervention? Could U.S. ground troops or aircraft repel an attack on Saudi oil fields without destroying the facilities themselves?

There was also the more perplexing problem of how to use military force to prevent or to control radical political change motivated by religious or social discontent. It is far more difficult to fight against ideas or popular sentiment than against an enemy's physical structure. The United States confronted this quandary during the fundamentalist revolution in Iran. Could the use of force effectively prevent the Shah's demise? Or would the intervention of Iranian forces or the overt presence of U.S. troops only exacerbate the social upheaval? The tension between strategy and capability is thus a function of the need both to define means sufficient to achieve specific objectives and to define objectives within the context of limited means.

The second strategic dilemma is related to the problem of defining means and ends. It concerns the tension between globalism and regionalism, between America's broader strategic concerns and the political realities of the Gulf. The United States has two principal objectives in the Persian Gulf area: to maintain access to oil and to contain the Soviet Union. Policies molded to pursue these objectives must cultivate a fruitful dialogue between Gulf regimes and the Unit-ed States while simultaneously imposing restraint upon the Soviets. Some of the measures appropriate to achieve these goals indeed overlap; the stability of pro-Western oil-producing states in the Gulf assures the continued flow of petroleum and serves as a hedge against Soviet influence. From this perspective, the princi-pal challenge facing U.S. decision-makers is to formulate a security policy that is sensitive to both Soviet and intraregional threats to political stability.

The tension between globalism and regionalism, however, is not simply a product of the need to take both external and internal threats into consideration in the formulation of policy. The deeper problem is that U.S. efforts to imple-ment containment at times conflict with the political objectives of Gulf states and stimulate, rather than arrest, regional instability. Global and regional concerns then become incompatible. To focus on intraregional considerations is to leave the United States strategically vulnerable. To focus on the Soviet threat is to subsume local dynamics within an East–West context and to place considerable limitations upon America's political—and hence its strategic—position in Southwest Asia. Furthermore, the United States has had difficulty distinguishing between Soviet and intraregional threats to U.S. interests. As a result, U.S. security policy has been oriented primarily toward dealing with the Soviet Union and U.S. initiatives have reflected this global bias.

To meet the direct military threat posed by the Soviets, the United States needs strategic access to the Gulf and the political cooperation of host states. Regional actors, however, have been very reluctant to accept more than a nominal U.S. military presence in the area. On the one hand, states in the Gulf have welcomed U.S. assistance in meeting threats to their security. On the other, within the context of an Arab world divided by intraregional and East–West tensions, they fear the political repercussions of close cooperation with the United States. The very factor that brings America to the Gulf to protect the West's oil supplies and to contain the Soviets—its superpower status—is also a severe political liability. The legacy of anti-imperialist sentiment and fear of embroilment in the Cold War have led to Arab hesitancy to cooperate with the United States. America's role in the Arab–Israeli conflict has further impaired U.S. relations with the Arab world. Deterioration of the dialogue between the United States and Gulf powers not only undermines U.S. leverage in the region, it also calls into question the feasibility of America's strategy for containing the Soviet Union. The difficulty in forging a link between military strategy and political reality is reflective of the broader tension between global and regional perspectives within U.S. policy.

The third strategic dilemma facing U.S. policymakers concerns the relationship between unilateral and collective approaches to Gulf security. The conceptual problem is logically very straightforward. From one perspective, the Middle East clearly lies beyond the scope of NATO's geographic responsibility and should therefore be dealt with outside the alliance framework. From another perspective, a cutoff of Persian Gulf oil poses one of the more immediate and plausible threats to the collective security of the West and should therefore be addressed on an alliance-wide basis.

The record of alliance cooperation on Middle East policy has reflected this conceptual problem. Repeated attempts at coordination have produced, at best, mediocre results. The Suez crisis of 1956, the oil crises in 1973–1974 and 1978–1979, and the Soviet invasion of Afghanistan in 1979 each raised expectations within the alliance about the prospects of cooperation on Middle East policy. Yet in each case, expectations fell far short of reality. Shared recognition of the benefits of a coordinated response was not accompanied by the political will necessary to achieve substantive cooperation. The consequent oscillation and tension between unilateral and collectivist impulses is the third strategic dilemma that the United States and the Western alliance more generally face in the Persian Gulf.

Overview

This study will investigate the dilemmas of Persian Gulf security by examining both the process of formulation and the content of Western security policy toward the region. The analysis will weave together the domestic context of decision-making and the international political and strategic variables that shape foreign policy. The aim is to identify what key military, political, and economic issues molded policy and how they interacted in determining the behavior of states (or organizations, in the case of NATO) in the international arena.[7]

Although the Gulf emerged as an arena of East–West competition immediately after the war, the study focuses principally on the post-1973 period. A series of events during the 1970s served to exacerbate Western perceptions of strategic vulnerability in the Gulf: the British withdrawal from the region, the October War and subsequent oil crisis, the Iranian revolution, and the Soviet invasion of Afghanistan. By the 1970s, the United States had also replaced the British and the French as the principal external power in the region. Because of its role as the chief arbiter in the Arab–Israeli conflict, its position as the dominant arms supplier to states throughout the region, and the political leverage and military strength associated with its superpower status, the United States emerged as the Western state primarily responsible for formulating and executing policies to protect Western interests. The singular importance of U.S. policy in shaping security arrangements in the Gulf narrows, and therefore simplifies, the task of examining a "Western" approach to the region.

The following chapter establishes an historical context for the study by presenting an analysis of the chief aspects of American policy toward the Gulf

---

7. In terms of the theoretical literature, this study integrates the rational actor and the bureaucratic models of decision-making. It assumes that organizational and bureaucratic dynamics indeed affect policy choices but also recognizes the importance of the stimuli and constraints in the international system that are at the core of realist analysis. For the rational state as unitary actor approach, see Stanley Hoffmann, *Contemporary Theory in International Relations* (Englewood Cliffs, NJ: Prentice-Hall, 1980). For the bureaucratic process model see Graham Allison, *Essence of Decision Explaining the Cuban Missile Crisis* (Boston: Little, Brown, 1971). The slant taken in this study is very similar to that described by Robert Keohane in *After Hegemony—Cooperation and Discord in the World Political Economy* (Princeton, NJ: Princeton University Press, 1984). See especially pp. 25–30.

between 1946 and 1973. The key parameters and concepts that have framed the
debate about Gulf security in the postwar years will be identified.

Chapter three assesses the impact of the October War in 1973 upon American perceptions of the political fabric in the Middle East. American policy
entered a new phase between 1973 and 1979. The United States turned to Iran
and Saudi Arabia as its principal surrogates in the Gulf. The goal of the chapter
is to understand the key assumptions that shaped policy by examining decision
making within its domestic and international contexts.

Chapters 4–6 present a more detailed analysis of the steps taken by the
United States to react to the revolution in Iran and the Soviet invasion of
Afghanistan. This section investigates the political and strategic rationale behind the formulation of the Carter Doctrine. The declared commitment to
defend U.S. interests in the Gulf and the consequent development of the Rapid
Deployment Force (RDF) and the Central Command (CENTCOM) marked the
abandonment of a policy of avoiding military intervention which, with few
exceptions, had held constant from 1945 to 1979.[8] With the advantage of over
five years of hindsight and documentation, it is now possible to examine both
the evolution of the Carter Doctrine and its implementation during the Carter
and Reagan administrations. The analysis will focus on the political, strategic,
and bureaucratic factors that shaped policy and military strategy.

Chapters 7 and 8 move away from exclusive concern with American policy
toward the Gulf, and focus on why and in what ways the United States and the
Europeans have attempted to cooperate on issues of Middle East security. Chapter 7 examines the sources of tension within NATO over Middle East policy.
The areas to be analyzed are: the Arab–Israeli conflict, and the Palestinian
question in particular; the management of the world oil market and the allocation and pricing of Middle East oil; and Western military posture in the Southwest Asian theater. The key questions concern why European and American
perspectives on these issues diverged, and whether such splits result more from
the structure and nature of the alliance than from different assessments of what
is politically and strategically expedient.

Chapter 8 presents a thorough treatment of the debate over the Persian Gulf
that emerged within NATO after the Soviet invasion of Afghanistan. Through
an examination of the sources and content of the "out-of-area" debate, the
chapter addresses the evolution of NATO military policy toward the Gulf and
examines the political and bureaucratic dynamics of the decision-making process. The analysis seeks both to determine those factors that constrain the ability

---

8. The United States did land troops in Lebanon in 1958 and has participated in peacekeeping
forces in the Middle East. As will be shown later, the operation in Lebanon was a response to a
specific set of developments. It did not signify a long term shift in American perspectives about the
use of force in the Middle East.

of the alliance to address conflict in the Third World and to expose the sources of tension between unilateralist and collectivist approaches to the Gulf.

The final chapter assesses the extent to which the West has been able to respond to the strategic dilemmas that it has faced in the Gulf. It argues that there is one fundamental weakness that has plagued America's approach to the Gulf: a globalism that has produced a persistent disjuncture between U.S. military policy and the political realities of the Middle East. The analysis traces American globalism to two key factors. First, the cognitive framework in which U.S. decision makers operate precludes sensitivity to and engenders misperception of political change in the Middle East and the Third World more generally. Second, the structure of the bureaucracy in Washington excludes the input of regional experts and drives planning toward demanding scenarios, producing policies that are focused on the Soviet threat and that are unresponsive to regional political realities. Stemming from this analysis, the study offers general recommendations for the formulation of security policy toward Southwest Asia.[9]

9. A conceptual omission warrants mention at this point. This study is primarily about Western policy and the strategic and political issues that determine how and when military force is used to achieve political ends. In this sense, the analysis focuses on decision making and the implementation of policy in the United States, in Western Europe, and in NATO as a collective institution. Any study of security in the Persian Gulf should devote considerable attention to the regional actors themselves, the stability of the regimes, the composition of the domestic populations, and the peculiarities of political culture in specific Arab states. These issues will appear throughout the study. Nevertheless, it should be noted that I do not attempt to present a thorough analysis of Gulf politics, which is indeed a crucial factor in the overall equation of Gulf security.

Chapter Two

THE SETTING, 1946–1973

The military and economic costs incurred by Britain during World War II did little to undermine her dominant position in the Persian Gulf region. By temporarily leaving Soviet troops in Iran after the war, Stalin did indicate a desire to exercise influence, if not control, in the territories bordering on the Soviet Union. Britain's dominance in the lower Gulf, however, went unchallenged. Despite an agreement between the United States and Saudi Arabia providing U.S. forces access to military facilities in Dharhan, the Arabian peninsula remained outside the realm of the emerging Cold War and was viewed by the Western powers largely in terms of its position in the British Empire and its large and valuable oil reserves.

By 1973, the situation in Southwest Asia had changed dramatically. British willingness to maintain its colonial posture in the Middle East had eroded steadily until 1968, when the decision was taken to withdraw from all positions east of the Suez Canal. While the United States gradually assumed responsibility for security arrangements in the Middle East, the Soviets steadily increased their political influence in and military access to the region. As a result, Southwest Asia emerged as a key arena for a superpower rivalry that was becoming increasingly global in scope. By the 1970s, the Middle East was considered to be one of the areas in which a clash between the United States and the Soviet Union was most likely to occur.

The goal of this chapter is to chronicle this change in the West's position in the Middle East and to examine how successive U.S. administrations have both defined American interests in the region and designed means of defending those interests. The security policy of the United States has been consistently based upon the concept of containing the Soviet Union. Yet, the task of defining and implementing containment has raised complex questions about how best to exercise military and political influence in areas far from reservoirs of American power. The answers to these questions have ranged from extending deterrence to the Middle East by threatening aggressive powers with nuclear retaliation to providing local states with the ability to defend themselves. In examining the evolution of policy options, the following analysis will define the key elements of the debate over Gulf security as they have emerged since 1946.

The Truman Administration

The three principal issues that have dominated American perceptions of "security" in the Middle East during the postwar years were well formulated by the end of the 1940s. American commercial interests in Middle East oil began to blossom after the war, both for economic and political reasons. Stalin's aggressive behavior toward Iran after the defeat of Germany indicated accurately that the Gulf—and the Middle East as a whole—would emerge as a key area of Soviet–American competition. And the establishment of the state of Israel in 1948, with its implications both for U.S. domestic politics and for political stability in the Middle East, became an increasingly important factor in the formulation of American policy toward the region.

Western powers became involved in the Persian Gulf well before World War II; the British established a permanent presence in the Gulf in the middle of the nineteenth century. Their primary motivation for forming political and military ties with the littoral states was to secure trade and communication links to India.[1] The economic importance of the Gulf itself began to emerge only after the discovery of large oil reserves just prior to World War I. The British quickly tapped these reserves, establishing the Anglo-Iranian Oil Company in 1914. American oil companies began operating in the Gulf during the interwar years and succeeded in capturing a large share of the market by 1945. At the time, the United States was a net exporter of oil; companies were attracted primarily by the low production costs and high profits envisaged. In 1947, Middle East crude, pumped from only 199 wells, represented some 10% of world production.[2] Following the war, the Western presence in the region became of increasing political importance. Commercial contacts served as a tool through which the United States and Britain could affect the political orientation of the major producing states. While the British remained the primary external power in Iran after the war, American companies concentrated their attention on Saudi Arabia.

1. See Alvin J. Cottrell, ed., *The Persian Gulf States—A General Survey* (London: Johns Hopkins University Press, 1980), 84.
2. Benjamin Shwadran, *The Middle East, Oil and the Great Powers* (New York: Council for Middle Eastern Affairs Press, 1959), 447. By comparison, there were some 440,000 operating wells in the United States.

The Iranian crisis of 1946 proved to be an important event shaping the approach of the Western powers toward the Gulf. Early in 1942, British and Russian troops were stationed in Iran to ensure access to the region's oil and to secure a corridor for sending military aid to the Soviet Union. Despite an agreement between Britian and the Soviet Union that each would withdraw its troops within six months of the cessation of hostilities, Stalin left Soviet forces in Iran past the March 2, 1946 deadline. The British and Americans feared that Stalin was attempting to partition the country by effectively annexing the northern province of Azerbaijan, and they reacted with anger and firm demands for the withdrawal of Soviet troops.[3]

In understanding America's response to Stalin's behavior, it is important to look in more general terms at the relationship between the Soviet Union and the Western powers that was developing after the war. Although the mutual distrust and abrasive rhetoric that have characterized the Cold War were not yet in full bloom by 1946, it was at that time that the allied governments, and especially the Truman administration, were seeking a consistent lens through which to view Soviet behavior.[4] The image that emerged in Washington was shaped by certain key officials, including George Kennan, a Soviet expert working in the American embassy in Moscow. Kennan's theory of containment emerged as the blueprint for the Truman administration's foreign policy, and although it has undergone successive changes, it has remained at the core of American thinking about national security. He based his concept of containing the Soviet Union on three points. First, the United States had to cultivate alliances with the primary industrial centers outside the Soviet Union and attempt to restore their economic vitality and military strength. Second, splits within the communist world had to be utilized as a means of weakening Moscow's aspirations toward global power. Third, the West had to work to modify Soviet behavior through both direct negotiations and indirect political and economic pressure.[5]

In its essence, Kennan's theory of containment was not based upon the encirclement of the Soviet Union or the restraint of Moscow's behavior through coercion. His approach emanated from the perception of an aggressive and dangerous Soviet leadership, yet one that could be controlled through psychological, economic, and political, as well as military means. In terms of strategic posture, Kennan favored "strongpoint defense" over "perimeter defense"; that is, he felt that the United States had to identify and be willing to defend with force

3. John Lewis Gaddis, *The United States and the Origins of the Cold War 1941–1947* (New York: Columbia University Press, 1972), 310.

4. See Daniel Yergin, *Shattered Peace: The Origins of the Cold War and the National Security State* (London: Andre Deutsch, 1978).

5. John Lewis Gaddis, *Strategies of Containment—A Critical Appraisal of Postwar American National Security Policy* (New York: Oxford University Press, 1982), 36–37.

certain strategic and industrial centers rather than to respond to Soviet intervention wherever it might occur. To this end, Kennan favored the construction of an elite military unit that could be rapidly deployed to aid in the defense of these strategic strongpoints.[6] This proposal of a versatile strike force was attractive not only because it suited Kennan's concept of selective defense, but also because it was a means of assigning to a single force different geographic missions, thereby reducing manpower requirements. After the end of the war, the American defense budget and the size of the U.S. Army decreased rapidly. The military budget for fiscal year 1945 was $81.6 billion; by 1947 this figure had declined to $13.1 billion.[7] Despite its economic appeal, however, the quick strike unit was never established. The center of action was in Europe and the services were reluctant to devote their dwindling resources to a special strike force for peripheral missions.[8]

When translated into policy toward Southwest Asia, Kennan's brand of containment led to a reliance on the so-called northern tier nations. In strategic terms, Iran was the regional strongpoint. President Truman insisted that Stalin withdraw his troops from the northern provinces and renounce his claim to territories in both Iran and Turkey. Although the Soviets eventually agreed to withdraw by early May, the Iran crisis induced the Truman administration to take a harder line toward Stalin. It heightened concern about Stalin's intentions and thus about Soviet expansion in forms short of actual military aggression or territorial claim.[9] Truman feared that growing communist and pro-Soviet groups in Greece and Turkey could eventually topple their governments, sending those countries into the Soviet bloc. The administration responded in 1947 by introducing the Truman Doctrine, asserting that the United States must "support free people who are resisting attempted subjugation by armed minorities or by outside pressures."[10] The formal declaration of this policy as well as the large assistance packages that accompanied it were to make highly visible America's commitment to preserve the pro-Western orientation of the northern tier states. Furthermore, the United States secured military access to the Gulf itself by arranging for the use of an airfield in Saudi Arabia in 1947 and a port in Bahrain in 1949. In general, Truman's principal objective in the Middle East was to pre-

6. Ibid., 39.

7. Ibid., 23.

8. Kennan in the late 1940s argued for two divisions to be earmarked for rapid deployment purposes. Similar proposals were put forth and rejected during the Eisenhower and Kennedy administrations. During the Eisenhower administration the Army temporarily supported the establishment of quick strike units. But this was largely a response to the doctrine of Massive Retaliation and the growing importance of the Air Force. See Samuel Huntington, *The Common Defense-Strategic Programs in National Politics* (New York: Columbia University Press, 1961), 41, 343–353.

9. Gaddis, *Origins of the Cold War*, 312–315.

10. Ibid., 351.

serve the political status quo, allowing him to devote attention to the emerging alliance in Western Europe and to the problems brewing in East Asia.

It is important to note that U.S. concern about the strategic importance of the Persian Gulf was relatively new. It was essentially a by-product of the war and the need to expand energy resources to fuel European recovery. As a result of the emerging conception of an expansive Soviet Union, the political orientation of states in Southwest Asia became of growing importance. Yet, with the exception of northern Iran, the question of Soviet expansion and territorial control was not an issue. The Soviets did not have the capability to project significant power into the Gulf area or the eastern Mediterranean, nor were there surrogate communist forces in the region threatening to invade pro-Western states. This explains the relatively low priority initially assigned the Middle East within America's emerging global strategy.

The situation in East Asia presented a clear contrast. The impact of the Korean War upon both the essential assumptions of containment and America's global strategy was dramatic. Not only was there a sudden reversal of the trend toward reduced military expenditures, but the core principles of Kennan's brand of containment—through the influence of others such as Paul Nitze—was altered as well. In Korea, the United States faced what it considered to be the growing peril of unchecked international communism instigated by the Soviet Union. The North Koreans and the Chinese represented more than physical enemies; they encapsulated what the Americans feared most about the volatile mix of military power and communism.

Before the war began, the National Security Council had produced a review of global security (NSC-68) that challenged Kennan's basic conception of containment. Largely in response to the crisis in Korea, the Truman administration reoriented its foreign policy on the basis of the assumptions presented in NSC-68. The document stated with chilling clarity that "in the context of the present polarization of power a defeat of free institutions anywhere is a defeat everywhere."[11] This one sentence contained a repudiation of key elements of Kennan's thinking. It pointed to a return to perimeter defense, to a commitment to contain the Soviets on a global scale. In doing so, it blurred the distinction between interests in one region versus those in another. NSC-68 established a global strategic perspective in which the policy formulated to defend U.S. interests in one area was thought to be equally valid to serve the same purpose in others. And the principal objective was universal: to meet the Soviet threat. Finally, this sentence emphasized the ideological threat posed by the Soviet Union and suggested that it was "free institutions" that must be defended, not only the independence of strategic and industrial centers. All three of these tenets led to the conclusion that the United States must return to a strong

11. NSC-68 cited in Gaddis, *Strategies of Containment*, 91.

military posture and increase industrial production to support a new buildup of the armed forces. From fiscal year 1947 to fiscal year 1952, the defense budget increased from $13.1 to $44.0 billion.[12]

This shift in the general orientation of American policy toward the periphery had no immediate implications for the Middle East. Yet two decisions concerning strategy in the European theater were to color significantly the legacy passed on to the Eisenhower administration. First, Truman deployed American divisions in Europe as a permanent contribution to the force structure of NATO. At a time when the loss of American troops in Europe and Asia was still a fresh memory, this was a bold symbolic statement of the breadth of America's global policy. Second, Truman also decided to send the Sixth Fleet to the Mediterranean to establish a permanent naval presence. This clarified his commitment to Greece and Turkey and was to become an important strategic factor in the Middle East in coming years. Though the Eisenhower administration made a rhetorical retreat from Truman's willingness to assume comprehensive global responsibility, these permanent changes in military posture constituted a de facto extension of American power to Western Europe and the Mediterranean.

One final element of U.S. policy that was taking shape during the Truman administration was the nature of America's relationship with Israel. During the U.N. debate in 1947–1948 about the partition of Palestine, the administration was deeply divided over the question of establishing an independent Jewish state. The State and Defense Departments were generally opposed to the idea, making arguments that have been heard repeatedly in the ongoing debate about Middle East policy in Washington. The State Department feared that the establishment of Israel would jeopardize American relations with the Arab world and potentially lead to the interruption of the flow of oil to Europe—an energy source essential to the viability of the Marshall Plan. Many officals also argued that the regional instability caused by partition would serve as an opening for the Soviets. The Defense Department voiced concern about losing military access to the airfield in Dharhan, Saudi Arabia.[13]

President Truman himself vacillated between accepting these arguments and showing sensitivity to the pressures of public opinion. There was strong support within the American public for the establishment of a Jewish state, and little opposition. American Jews, though not yet as politically powerful an electoral bloc as they were soon to become, did influence the administration's policy. In the late 1940s, there were some 5,600,000 Jews in the United States, many of whom were concentrated in states with a large number of electoral votes—such as New York, Illinois, and Ohio.[14] Truman's stance on the question of establish-

12. Ibid., 359.

13. Steven Spiegel, *The Other Arab–Israeli Conflict: Making America's Middle East Policy, from Truman to Reagan* (Chicago: University of Chicago Press, 1985), 26.

14. John Snetsinger, *Truman, the Jewish Vote, and the Creation of Israel* (Stanford: Hoover

ing a Jewish state seems to have been determined by electoral considerations more than any other single factor. In October, 1946, he publicly supported the creation of a Jewish state largely to aid the Democratic party in the upcoming congressional elections.[15] In 1948, however, Truman decided to vote against the Palestine partition plan in the United Nations. He again switched his position shortly thereafter as the presidential election neared. Convinced by his aides of the importance of winning the Jewish vote, Truman recognized the establishment of the state of Israel almost immediately after the end of the British trusteeship.[16] So began America's close, yet hesitant relationship with Israel that was to become an increasingly important factor shaping U.S. security policy toward the Middle East.

The Eisenhower Administration

A central component of General Eisenhower's campaign platform for the presidency focused on the need for a retrenchment in foreign policy and a reduction in America's reliance on sending ground troops to all corners of the world. In the aftermath of World War II and the Korean War, his call met eager ears. Eisenhower's determination to decrease defense expenditure and to reduce the size of the armed forces was not, however, accompanied by a willingness to relax the aggressive posture toward the Soviet Union that had emerged under Truman. In order to balance his budgetary goals with his commitment to the tenets spelled out in NSC-68, Eisenhower, with the help of his Secretary of State John Dulles, opted for greater reliance on nuclear deterrence, both in Europe and in outlying areas. Dulles' concept of massive retaliation meant that in Europe, NATO could tolerate an imbalance in conventional forces by threatening to retaliate with nuclear weapons should the Soviets cross the central front. On a global scale, the United States would use its nuclear capabilities to deter communist states from encroaching upon their "free" neighbors. At the same time, however, Eisenhower realized that the threat of massive retaliation lacked credibility, especially in peripheral areas. He therefore redoubled efforts to create pro-Western alliances outside Europe and relied heavily on covert operations to influence events in the Third World.

Institution Press, 1974), 12. See also Zvi Ganin, *Truman, American Jewry, and Israel 1945–1948* (New York: Holmes and Meier, 1979), and Nadav Safran, *The United States and Israel* (Cambridge, MA: Harvard University Press, 1963), chap. 4.

15. Snetsinger, *Truman*, 42–44.

16. Ibid., 138. For details of the debate within the Truman administration about the recognition of Israel, see William Roger Louis, *The British Empire in the Middle East 1945–1951, Arab Nationalism, the United States, and Postwar Imperialism* (Oxford: Clarendon Press, 1984), 526–528.

Eisenhower's security policy toward the Middle East reflected a mix of his retreat from dependence on the use of American forces abroad with a reaffirmation of the aggressive, ideological interpretation of containment that emerged late in the Truman administration. The result, however, was not one of continued restraint in the Middle East. By the time he left office, Eisenhower had greatly increased America's involvement in the region and had reshaped the guidelines within which U.S. policy toward the area was to be formulated after the 1950s.

Eisenhower's two terms in office were punctuated by a steady series of crucial decisions concerning policy in Southwest Asia. In 1951, Iranian Prime Minister Mossadeq nationalized the Anglo–Iranian Oil Company. In retaliation, Western European and American oil companies refused to distribute Iranian oil. The British and Americans interpreted this course of events as posing a threat to the stability of the northern tier. The nationalization of the oil company reduced Western leverage in Iran by terminating the principal source of commercial contact. The move was also a clear challenge to Britain's imperial power, a challenge to which she was not yet prepared to succumb. The boycott itself could have further damaged Iran's commercial ties with the West and forced the Iranians to increase their trade with the Soviets. Based on these considerations, the British and the Americans decided to remove Mossadeq, placing power in the hands of Mohammed Reza Shah Pahlavi.[17] This episode clearly indicated America's willingness to use coercion to influence the internal politics of other nations and reflected the attitude prevalent in the West that the Europeans and Americans had a "right" to Gulf oil. The coup in Iran was only the first of several similar operations to be sanctioned by the Eisenhower administration. The CIA orchestrated a successful coup in Guatemala in 1954, and then failed in both Indonesia (1958) and Cuba (1960–1961).

With the Shah in power, the potential to solidify the pro-Western orientation of the northern tier nations increased. The first step toward collective security was taken in 1955 when Turkey, Iran, Iraq, Pakistan and Britain signed the Baghdad Pact. The Pact was to facilitate political and military cooperation among the signatories and to provide for collective defense should a member state be attacked. It ended abruptly in 1958 following a coup in Iraq that displaced a pro-Western leadership. In August, 1959, however, the Central Treaty Organization (CENTO) was formed with Turkey, Iran, Pakistan, and the United States as signatories. As a result of the coup in Iraq, CENTO maintained its headquarters in Ankara rather than in Baghdad. Although CENTO lacked the cohesion, credibility, and military strength characteristic in an alliance such as NATO, it was of considerable symbolic significance in terms of Eisenhower's plan to proliferate pro-Western pacts throughout the Third World. Even after

17. Robert Divine, *Eisenhower and the Cold War* (New York: Oxford University Press, 1981), 74.

Pakistan effectively withdrew from CENTO following the Indo-Pakistan War in 1965, the United States was not willing to allow the dismantling of the organization because of the potential signal that such a move would send to the Soviets.[18]

The history of the Baghdad Pact and CENTO illuminates several key problems that the Western powers were to face repeatedly in the Middle East. To begin, the British and Americans had differing conceptions of what purpose a security pact in the northern tier was to serve. While the British were concerned primarily about protecting their economic interests in Iran and their access to military bases in Iraq, the Americans viewed the Pact more in terms of its role in implementing containment.[19] The British perceived their interests in a regional context; American interests were more closely wedded to a certain conception of U.S.–Soviet global competition. The French were also involved: They were not included in either the Baghdad Pact or CENTO and were affronted by what they perceived as their exclusion from security arrangements in the northern tier. As will be discussed shortly, these differing perceptions and interests were to hinder effective cooperation among the Western allies on Middle East policy issues.

The coup in Iraq was also indicative of a second recurring problem facing external powers: the volatility of political developments in the Middle East. The impact of the revolution in Iran in 1978–1979 had many similarities with the consequences of the events in Iraq in 1958. In both cases, domestic political developments altered radically the alignment of these states with external powers. Britain and the United States relied on Iraq and Iran both for providing military access and for serving as a stabilizing political force in the region. Not only did these states suddenly become unwilling to act on behalf of Western interests in the region, they became aggressively anti-Western. The coup in Iraq was an early indication of just how fragile and unpredictable Western relations with regional powers were to become in the changing political context in Southwest Asia.

The spread of anti-Western sentiment in the Middle East was fueled by the emergence of Egyptian President Gamal Abdel Nasser as the predominant leader in the Arab world. This development eventually diverted the Eisenhower administration from its exclusive concentration on the northern tier. Nasser's rise to power stimulated the forces of change in the Middle East that were to alter profoundly Western perceptions of and policies toward the region. As an Egyptian nationalist, Nasser firmly opposed the long-standing British presence in his country, eventually causing London to withdraw its troops and to rethink its commitment to the region as a whole. As an Arab nationalist, he envisaged a pan-Arab community to be united by common ethnicity and shared political

18. Interview with Robert Komer.
19. Personal communication with Sir Anthony Parsons, 23 October 1984.

perspectives. He urged other Arab states to loosen their ties with colonial powers as a means of stimulating nationalism. Finally, Nasser was the first Arab leader to invite direct Soviet involvement in the Middle East. In 1955, he accepted a shipment of arms from Czechoslovakia, thereby confirming a new military relationship with the Soviet bloc. Nasser's decision to turn to the Soviets for arms was based primarily on pragmatic rather than ideological considerations. The Tripartite Declaration signed in 1950 by Britain, France, and the United States limited the amount of arms to be sold to the region by Western nations.[20] The purpose of the agreement was to prevent the rapid militarization of the area and to stabilize territorial boundaries, but it unintentionally drove Nasser to look elsewhere for armaments. Nasser also voiced irritation about the Baghdad Pact, perceiving it as a reassertion of "British Imperialism" and a strengthening of Iraq's position in the Middle East.[21] An Israeli raid in the Gaza Strip in 1955 also stimulated his search for a new source of arms.

By involving the Soviet Union in the arms trade in the Middle East, Nasser was ensuring that regional issues were to be submerged within the broader guise of East–West or Soviet–American confrontation. The introduction of Soviet weaponry into Egypt and the tacit influence that accompanied it encouraged the United States to perceive Nasser's behavior as either manipulated by the Soviets or shaped to enhance Moscow's stance in the region. Of particular importance in this respect was the tendency of the Eisenhower administration to associate Arab nationalism with Soviet involvement and communist ideology. This tendency complicated the task of distinguishing between events of only isolated regional significance and those of broader importance to U.S. interests. This perceptual problem became manifest in America's reaction to the Suez crisis in 1956 and the Lebanon crisis in 1958.

In July 1956, Nasser unilaterally nationalized the Suez Canal Company. Britain, France, and Israel collectively planned for an Israeli attack on Egyptian positions in the Sinai to serve as a pretext for British and French forces to intervene and seize the canal. The British and the French interpreted Nasser's unilateral act as an outright challenge to their power and influence; they responded accordingly. The United States, on the other hand, argued against a military response. Its forces did not participate in the operation and the Eisenhower administration was not even informed that it was to take place. The United States viewed the central issue to be the maintenance of free passage through the canal for ships of all nations. As Nasser did not actually deny any vessels access to the waterway, Washington saw no need to intervene. Eisenhower was also reluctant to send troops because he questioned "whether such

20. Geoffrey Kemp, "Strategy and Arms Levels, 1945–1967," in J.C. Hurewitz, ed., *Soviet–American Rivalry in the Middle East* (New York: Praeger, 1969), 31–32. See also Louis, *The British Empire*, 583–590.

21. Elie Kedourie, "Britain, France and the Last Phase of the Eastern Question," in Hurewitz, *Soviet–American Rivalry*, 194.

action would not outrage world opinion and whether it would achieve permanent, soundly based stability."[22] The administration feared that U.S. involvement might lead to a major conflict in the Middle East and could even stimulate
Soviet intervention. Dulles was particularly concerned about how the Arab
states would perceive American involvement: "Let us remember that while *we*
think first of the danger that stems from international communism, many of
them [the regional states] think first of possible encroachments from the West,
for that is the rule that they have actually known at first hand."[23] In short,
Eisenhower was willing to let the matter rest; he felt that the dangers of military
intervention far outweighed the potential benefits.

The unfolding of the Suez crisis had numerous implications for the policies of
the Western powers in the Middle East. For obvious reasons, a serious rift
developed between the Americans and the British and French. The Americans
were angered over the lack of consultation and the British and French resented
Washington's lack of support both before and after the unsuccessful operation.
The implications for alliance relations will be discussed in depth in Chapter 7.
At this point, it is sufficient to point out that the episode clearly diminished
British willingness to maintain a presence in the region. London had faced a
steady series of setbacks: her inability to solve the Palestine question in 1948; her
expulsion from Egypt in 1955; and now her failed military response to the
nationalization of the canal company. That the attack was even mounted,
however, was a clear indication that neither the British nor the French were
ready to let threats to their economic interests or their prestige go unchallenged.
The decision to use force reflected that both Paris and London viewed the
seizure of the canal as morally acceptable, strategically feasible, and politically
expedient in terms of relations with both the United States and the Arab
countries in the Middle East.

Three points follow. First, the issue of moral justification points to the extent
to which colonial attitudes still prevailed in Britain and France: The canal was
privately owned and should remain so. Second, the question of strategic feasibility highlights European willingness and ability to project power over long
distances. The operation was also an indication that the major European powers
did not perceive Nasser's military strength as a significant challenge to their own
regional role. Third, the issue of political expediency shows that the French and
British were willing to act without American approval and, in fact, against
Eisenhower's better judgment. These three observations have been stressed primarily because they were to become obsolete by the 1960s, a development with
important implications for U.S. policy.

22. Dwight Eisenhower, *Waging Peace* (Garden City, NY: Doubleday, 1965), 37.
23. John Foster Dulles, radio-television address, 23 March 1956, cited in Gaddis, *Strategies of Containment*, 179.

The Suez crisis had one additional impact on regional security considerations. For the first time, Israel was directly involved in a military operation that was jointly planned and executed with Western powers. For the Israelis to buy French arms was one matter; many other states in the region did so as well. Yet, for Israel to participate in a coordinated attack against an Arab state was a different matter altogether. This was a further step toward casting the Arab–Israeli conflict into a context of East–West confrontation.

Though Eisenhower exercised restraint during the Suez crisis itself, the episode did lead him to reassess America's position in the Middle East. After the furor surrounding the Suez affair subsided, two factors compelled him to unveil the Eisenhower Doctrine as a means of publicly reaffirming America's willingness to intervene in the region if necessary. First, he did not want either the Soviets or the Arabs to believe that the West was incapable of effectively using force in the Middle East. In Eisenhower's own words, "[t]he existing vacuum in the Middle East must be filled by the United States before it is filled by Russia."[24] The British and French mission had failed and they would no doubt think twice before attempting another operation in the area. The United States had unequivocally exhibited its hesitation to send troops to the region. Eisenhower therefore wanted to preempt those who might have concluded that the West's position in the Middle East was eroding. His second motivation for setting forth the Eisenhower Doctrine in January, 1957 emerged from fear that Nasser's victory in the Suez affair would both bolster his image in the Middle East and fuel the spread of Arab nationalism.

Both concerns, as it turned out, were quite accurate. Nasser stepped up his exhortations to other Arab countries, and in 1958, Egypt and Syria formed the United Arab Republic. Nasser's dependence on Soviet arms and his surging political power in the region confirmed the tendency in Washington to see the growth of Arab nationalism as a sign of increasing Soviet influence in the Middle East. This perspective was evident in the wording of the Eisenhower Doctrine: The United States must be prepared to use armed force "to secure and protect the territorial integrity and political independence of such nations, requesting such aid, against overt armed aggression from any nation controlled by International Communism."[25] At the same time, Eisenhower asked for and received from Congress the authority to deploy forces to the Middle East. These moves were to make clear "the American view of the current situation and our intentions . . . so that all, including the Soviets, would understand that . . . we were fully determined to sustain Western rights in the region.[26]

24. Eisenhower, *Waging Peace*, 178.
25. Text in U.S. Department of State, *United States Policy in the Middle East, September 1956 - June 1957* (Washington, DC: GPO, 1957), 15–23.
26. Eisenhower, *Waging Peace*, 178.

The aggressive wording and ideological content of the Eisenhower Doctrine served two purposes. On the one hand, it was to reassure threatened regimes sympathetic to the West that the United States would defend them. On the other, it was to deter radical leaders from attempting to overthrow moderate regimes in contiguous states. Yet, the Eisenhower Doctrine also had one unintended ramification: It forced regimes in the Middle East to choose between East and West, and to suppress indigenous political forces out of fear that the United States would see nationalism as a force leading the country into the Soviet camp. The rise of "radical" regimes in Syria and Iraq did, in fact, pose a threat to Western ties with those countries. Yet, their eventual links with the Kremlin were the result of Western hostility toward them as much as any ideological affinity for Soviet communism.[27] Whereas Kennan had once seen the resurgence of nationalism in the Third World as crucial to containing Soviet expansionism, Eisenhower saw it as paving the way for international communism. Missing was the emphasis on strengthening strategic centers through political and economic development. Absent from public debate was the need to distinguish between communism as an economic system and Soviet ideology as a subversive force sweeping the Third World. Instead, the United States declared a commitment to use armed force to "roll back" Soviet communism and military power.

The difficulties inherent in imposing such a rigid model of regional conflict on the Middle East became evident during the Lebanon crisis of 1958. In July, a coup in Iraq led by General Qassim replaced the pro-Western leadership with a regime sympathetic to the Syrian–Egyptian alignment. American anxiety about the coup was exacerbated by Iraq's long-standing diplomatic ties with the Soviet Union (since 1944) and the presence of a large communist party in the country. In Lebanon, a similar rift was developing between Christian President Camille Chamoun and a more radical Moslem group. In its origins, the crisis in Lebanon was a domestic affair; it was the culmination of festering tension between Christian and Moslem leaders. Yet, in part because of the strictures imposed on the region by the Eisenhower Doctrine, the rift developed into an overt struggle between pro-American forces and a nationalist opposition. When faced with the collapse of his regime, Chamoun called upon the Americans for military assistance. Eisenhower responded by sending 14,000 marines to Beirut.

The nature of the U.S. response to Chamoun's request indicated that Eisenhower's goals went far beyond simply supporting the pro-Western government. The internal rivalry in the country appeared to serve as the excuse for military intervention for which Eisenhower had been waiting. In his own mind,

27. This is obviously a controversial point bearing much relevance for American policy toward Latin America in the 1980s. The perspective expressed here takes into consideration the unfolding of the crisis in Lebanon in 1958 as well as the lack of ideological sympathy for Soviet communism in those Arab countries receiving arms from the Soviet Union.

the landing of Marines was to deter Soviet advances as well as to "stop the trend toward chaos" and was "only one step in our efforts to restore reasonable stability to the Middle East."[28] That the U.S. presence was more than symbolic was made certain by the placement of tactical air units in Turkey and the movement of a seaborne Marine combat team from Okinawa to the Persian Gulf. The size of the unit in Beirut was also determined by contingency plans to invade Iraq if Baghdad made threatening moves toward Jordan, Kuwait, or Saudi Arabia.[29] In short, the intervention was to serve as a makeshift dam, arresting a process of radicalization that Eisenhower feared would flood the entire region from Egypt to the Gulf states.

The U.S. operation did, in fact, achieve its immediate goals; the political challenge to Chamoun subsided without the Marines engaging in combat or leaving the limits of Beirut. The United States intervened in response to a specific set of circumstances and with certain objectives in mind. Eisenhower chose to demonstrate the degree of his commitment, but wanted to enter and to withdraw from the region as smoothly as possible; there was never any question of a permanent presence. Yet, the change in policy since 1956 was evident. In Eisenhower's mind, the unilateral nationalization of the canal company had limited implications for the Arab world; its impact upon Nasser's behavior and that of other Arab leaders was not yet clear. During the next two years, however, Eisenhower's fears about the spread of communism and the loss of the region as a whole escalated. By 1958, he saw a close and indelible link between pan-Arab nationalism and Soviet infiltration. The intervention in Lebanon raised markedly the level of direct Soviet–American competition and, in juxtaposition to the British and French failure in 1956, meant that the responsibility for defending Western political and economic interests in the region fell increasingly, by default as well as by design, upon American shoulders.

Was the Eisenhower administration justified in calibrating its policy to meet the Soviet challenge and in associating events in the Middle East with the rampant spread of communism? While the Soviet Union may indeed have benefited from the loss of Western influence in Egypt, Syria, Iraq, and Lebanon, there is little evidence that suggests that the Soviets were involved in orchestrating events in these states or that the new regimes were either communist or overtly pro-Soviet in orientation. On the contrary, the evidence suggests that the "radical" regimes that emerged during this period were openly hostile to communism, and were pushed into reluctant and distant alignment with the Soviet Union by Eisenhower's insistence that they choose between East and West.

Nasser himself moved closer to the Soviets and turned to them for arms and

28. Eisenhower, *Waging Peace*, 270, 274.
29. William Quandt, "Lebanon 1958 and Jordan 1970," in Barry Blechman et al., eds., *Force Without War—U.S. Armed Forces as a Political Instrument* (Washington, DC: Brookings Institution, 1978), 232–248.

financial assistance only after being isolated by his exclusion from the Baghdad Pact, affronted by U.S. unwillingness to fund the Aswan Dam project, and angered by the Eisenhower Doctrine.[30] The United Arab Republic (UAR) was anything but the product of a communist conspiracy; the Syrian leadership pressured a reluctant Nasser to assist them in suppressing growing communist influence in Syria.[31] The coup in Iraq was similarly devoid of pro-communist sentiment and Soviet meddling. It was the result of long-term splits within the military and Iraq's withdrawal from the Baghdad Pact reflected Qassim's desire to pursue a policy of neutralism, not to ally with the Soviet Union.[32] The civil war in Lebanon was also the result of internal political rifts—stemming from the National Pact of 1943 between the Christians and Moslems—that were stimulated neither by communist sympathizers nor external meddling. While the opposition did receive supplies from the UAR, a U.N. commission found almost no evidence to support President Chamoun's claim that the UAR had undertaken "massive intervention" in Lebanon.[33]

In short, the Eisenhower administration's suspicions that international communism was sweeping the Middle East were simply unfounded. The spread of Arab nationalism and anti-imperialism indeed made alignment with the United States a less popular proposition (and in some cases a dangerous one). Washington was understandably concerned about its eroding influence. And the decline of Western leverage in the Middle East after 1956 was a development upon which the Soviets might be able to capitalize. But this was not a movement orchestrated by the Soviets nor one which professed any particular affinity for Soviet communism. To base policy on these assumptions was misguided and led to the formulation of inappropriate and, at times, counterproductive initiatives.

The impetus behind this exaggerated perception of the communist threat between 1956 and 1958 was in part provided by events in other parts of the world and by pressure at home. In the first six years of his administration, Eisenhower witnessed a steady series of leftist regimes emerge in Iran, Guatemala, Indochina, Egypt, and Iraq. He was coming under pressure in Washington for having neglected the Third World, for shrinking from America's responsiblity to contain the spread of Soviet influence. The intervention was a response to these

---

30. Gail Meyer, *Egypt and the United States* (Rutherford, NJ: Fairleigh Dickinson University Press, 1980), 184–187. See also Robert Stookey, *America and the Arab States: An Uneasy Encounter* (New York: John Wiley, 1975), 147–149 and Spiegel, *The Other Arab–Israeli Conflict*, 66–71.

31. Richard Nolte, "The United States Policy in the Middle East," in The American Assembly, *The United States in the Middle East* (Englewood Cliffs, NJ: Prentice Hall, 1964), 168.

32. Phebe Marr, *The Modern History of Iraq* (Boulder, CO: Westview Press, 1985). On the coup see 116–125; on the orientation of the new regime see 153–155.

33. Nolte, "The United States Policy in the Middle East," 169.

critics as well as a warning to areas outside the Middle East of America's willingness to intervene on behalf of its interests.

During the years between 1950 and 1958, the Cold War in Southwest Asia spread geographically and escalated in intensity. In 1950, the Truman Doctrine was considered sufficient to secure the anti-Soviet orientation of the northern tier states; the rest of the Middle East was of considerably less concern to either superpower. The Eisenhower Doctrine, on the other hand, was concerned with the Middle East as a whole. The scope of containment was no longer restricted to the periphery of the Soviet Union. By 1958, the United States had sent 14,000 Marines to Beirut, the Soviets had solidified ties with Egypt, Syria, and Iraq, and no portion of the region was left unwatched. Eisenhower focused on preventing the spread of Soviet ideology and the repetition of what had happened in Egypt—the emergence of a powerful regional state sympathetic to the Kremlin. The meaning of containment had not changed, but the instruments required to implement it had. By 1958, most of the states in the Middle East had fallen into either the Eastern or Western camp. A new period of Soviet–American rivalry emerged in which both superpowers attempted to use arms sales to seek and strengthen ties with regional surrogates.

The Kennedy and Johnson Administrations

The Kennedy administration attempted to move away from the rigid version of containment that had dominated America's approach to regional security during both the Truman and Eisenhower administrations. Kennedy hoped to mold a more flexible, selective policy toward the Third World, one that would fill the existing gap between neglect and the use of large-scale military force. This increase in the range of available options was to be obtained by initiatives in both the military and nonmilitary realms. The concept of flexible response emerged, predicated upon the need to react to specific contingencies with appropriate and proportional means. In the periphery, flexible response meant not only a repudiation of the doctrine of massive retaliation, but also a reliance on developing the capability to wage unconventional war and to deal with insurgency movements in the Third World. Accordingly, new emphasis was placed on counterinsurgency training, and there was again consideration of the establishment of a quick strike force for rapid deployment in the periphery. Although the services continued to resist the creation of such a special unit, the Strike Command was established in 1961 to deploy troops to and coordinate operations in remote areas.

In the nonmilitary realm, Kennedy hoped to contribute to stability in developing states and improve America's position in the Third World by expanding foreign aid programs, encouraging economic development, and offering support for national self-determination movements. Numerous mechanisms emerged to carry out this plan; the Peace Corps and the Alliance for Progress—a development scheme for Latin America—were cases in point.

The implications of these initiatives and, consequently, their continued support in the administration, were tempered by several factors. First, America's growing involvement in Vietnam challenged the practicality of implementing flexible response in the periphery. The advisers and special units initially sent to Vietnam were quickly supplemented by large numbers of regular troops. Hopes of fighting a small counterinsurgency war gave way to steady calls for the application of large-scale offensive forces. And despite the existence of the Army Special Warfare School, training in counterinsurgency rarely meant its implementation in the field. One officer revealed the widespread neglect of counterinsurgency doctrine in Vietnam: "I was surprised to discover that my immediate superiors were only interested in classical combat intelligence, not the 'new' counterinsurgency varieties. . . . [I]n June 1964 it was already obvious that enforcement of physical security—convenient rhetoric for violent repression— had become the overwhelming theme in counterinsurgency."[34]

Finally, the war itself raised some problematic questions about the notion of selective defense. Was the vision of falling dominoes in Southeast Asia sufficient justification for U.S. involvement in Vietnam? What U.S. interests were at stake other than prestige and credibility? Had the administration unveiled a policy of restraint that it was unwilling or unable to implement? These issues challenged not only the reasons behind America's involvement in Vietnam, but also the administration's broader notion of when and how to use force in the Third World.

Kennedy's initiatives in the nonmilitary realm did not meet with such immediate obstacles. Rather, the problem was that the principal benefits of foreign aid became apparent only over the long term. Development schemes were simply inadequate to deal with the apparent threats that Soviet-backed communism posed to U.S. interests in the Third World. This did not detract from the importance of aid programs, but it did mean a continuing reliance on the military components of regional security policy.

United States security policy toward the Middle East in the 1960s was, for obvious reasons, overshadowed by events in Southeast Asia. The legacy left by the Eisenhower administration was a reliance on "influence through arms" as the chief source of political leverage in the region. The Lebanon invasion served as a watershed in this respect; it forced regional states to choose between alignment with either the East or West and established the status quo as the situation prevailing after the withdrawal of the Marines.

---

34. David Marr cited in Richard Betts, *Soldiers, Statesmen, and Cold War Crises* (Cambridge, MA: Harvard University Press, 1977), 131–132.

Table 1
VALUE OF ARMS IMPORTED, 1961–1970 (MILLIONS OF DOLLARS)

Country	1961	1962	1963	1964	1965	1966	1967	1968	1969	1970
Iran	22	10	27	26	34	56	104	135	222	160
Iraq	60	114	107	28	44	35	90	133	69	45
Israel	15	19	20	69	46	37	23	55	163	232
Jordan	7	7	3	18	16	23	17	25	72	48
Kuwait	2	1	5	2	1	1	3	Negligible	26	1
Lebanon	2	3	1	Negligible	1	2	Negligible	34	20	4
Saudi Arabia	2	2	5	7	27	25	47	79	83	26
South Yemen	—	—	—	—	—	—	—	2	6	4
Syria	15	35	35	16	10	15	58	40	48	61
Yemen	—	20	25	13	6	4	10	5	1	2

Source: U.S. Arms Control and Disarmament Agency, The International Transfer of Conventional Arms (Washington, DC: September 1973), A-9.

Table 2
U.S. FOREIGN MILITARY SALES DELIVERIES, 1964–1970
(VALUE IN THOUSANDS OF DOLLARS)

Country	FY 1964	FY 1965	FY 1966	FY 1967	FY 1968	FY 1969	FY 1970
Iran	191	12,896	52,188	38,866	56,717	94,894	127,717
Iraq	1,290	949	4,256	5,564	205	29	—
Israel	1,139	17,501	20,644	14,487	29,372	61,910	221,782
Jordan	1,528	943	25,329	11,446	12,402	24,773	56,516
Lebanon	32	23	58	25	559	735	1,126
Saudi Arabia	4,382	5,839	9,200	38,854	23,356	5,586	4,937

Source: U.S. Defense Security Assistance Agency, Foreign Military Sales and Military Assistance Facts (Washington, DC: Data Systems and Reports Division, April 1974), 16–17.

The Kennedy and Johnson administrations, in an effort to maintain this status quo, quickened the pace of arms sales to the Middle East. The flow of arms to the region as a whole increased steadily throughout the decade (see Tables 1 and 2). In the early 1960s, the United States enlarged its military assistance program to Israel and assisted Saudi Arabia in developing a modern military infrastructure. The Soviets, meanwhile, continued to supply arms to Egypt and secured their ties to Iraq and Syria. The principal goal of both the Soviet Union and the United States was to solidify their respective spheres of influence in the region and to tighten their relationships with recipient states. Less attention was devoted to the strategic implications of these sales and to the military balance among regional states. This neglect of strategic considerations was partly due to the fact that the region was still dominated by Western powers. The northern tier states were overtly pro-Western, the British maintained stability and protected communications in the Gulf, and the Americans maintained naval superiority in the eastern Mediterranean. Through the mid-1960s, the battle between the superpowers for surrogates in the Middle East was primarily a battle for political supremacy, a race to secure regional influence.

By the late 1960s, however, several factors compelled the Johnson administration to look more carefully at the strategic situation in the Middle East. Four developments are of particular importance: the 1967 Arab–Israeli War, the emerging economic and political power of the Arab oil-producing states, the British decision of 1968 to withdraw from the Persian Gulf, and the budding U.S.–Soviet naval rivalry in the Indian Ocean.

The Middle East War in 1967 furthered the transformation of the Arab–Israeli conflict into an integral component of the Cold War. By 1967, the Americans had replaced the French as Israel's principal arms supplier. In terms of rhetoric and of military and economic aid, American support for Israeli security was becoming highly visible and thus essential to Washington's image, both at home and abroad. The Soviet Union, on the other hand, broke diplomatic relations with Israel in 1967 and publicly supported the Palestine Liberation Organization (PLO). The Arab–Israeli conflict offered the Soviets another point of entry into the region; they began to realize the extent to which association with the Palestinian national liberation movement would increase their popularity and leverage in the Middle East. It was not only the radical Arab states that took notice of the Kremlin's new position. Moderate regimes could not afford to ignore that one superpower was now supporting the Palestinian cause and that alignment with the West would therefore be a more dangerous proposition. The United States was forced to reassess its own position on the Palestinian question, as well as to offer increasing protection and support to the Saudis and other moderate regimes who were coming under pressure from the Arab left.

The war also led to a distinct shift in the motivation behind arms sales to the region. Before 1967, arms sales were offered primarily as a means of securing political influence and access to bases. After the war, however, transfers were directed more at building up the regional military capabilities of the Soviet-backed Arabs and the American-supported Israelis.[35] The superpowers had clearly chosen sides in the Arab–Israeli dispute. This meant that even conflicts confined to local actors had global implications. American and Soviet surrogates were confronting each other, pitting American against Soviet weaponry. As in Europe, the strategic calculus was beginning to take shape around two distinct spheres of military and political influence.

The second factor leading to a reassessment of policy was the growing dependence of the industrialized West upon Middle East oil. Throughout the 1950s and 1960s global consumption of oil rose steadily. In Europe, industries shifted from coal to petroleum products to meet their energy needs.[36] Despite the continuing rise in U.S. domestic production through the late 1960s, the West was becoming increasingly dependent on imported oil. Several events bred fear that the oil flow from the Persian Gulf could be jeopardized by political developments in the region. In response to the 1967 War and the Israeli seizure of territories, including East Jerusalem, Arab states attempted to reduce oil exports to the United States and Europe. Loose market conditions prevented the embargo from seriously affecting supplies.[37] Yet, the attempt itself revealed clearly that the Arab–Israeli conflict was integrally linked to developments in the Persian Gulf and that the Gulf states were willing to use their oil reserves as a source of leverage over the West. Attacks on Jews in Aden following the war confirmed

35. Kemp, "Strategy and Arms Levels," 33–35.

36. Wolfgang Hager, "Western Europe: The Politics of Muddling Through," in J.C. Hurewitz, ed., *Oil, the Arab–Israel Dispute and the Industrial World—Horizons of Crisis* (Boulder, CO: Westview Press, 1976), 34–37.

37. Hans Maull, "The Strategy of Avoidance: Europe's Middle East Policies after the October War," in Hurewitz, *Oil*, 111.

the spread of pan-Arab sentiment to the Arabian peninsula.[38] The embargo also set the stage for repeated challenges to the structure of Western oil interests in producing countries. Algeria in 1968 and Iran in 1969 attempted unsuccessfully to increase their percentage interest in oil companies operating in their territories. Then, in 1971, the Algerians and Libyans succeeded in partially nationalizing the oil industry on their territories, claiming the shares of French and British companies, respectively.[39] This set in motion a chain of nationalization efforts, most of which came to fruition after the 1973 October War. In any case, it was becoming increasingly clear to the major oil companies and to Western governments that the task of securing access to Middle East oil was no longer under the firm control of the importing states.

Closely related to the issues of controlling oil production and the ultimate political independence of the Gulf states was the British decision of 1968 to withdraw its forces from the Persian Gulf. Stimulated by its failure to reach a peaceful solution to the Palestinian question in 1948 and by the Suez debacle, Britain during the 1960s was forced to rethink the feasibility of maintaining a permanent presence in the Gulf. The British also faced increasingly violent resentment of their presence on the peninsula. These successive setbacks, combined with domestic economic problems, led the Labour government under Harold Wilson to announce that Britain would withdraw its troops from the Persian Gulf by 1971.

As far as the United States was concerned, removal of British troops was not in itself the most crucial consequence of Britain's decision. It was the network of political relationships that the British had developed in the Gulf that would be the most difficult to replace. The key question was whether the Gulf states would plunge into war as a result of the numerous territorial and religious disputes that had been held at bay by an external third party. Had a "power vacuum" been created? Would either the United States or the Soviet Union attempt to move into the Gulf after the British withdrawal? Could U.S. initiatives maintain the stability that quiet British diplomacy had achieved? Whatever the answers to these questions, a change in the status quo was unavoidable, and officials in Washington became a captive audience of events in the Gulf.

The fourth development highlighting the strategic importance of the Gulf area was the increasing attention devoted by both superpowers to the Indian Ocean. In 1968, the United States, through the deployment of the Polaris A-3 submarine-launched missile, acquired the capability to target the Soviet homeland from submarines operating in the Indian Ocean. Although it is not clear that the Soviets were reacting specifically to the new U.S. capability, the

38. See Sir David Lee, *Flight from the Middle East—A History of the Royal Air Force in the Arabian Peninsula and Adjacent Territories 1945–1972* (London: HMSO, 1980) 234–240.

39. Stephen Krasner, *Defending the National Interest* (Princeton, NJ: Princeton University Press, 1978), 248.

Kremlin did increase its naval activity in the region. In 1968, Soviet vessels spent 1900 ship-days in the Indian Ocean. This figure increased steadily in successive years: 4100 ship-days in 1969, 5000 in 1970, and 9000 in 1973.[40] The logistical difficulties in maintaining a forward presence led the Soviet Union to comb the region for forward bases and ports of call. It succeeded in the late 1960s and early 1970s in securing access to naval facilities in Aden, Somalia, and Mauritius. The United States responded primarily by expanding its facilities on Diego Garcia.

The key point is that at the same time that the British decided to withdraw from the Gulf, Soviet–American naval rivalry expanded to the Indian Ocean. The issues at stake were no longer limited to gaining political influence in the Gulf area or establishing a regional balance of power, but now potentially included the defense of the Soviet homeland from sea-based nuclear forces. The Persian Gulf and Indian Ocean littoral were simultaneously placed into the strategic mainstream of the Cold War and given top priority as an area of growing political uncertainty. It was under these volatile conditions that the Soviet Union and the United States approached the Gulf after 1968.

The Nixon Administration

When Richard Nixon became President in 1969, the internal political structure of the Middle East as well as the region's role in global affairs were in a great state of flux. One of the tasks facing his administration was to incorporate the four considerations just discussed into a new policy toward Southwest Asia. Yet, in light of America's involvement in Vietnam, America's global security posture was changing as well. And, as during the administrations of his predecessors, Nixon's approach to the Middle East was heavily influenced by U.S.–Soviet relations and by developments in other areas. Thus, before looking at the details of his Middle East policy, it is necessary to examine the impact of both the Vietnam War and the emergence of détente upon America's military strategy in the Third World.

By 1970, there was widespread support throughout the U.S. government as well as the populace at large for the total withdrawal of American troops from Vietnam. America's looming failure in Southeast Asia had also seriously damaged the country's image both at home and abroad. This perceived decline in American power and influence meant that Nixon could not politically afford to withdraw into an isolationist position as America withdrew from Vietnam. To reassure allies about the strength of Washington's commitment and to re-

40. Gary Sick, "The Evolution of U.S. Strategy toward the Indian Ocean and Persian Gulf Regions," in Alvin Rubinstein, *The Great Game: Rivalry in the Persian Gulf and South Asia* (New York: Praeger, 1983), 56.

build domestic confidence, President Nixon in 1969 formally expressed the new direction of American foreign policy for the 1970s. Embodied in the Nixon Doctrine, the formulation contained three central points:

> First, the United States will keep all of its treaty commitments.
> Second, we shall provide a shield if a nuclear power threatens the freedom of a nation allied with us or of a nation whose survival we consider vital to our security.
> Third, in cases involving other types of aggression, we shall furnish military and economic assistance when requested in accordance with our treaty commitments. But we shall look to the nation directly threatened to assume the primary responsibility of providing the manpower for its defense.[41]

Made perfectly clear was Nixon's commitment to maintain a nuclear capability sufficient to deter outright aggression by the Soviet Union or China. Made equally evident, however, was that with the exception of its contribution to NATO and its permanent presence in the Pacific, the United States was recalling its troops and turning to the state directly threatened to "provide manpower for its defense."

It is as illuminating to examine what the Nixon Doctrine omitted as to study what it contained. Missing from the rhetoric of the Eisenhower days was the preoccupation with "International Communism." In its place was a pledge to defend areas "vital to our security." Nor was Nixon specifying new areas of crucial concern to the United States, as both Truman and Eisenhower had done. Rather, he was reaffirming America's intention to act according to existing treaty commitments. Finally, the emphasis on using surrogates to maintain the status quo presented a stark contrast to Eisenhower's declaration to use armed force "to secure and protect the territorial integrity and political independence" of friendly nations. The use of what appears to be language of appeasement is in part a reflection of the plight of the Nixon administration in Vietnam. A far greater force shaping the wording of the doctrine, however, was the nature of America's changing relationship with the Soviet Union.

It is difficult to pinpoint when the concept of détente became a motive force in American foreign policy. There is no doubt, however, that the establishment of a new dialogue with Moscow was a primary objective of the new administration under President Nixon and his national security adviser, Henry Kissinger. The conditions allowing for a relaxation in relations between the two superpowers were numerous: Relative nuclear parity, America's embroglio in Vietnam, weakness in the Soviet economy, and the Kremlin's concerns about China's tilt toward the United States were all key factors. The fabric of détente itself was equally broad; increased trade, numerous summit meetings, and the SALT I agreement were some of the more visible consequences.

41. For the full text of the policy statement, see Richard Nixon, *United States Foreign Policy for the 1970s: A New Strategy for Peace* (Washington, DC: GPO, 1970).

To draw links between these developments and U.S. policy toward the Middle East is, on the first level of analysis, quite straightforward. A reduction in U.S.–Soviet tension on a global scale meant a similar reduction within specific theaters. The United States and the Soviet Union did sign the Basic Principles Agreement in 1972 in which both parties agreed to exercise restraint in third area conflicts. And given the extent to which U.S. policy in the Middle East had fluctuated with perceptions of Soviet intentions, détente, at the least, made possible a more flexible American stance.

It is also possible, however, to identify those specific aspects of détente that affected the Nixon administration's approach to Southwest Asia. Central to Kissinger's understanding of the process of détente was the concept of linkage: that Soviet–American rapproachment could take place only through a comprehensive restructuring of the relationship between the superpowers. To negotiate on nuclear arms reduction while ignoring superpower competition in the Third World would be futile. By insisting upon this point, the United States hoped to impose an element of restraint upon the Soviets in areas outside Europe. The Soviets were more interested in arms negotiations and grain deals than they were in solidifying their influence in the Arab world. By placing such disparate issues in the same basket, as it were, the concept of linkage was to ensure a more restrained Soviet approach to the Middle East. The Nixon Doctrine, in return, was an indication to the Soviets that American troops would be spending less time in the Third World than in the 1960s.

The noticeable reduction in confrontational statements and actions associated with détente also provided the Nixon administration an opportunity to clarify the distinction between threats and interests. Although the level of America's involvement and hence its stakes in the Middle East rose steadily after the mid-1960s, its key interests changed only in emphasis. The United States in 1970 still wanted to contain the Soviet Union, secure access to oil supplies, and maintain Israeli military superiority. Yet, in the 1950s and 1960s, these specific interests were too often submerged in a preoccupation with the perceived spread of Soviet-backed Arab nationalism. There was a chronic tendency to base policy on directly containing Soviet influence and isolating radical regimes rather than on addressing the regional political divisions that ultimately gave the Soviets footholds in the Middle East. As the perceived Soviet threat subsided with the emergence of détente, the Nixon administration was able to focus on American interests more within the context of regional politics than under the shadow of Soviet expansionism.

Finally, the flood of negotiations and summit meetings that were at the core of détente restored American confidence in the potential for initiatives in the political realm. Success in negotiations with Moscow was reflected in increased diplomatic efforts in the Middle East. The Rogers Plan, the Israeli–Egyptian disengagement, Kissinger's shuttle diplomacy, and the Camp David Accords—

these were all manifestations of an unprecedented effort on the part of the United States to maintain stability in the region through political means.

How were these more abstract considerations reflected in Nixon's approach to security in the Middle East? When the President proclaimed that the United States "shall look to the nation directly threatened to assume the primary responsiblity of providing the manpower for its defense," he was laying the foundation for the "Vietnamization" of the war in Southeast Asia. The task of fighting the Viet Cong was to fall increasingly on the shoulders of the South Vietnamese themselves. Yet, this component of the Nixon Doctrine also formed the core of U.S. policy toward the Persian Gulf. Nixon's "twin pillar" policy centered on providing military and economic assistance to pro-Western states in the Gulf, with Iran to assume chief responsibility for regional security.

One of the most remarkable aspects of recent history in the Gulf was that the British withdrawal was followed by a period of relative peace. The departure of British political advisers and troops exposed numerous festering disputes, leading many in the West to believe that a series of local wars would break out. The principal disputes, most of which were over territory, were between Iran and Iraq, Iran and Bahrain, Iraq and Kuwait, and Saudi Arabia and Abu Dhabi. Two considerations kept these sources of conflict from exploding. First, the regional actors themselves were acutely aware of the potential for outside intervention. They therefore wanted to avoid the outbreak of hostilities, as conflict could well have stimulated superpower involvement.[42] This factor led Gulf leaders to take more conciliatory approaches to their disputes and, in some cases, to resolve them through negotiation.

Second, success in reaching negotiated settlements was in large part due to the diplomatic efforts of Britain. Not only did the British leave behind an extensive communications and intelligence infrastructure, but they also served as arbitrators in many of the disputes.[43] In addition to addressing specific grievances, the British sought to encourage cooperative security agreements among local states in order both to temper animosities and to reduce competition among neighboring states for military supremacy. This approach was most successful in the lower Gulf, where the British were able to secure a degree of political cohesion through the formation of the United Arab Emirates. As far as Iran, Iraq, and Saudi Arabia were concerned, however, such attempts at regional cooperation were far less successful. The obstacles to effecting joint security arrangements among these states were formidable; relations were strained by deep-rooted religious and political divisions. Each feared domination by the other and sought to increase its own military strength. The Iraqis proposed an

42. James Noyes, *The Clouded Lens—Persian Gulf Security and U.S. Policy*, Hoover Publication 206 (Stanford, CA: Hoover Institution Press, 1979), 26–27.

43. See Rouhollah Ramazani, "The Settlement of the Bahrain Dispute," in *Indian Journal of International Law*, vol. 12, no. 1, 1972. See also Noyes, *The Clouded Lens*, 26.

Arab Defense Organization in 1970, yet the smaller states feared being swept into broader regional conflicts. Because of their common ties to the United States, a pact between Iran and Saudi Arabia was a logical proposition. Yet, Iran's relationship with Israel, its non-Arab population, and its membership in CENTO were chief obstacles preventing the Saudis from gaining wider Arab support for such formal cooperation.

The most telling hindrance to a cooperative regional system initiated by the British was that they could not offer what many Gulf states wanted most: security. Britain was departing from, not moving into, the region. She had neither the political leverage nor the sheer military power to provide threatened regimes with the assurances they sought. The Gulf states trusted neither their neighbors nor the durability of political solutions; they wanted the military capability to defend themselves. This yearning was ripe for exploitation by the Soviets and Americans, both of whom were seeking to secure allies in a region that was of growing strategic importance following Britain's departure. As a result, the arms race that the British had so carefully tried to prevent gradually took shape in the Gulf between 1967 and 1973, fueled by America's new policy toward the region.

The earliest formulation of Nixon's twin pillar policy was contained in National Security Study Memorandum (NSSM) 66 (1969). During the 1960s, both Iran and Saudi Arabia had made requests for U.S. weaponry to meet their local security needs. NSSM 66 recommended increased sales to Iran and Saudi Arabia to enable them both to deter Soviet advances into the region and to maintain stability among the littoral states. Although U.S. sales to these two countries began well before the twin pillar policy, in 1969 the amount of weaponry sold to Iran and Saudi Arabia began to mount. Despite the reference to two "pillars," Iran was clearly the favored recipient and received weaponry of a much higher quality than did Saudi Arabia. In 1972, President Nixon issued a carte blanche to the Shah, allowing him to purchase virtually any type of armament that he desired.[44] During 1973 and 1974, for example, the Shah purchased from the United States 108 F-4s, 141 F-5Es, 4 surveillance aircraft, 6 tankers, and a number of other smaller planes and helicopters. Over the same period, U.S. sales to the Saudis included 30 F-5Es, 20 F-5Bs, and 4 transport aircraft.[45] This clear preference for Iran emerged for two reasons. First, the Shah was indebted to the CIA for returning him to power and since 1953 had become a trusted ally of successive administrations. Second, Iran's high level of modernization and large population allowed for more rapid and broad military growth than was possible in Saudi Arabia. While a large Iranian military did not significantly

---

44. U.S. Congress, Senate, Foreign Relations Committee, *U.S. Military Sales to Iran* (Washington, DC: GPO, 1976), 5.

45. See Stockholm International Peace Research Institute, *World Armaments and Disarmament, SIPRI Yearbook 1974* (Cambridge, MA: MIT Press, 1974), 267–271.

threaten the Shah, rapid growth in the Saudi armed forces could have presented a challenge to the ruling family.

In an interview in 1973, the Shah enumerated his forces' main military responsibilities: to combat domestic opposition, to deter a Soviet advance into Iran, to maintain the political status quo in the Gulf, to suppress radical Arab elements, and to guard the sea lanes vital to the continued flow of oil.[46] Though the Shah was speaking to an American audience and no doubt clearing the way for his unimpeded arms purchases, he did substantially increase Iran's military presence throughout the Gulf. Iranian ships began to patrol the Straits of Hormuz and the Shah sent forces to Oman to assist in repressing a leftist rebellion in the Dhofar region.[47] As far as Iran's relationship with the Soviet Union was concerned, the Shah was wary of Soviet unwillingness to abrogate a treaty signed in 1921 which gave Moscow the right to intervene should Iranian territory be threatened by a foreign power. Under these circumstances, the Shah demonstrated that he could and indeed would make good use of American weaponry, encouraging the United States to continue what appeared to be a favorable arrangement providing for Gulf security without the presence of American soldiers.

Though Iran was the primary beneficiary of the twin pillar policy, requests from other Gulf states were by no means neglected. Saudi Arabia received substantial assistance in the modernization of its forces. The aim was not to build a second state capable of policing the Gulf, but to enhance the Saudis' ability to confront both internal and external threats to their security. To prevent the emergence of a military elite that could challenge the authority of the ruling family, two separate institutions—the armed forces and the national guard—were developed. Kuwait and Oman also received American weaponry in the early 1970s, although the Kuwaitis were careful to maintain a concurrent arms relationship with both France and the Soviet Union. By arming only Iran and Saudi Arabia, the United States might have pushed other states in the region to rely exclusively on Soviet weaponry. Thus, while Iran was America's main card, sales to other Gulf states were meant to foster regional stability and prevent the Soviet Union from gaining further points of access.[48]

The twin pillar policy incorporated several key assumptions that were prevalent in American strategic thinking at the beginning of the 1970s. The impact of America's involvement in Vietnam was evident. The cost of the war in terms of lives and dollars and its emerging futility virtually precluded any direct escalation of America's military commitment to the Gulf. On the other hand, the British withdrawal, the West's rising dependency on Middle East oil, the deploy-

46. Interview with the Shah in *Newsweek*, 21 May 1973, 40–44.
47. For details of the Dhofar revolt see Gulf Committee, *Documents of the National Struggle in Oman and the Arabian Gulf*, 9 June Studies (London, 1974).
48. U.S. Congress, House, Foreign Affairs Committee, *The Persian Gulf, 1974: Money, Politics, Arms and Power* (Washington, DC: GPO, 1974), 64–66.

ment of the Polaris A-3 missile, and the impact of the 1967 War meant that the region was of growing strategic importance.

The initiatives devised by the Nixon administration reflected increasing concern about the strategic situation in the Gulf, yet also showed a rising awareness of political nuances within the Middle East. Iran was to maintain regional stability through its military power while Saudi Arabia was to become a more dominant force in moderate Arab politics. The administration also exhibited an adroit diplomatic approach to the Arab–Israeli conflict. The 1967 War had led to two key changes in the situation: The Soviets aligned themselves with the Palestinian cause and the Israelis seized considerable territory. Although the administration introduced the Rogers Plan to stimulate negotiation on the return of the occupied territories, Nixon's overall strategy, partly because of disagreements in Washington, turned out to be one of delay. Henry Kissinger and others argued that the Soviets would not be able to provide the Arabs what they most wanted: the return of territories. Over time, Soviet impotence would become evident to those states relying on the Kremlin's political weight. The United States, therefore, need only wait for Soviet influence in the region to wane. In Kissinger's own words, "a prolonged stalemate . . . would move the Arabs toward moderation and the Soviets to the fringes of Middle East diplomacy."[49] Given the split that emerged between Egypt and the Soviet Union in the early 1970s, this assessment proved to be quite accurate.

As arms sales were one of the key instruments of American policy after 1968, it seems appropriate to digress momentarily on the nature of military sales as a foreign policy tool. Until 1967, there were three principal motives for sales to the Middle East: to foster political ties, to serve as a quid pro quo for bases, and to improve the seller's balance of trade while lowering production costs per unit. Increasingly throughout the 1950s and 1960s, financial considerations were the primary stimulant for British and French sales.[50] The Soviets and Americans, however, sought to enlist client states and to pressure recipients into granting access to military bases. The Soviet Union pressed much harder on the bases issue, building facilities in Yemen, Egypt, Syria, and Iraq, while the United States had limited access agreements for the use of Dhahran and Bahrain. This imbalance was partly a result of the lower long term sustainability of Soviet ships as well as Moscow's desire to counter America's capability to deploy strategic submarines in both the Mediterranean and the Indian Ocean.[51]

49. See Henry Kissinger, *Years of Upheaval* (London: Weidenfeld and Nicholson and Michael Joseph, 1982), 195–205. The quotation is from p. 196.

50. Robert Harkavy, "Strategic Access, Bases and Arms Transfers: The Major Powers Evolving Geopolitical Competition in the Middle East," in Milton Leitenberg and Gabriel Sheffer, eds., *Great Power Intervention in the Middle East* (New York: Pergamon, 1979), 181.

51. Michael MccGwire and John McDonnell, eds., *Soviet Naval Influence—Domestic and Foreign Dimensions* (New York: Praeger, 1977), 653.

Between 1967 and 1973, both the motivations behind arms sales and their impact on regional politics became increasingly complex. Rather than focusing primarily on the leverage derived from arms sales, U.S. policy sought to achieve closer integration between political aims and strategic requirements. In American military jargon, the goal of "influence through arms" was superseded by the ambiguous concepts of "stability" and "balance of power." As these terms consistently appear in American policy statements on the Middle East, it is worth attempting to decipher them.[52] Stability adopted four distinct meanings. First, weapons were sold to a pro-West regime to improve its defense capabilities against a radical or pro-Soviet regime. Stable conditions prevailed when an American ally could deter if not repel an aggressor. Second, stability referred to the political durability of a specific regime. The Saudi government, for example, was given arms to strengthen its forces and hence its legitimacy in the eyes of the public. It was not the capability of the forces itself that was important, but that the government be able to make visible its military power. Third, stability entailed the ability to counter subversion or sabotage, whether by foreign elements or domestic opposition. This usually involved training and equipping the security forces of the recipient state. Finally, the term referred to the maintenance of a consistent relationship between patron and client. An example of this usage involved U.S. arms sales to Saudi Arabia and North Yemen in the mid-1970s. At the time, the United States was selling weaponry to both states. When North Yemen felt that its security needs had been subordinated to those of the Saudis, however, it turned to the Soviet Union for armaments.[53]

The term balance of power was also used to connote a wide range of meanings in the context of the Middle East. First, it referred to the emergence of pro-Western and pro-Soviet spheres in Southwest Asia and the political equilibrium that was achieved between them. It was analogous to the NATO–Warsaw Pact relationship, not in the sense of which side has how much power, but in the recognition that such spheres existed and served as a stabilizing force in the Middle East and in American and Soviet policy. Balance of power also referred to strategic competition among regional states.[54] The United States wanted to build local balances and to allow pro-West regimes to have countervailing force against pro-Soviet states. In the 1960s, the areas receiving most attention on this score were on the rim of the Gulf: the northern tier, the choke points at the Straits of Hormuz and Babel-Mandeb, and the northern Indian Ocean. Yet, after the 1967 War, such competition spread throughout the Middle East. Finally, the balance of power concept was used with respect to the Arab–Israeli

52. The following analysis reflects how these terms were used in congressional documents on Middle East policy after 1973. See the bibliography for specific citations.
53. U.S. Congress, House, Foreign Affairs Committee, *U.S. Interests in, and Policies toward the Persian Gulf, 1980* (Washington, DC: GPO, 1980), 102.
54. William Quandt in ibid., 166.

conflict. An overriding goal of U.S. arms transfer policy was to give Israel a significant edge in military capability. This consideration did not present a problem in the early 1970s, largely because those countries receiving top American weaponry were not direct opponents of Israel. Thus, the United States could maintain Israel's security while fulfilling its commitments to other states in the region. Yet, as the quality of arms sold to Saudi Arabia, Jordan, and Egypt increased later in the decade, friction emerged among these contradictory commitments.

One final point warrants mention. Though the Nixon Doctrine relied upon arming surrogates as the core of its security policy for Southwest Asia, it did not preclude the possibility of deployment of U.S. military assets to the Gulf area. The Middle East Force (MIDEASTFOR), a small flotilla stationed at Bahrain since 1949, continued to operate in Gulf waters. Though its military potential was limited, it did constitute a permanent, albeit symbolic, presence. Further, National Security Study Memorandum 104 led to the periodic deployment after 1970 of a carrier task force in the Indian Ocean. This deployment became a regular responsibility of the Atlantic Fleet and was maintained throughout the decade. There was also discussion of establishing a large naval presence in the Arabian Sea area, yet this option was rejected because of domestic opposition, the potential backlash of anticolonial sentiment following the British withdrawal, and the lack of sufficient bases for home porting.[55] It is also important to realize that the sale of arms itself established a small American presence in the region because of the technicians that accompanied any transfer. Technical Assistance Field Teams (TAFTS) brought several thousand civilians and military personnel to the Gulf states.[56] Their presence served as a psychological tie between the United States and the recipient state, if not an explicit means through which Washington could exercise influence over military operations in the host country.

Between 1968 and 1973, the United States made significant progress in developing a coherent security policy toward the Middle East. The Shah was more than willing to protect the flow of oil to the West; numerous disputes in the Gulf had been settled without hostilities; Israel had demonstrated its overwhelming military superiority in 1967; and the Soviets seemed to have gained little despite the British withdrawal. In the early 1970s, the Soviets did sign a Treaty of Friendship with Iraq and improved their relations with Kuwait. Yet, their ability to influence events in the Middle East remained limited.[57] Ameri-

55. Noyes, *Clouded Lens*, 55.
56. The number of advisers has varied greatly. In 1981, for example, there were 45,000 Americans living in Saudi Arabia with over 1,000 working directly with the Saudi armed forces (*Guardian Weekly*, 8 March 1981).
57. Aryeh Yodfat, *The Soviet Union and the Arabian Peninsula—Soviet Policy Toward the Persian Gulf and Arabia* (London: Croom Helm, 1983), 26.

can officials continued to doubt that the Soviets would risk direct confrontation over the Gulf, and Moscow likewise was well aware of America's post-Vietnam retreat. The attitude of the Nixon administration was reflected in a National Security Study Memorandum issued in 1972. This document stressed nonintervention in the affairs of other nations, support of regional friends, and adherence to the Moscow Summit principles to avoid confrontation with the Soviets.[58] As late as 1973, conventional wisdom in the State Department was that "we do not think the Soviets are seeking any direct confrontation with us in the Gulf area."[59]

Conclusions

Between 1946 and 1973, America's interests in the Middle East remained quite consistent: to contain Soviet political and military advances into the region, to secure access to adequate supplies of oil from the Persian Gulf, and to support Israeli security. The United States pursued these aims through four broad policy instruments: the use of diplomatic and economic incentives to mold the political orientation of local states; the offering of military hardware both to gain influence in the region and to shape the regional balance of power; the creation of regional security pacts and alliances to foster stability; and the use of American military power both to support allies and to deter intraregional aggression. Given the consistency of America's national interests over this period, the challenge that emerges is to explain the shifts in policy that occurred to protect those interests. This will be done by examining policy within the context of two conceptual issues set forth in the introduction: strategy versus capability and globalism versus regionalism.

During the first two postwar decades, American security policy toward Southwest Asia was not constrained by limited military capability. There was a consensus within successive administrations that the preservation of "stability" in the Middle East required a minimal direct allocation of military resources. This consensus emerged for several reasons. The British presence in the Persian Gulf, though a budding source of anticolonial sentiment, played a key role in suppressing regional strife. Among the eastern Mediterranean states, Israel managed to maintain military superiority over its Arab neighbors; the United States engaged in the arms trade primarily to secure political leverage and did not, until the late 1960s, play a crucial role in shaping the intraregional balance of power. The United States perceived the Soviet Union as presenting the key threat to American interests in the region, but was concerned primarily about the spread of

58. Noyes, *Clouded Lens*, 53.
59. Joseph Sisco in U.S. Congress, House, Foreign Affairs Committee, *New Perspectives on the Persian Gulf* (Washington, DC: GPO, 1973), 7.

political influence, not the potential for military intervention. Increasing Soviet leverage could indeed have led to adverse strategic and economic consequences. Yet, the measures required to address indirect Soviet advances differed from those required to cope with Soviet forces.

This preoccupation with the political nature of the Soviet threat clearly emerges when comparing America's response to the nationalization of the Suez Canal with its reaction to the crisis in Lebanon in 1958. Nasser's decision to nationalize the canal had potentially important strategic consequences: He had control over what vessels could use the waterway. Nevertheless, Eisenhower argued against any military countermeasures. In Lebanon in 1958, no specific strategic assets were at stake. Rather, the American decision to intervene was based upon a vision of Soviet-inspired Arab nationalism sweeping the Middle East. The purpose of the Marine contingent sent to Beirut was to offer visible support to Chamoun, not to secure strategic objectives. As long as the political orientation of the region as a whole was not at stake, the Eisenhower administration saw no need to commit U.S. troops. Throughout the 1950s and 1960s, then, successive administrations assumed that they could secure their objectives in the region without, except in extreme circumstances, calling upon U.S. forces.

It is important to note that the United States, if it had desired to commit more forces to the Middle East, had the capabilities to do so. In broad terms, the two Democratic administrations examined above favored higher defense spending and a more aggressive U.S. role in the periphery, while the Republican administrations favored a decrease in the manpower and resources allocated to America's regional missions. This budgetary trend had a much greater effect on declaratory policy than on military capability. Eisenhower, despite his reliance on massive retaliation and his overall military retrenchment, was the one president to commit forces to the Middle East in the postwar area. Eisenhower's retrenchment did not diminish the ability of the armed forces to intervene globally; since the Korean War, the United States has maintained forces-in-being sufficient to support a major operation in the periphery. Budgetary constraints did, however, affect force structure. The Truman, Eisenhower, and Kennedy administrations each considered establishing an elite unit for intervention in the Third World. It was not until 1961 that Kennedy established the Strike Command. Even then, training and procurement for operations in the periphery were neglected; each service resisted assuming a regional role, preferring to devote its expenditures toward central front missions. The United States had sufficient forces to fight in the Middle East. The problem, soon to become apparent, was that few planners were addressing how to get forces to the area or what these troops would do upon arrival.

This relative complacency about America's strategic position in the Middle East lasted until the late 1960s. The 1967 War, the British decision to withdraw from the Gulf, and the militarization of the Indian Ocean meant that more attention had to be devoted to America's military posture in the region. The Nixon administration faced the options of strengthening the U.S. presence in the region—in effect attempting to replace the British—or appointing and arming regional surrogates. In choosing the latter option, Nixon was responding more to the political constraints placed on policy by the Vietnam War than to the emergence of new military missions in the Gulf itself. America's emerging strategic dependence on Iran was an extension to the Gulf of the strategy of "Vietnamization" devised to disengage the United States from Southeast Asia. Arming regional powers with sophisticated weaponry had inherent dangers that were to become manifest by the late 1970s. But this approach met America's immediate strategic objectives and fell within the confines of political acceptability as shaped by the war in Vietnam.

The picture that emerges of America's approach to the Gulf reveals a policy that is quite sensitive to shifts in U.S. grand strategy and global perspectives, yet significantly less attuned to shifts in the strategic and political environment within the Gulf itself. To restate the problem, U.S. policy was predominantly global rather than regional in its orientation. This meant that the single most important factor shaping policy between 1946 and 1973 was Washington's perception of Moscow's intentions and of the general state of U.S.–Soviet relations. The Truman Doctrine, the Baghdad Pact, CENTO, the Eisenhower Doctrine—the key policy initiatives—were all reactions to perceived shifts in the nature of the Soviet threat. American perceptions of political developments within the Arab world focused primarily on the orientation of the region as a whole, not on specific events at the state or substate level. The rise of Nasser was not perceived as a threat to American interests, but the spread of pan-Arabism was. Similarly, Washington viewed the coup in Iraq and the potential fall of Chamoun in Lebanon not in terms of the indigenous forces at play, but in terms of a shift in the ideological and political orientation of the region as a whole. The United States gradually cultivated a more delicate approach to internal Arab politics following the emergence of "radical" and "moderate" coalitions after the 1967 War. Yet, the key point is that Washington tended to view the region as the crucial unitary actor, not individual states. This tendency proved to be costly in the 1970s when the United States became more dependent upon the cooperation of specific Gulf states to secure its interests in the Middle East.

This neglect of intraregional considerations must also be understood within the context of the relative strategic importance of the Middle East to the United States. Southwest Asia was assigned a relatively low priority in comparison with other peripheral areas. While the United States established a permanent military presence and fought two wars in East Asia, it devoted few resources and relatively little attention to the Middle East. This is quite understandable in light of the guidelines set forth by the policy of containment. Communism never really took root in the Arab world; regimes aligned with Moscow accepted Soviet arms, but not Soviet ideology. Nor were there communist powers similar to the North Koreans or the North Vietnamese threatening to move into Southwest Asia. Furthermore, it was not until 1973 that the United States came to terms with the vulnerability created by Western dependence on Persian Gulf oil. Before the 1970s, Middle East oil was indeed seen as an essential commodity. The potential for producer states to deny the West access to this resource, however, had not been fully confronted. These considerations relegated the Middle East to an area of only peripheral interest until the October War.

Between 1946 and the late 1960s, U.S. security policy toward the Gulf reflected the consistency that characterized America's post-war grand strategy. The brand of containment that emerged under Truman found broad support in the following two administrations. Preoccupation with Soviet communism forged a bipartisan consensus on foreign policy that relied, with some degree of variation, upon symmetrical containment and perimeter defense. In the 1950s and 1960s, the United States indeed had a vision of grand strategy which informed its approach to the periphery. Until the 1970s, this strategy, and the means available to implement it, were sufficient to cope with the challenges to U.S. interests confronted in the Middle East. The long term problem, however, was that this strategy depended upon two assumptions: that the defense of U.S. interests in Southwest Asia required little direct allocation of military resources, and that the Soviet Union presented the dominant threat to those interests. Reliance on these assumptions meant that U.S. policy lacked a clear means of implementation if large numbers of U.S. forces were needed in the Middle East. It also left the United States ill-prepared to deal with threats other than those posed by the Soviet Union. By the end of 1973, the crucial threat to U.S. interests was not a shift in Soviet behavior, but rather the profound strategic and political implications of the October War. The challenge to American policy came from within the Gulf itself and in a way and on an order of magnitude never thought possible.

Chapter Three

THE OCTOBER WAR
AND ITS AFTERMATH

The 1973 Arab–Israeli War deeply altered both intraregional and superpower relations in the Middle East. This study is concerned specifically with how this event reshaped U.S. perceptions of its strategic position in the region and laid the foundation for American policy in the Middle East until 1979. Within this context there are four essential points that require elaboration: the emergence of the "oil weapon" and its economic and political impact on the Arab and Western world, the enhancement of American diplomatic leverage in the Middle East, the reaction of the Soviet Union to its strategic and political losses in the region, and the increasing political power of the Gulf states and their growing involvement in the Arab–Israeli conflict.

For reasons soon to be discussed, the Arab oil embargo and the oil crisis associated with it were the most important consequences of the October War. In the short term, the embargo furthered the process of political unification within the Arab world and demonstrated that such political unity could challenge effectively the economic and military power of the industrialized world. This altered thinking about both the vulnerability of U.S. interests in the Middle East and the suitability of containment to protect those interests. In the long term, the oil price rises and economic turmoil that resulted from the embargo continue to have a profound impact upon the international economy and the approach of the Western world to the Middle East. For these reasons, an examination of the oil weapon will form the core of the following discussion about U.S. and Soviet reactions to the war as well as about the new role that the Gulf states played in the Arab–Israeli conflict after 1973.

The Embargo and Its Impact on U.S.–Arab Relations

Although the Arabs were by no means military victors in the 1973 War, they indeed won a psychological battle in the ongoing Middle East conflict. Their military performance against the Israelis was far more coordinated and substantial than in 1948, 1956, or 1967. In the first days of the war, the Egyptians came close to inflicting irreparable losses on the Israelis in battles in the Sinai. This contributed to a climate of unity and confidence that the Arab world had never before experienced.[1] The years of military and political frustration that had for so long polarized Arab politics began at least temporarily to fade. The so-called moderate-radical split grew less pronounced, and a tentative alliance composed of Egypt, Algeria, Saudi Arabia, and Syria took shape.[2]

The 1973 War fostered Arab cohesion for two complementary reasons. First, the war served to subordinate political divisions among Arab states to a greater pan-Arab cause. Virtually every state in the region perceived crucial political issues at stake. Egypt was in a precarious position because of the proximity of Israeli troops in the Sinai. While the Syrians bristled over the Israeli presence in the Golan Heights, the war intensified pan-Arab anger over Israel's occupation of East Jerusalem, the West Bank, and the Gaza Strip. The large Palestinian populations in states such as Jordan and Saudi Arabia placed increasing pressure upon the ruling elites to work toward an Israeli withdrawal from these territories.

The second source of cohesion follows from the fact that shared political objectives led to greater communication and cooperation among Arab states after the war. Although political and economic development within the Arab world led to growing cohesion before 1973, the war served as an infusion of activism. As the current of Arab nationalism grew in strength, so did pressure on moderate states to play a more aggressive role in regional politics. So too was there a demand for greater economic autonomy. In short, the realization that greater cohesion was possible was itself a source of unity. The Arab states recognized that they had sufficient will and political power to take collective action against the West. They used their leverage as a means of influencing both the Arab–Israeli conflict and their broader economic relations with the industrialized world.

The Arab states took their first collective step in pursuit of these interests on October 17, 1973, when Saudi Arabia, Kuwait, Abu Dhabi, Bahrain, Qatar, Iraq, Syria, Egypt, Algeria, and Libya agreed to reduce their levels of domestic oil production by 5% per month until Israel withdrew from the territories taken in 1967. Not more than three weeks later, the terms of the embargo tightened. In addition to the monthly reduction, there was to be a 25% cut in production in November and a total stoppage of all shipments to the United States and The Netherlands. These measures were implemented until March of the following year, at which time, largely through the diplomatic efforts of the United States, the Arab states lifted the embargo.

1. Hisham Sharabi, "The Arab–Israeli Conflict: The Next Phase," in Gregory Treverton, ed., *Crisis Management and the Superpowers in the Middle East* (Farnborough: Gower for the International Institute for Strategic Studies, 1981), 14. See also Leitenberg, *Intervention*, 8.
2. Sharabi, "The Arab–Israeli Conflict," 14.

With the exception of the boycott of the United States and The Nether-lands, which was circumvented by redirecting shipments, the steps taken by the Organization of Arab Petroleum Exporting Countries (OAPEC) were felt on a global scale. Inadequate supplies in Western Europe and the United States led to temporary shortages of petroleum products and irritated consumers. More impor-tant in the long term, however, were the substantial price increases that accom-panied the cutbacks in production. Between October, 1973 and January of the following year, the price of oil rose some 400%. The impact of such substantial oil price increases—both in 1973 and 1979—on the international economy was dramatic. Among industrialized nations, the rising percentages of gross national product devoted to energy supplies contributed significantly to the high unem-ployment and inflation rates of the 1970s and 1980s.[3] After the first oil shock, average inflation rates among Organization of Economic Cooperation and De-velopment (OECD) members initially rose from 5% to 13%, while unemploy-ment rates rose from 3.5% to 5.5%.[4] The flow of large revenues to the oil producers has also profoundly altered the balance of trade between the Middle Eastern states and the Western world and has stimulated a reassessment of North–South economic relations in general.

Of more immediate importance to the concerns of this study, however, is how the embargo shaped American perceptions of its interests and sources of influence in the Middle East. In 1956 and 1967, Arab states had attempted to deny the West access to their oil supplies. Given the strength of the oil com-panies, the elasticity of supplies on the open market, and sharing among the Western powers, these attempted embargoes were unsuccessful. By 1973, the situation had changed dramatically. When the Saudis demanded an increase in their control over the Arabian–American Oil Company (Aramco), the U.S. government and the company itself were forced to acquiesce.[5] Tight market conditions at the time meant that cutbacks in production were readily translated into shortages of supply.[6] And most importantly, the American and European

3. David Deese and Linda Miller, "Western Europe," in David Deese and Joseph Nye, eds., *Energy and Security* (Cambridge, MA: Ballinger, 1981), 184–185.

4. Stanley Black, "Learning from Adversity: Policy Responses to Two Oil Shocks," Essays in International Finance, No. 160 (Princeton: Department of Economics, Princeton University, Dec. 1985), 5. After the second oil shock, the average inflation rate rose from 8% to 13% and the rate of unemployment from 5 to 8½%.

5. For specific examples of U.S. acquiescence to Saudi demands, see U.S. Congress, Senate, Foreign Relations Committee, *Multinational Corporations and United States Foreign Policy* (Wash-ington, DC: GPO, 1974), pt. 7.

6. Panic buying reduced stocks that could have cushioned the impact of the decreased produc-tion. See William Quandt, *Saudi Arabia's Oil Policy* (Washington, DC: Brookings Institution, 1982), 15. For an excellent study of the impact of demand on oil prices, see Daniel Badger and Robert Belgrave, "Oil Supply and Price: What Went Right in 1980?" Energy Paper No. 2 (London: Policy Studies Institute and the Royal Institute of International Affairs, 1982).

response to the looming crisis was both uncoordinated and ineffectual. In their attempts to secure access to oil, the members of the Western alliance acted more out of unbridled self-interest than concern for the collective welfare. The *sauve qui peut* attitude that prevailed served to enhance the impact of the embargo; consuming countries battled for supplies on the spot market, reducing stocks and driving prices higher. Even on a domestic basis, few corrective steps were taken to reduce consumption.[7] Part of the reason for this complacency was that between 1975 and 1979, the price of oil declined in real terms.[8] Further, U.S. oil companies benefited from the rise in OPEC's prices simply because it made domestic production much more profitable. Before 1973, the oil companies had pressed for high oil prices and import quotas to support the search for and tapping of domestic resources.[9] Nevertheless, the glaring absence of efforts in Western Europe and the United States to reduce dependence on Persian Gulf oil reflected the inability of the Western states individually or collectively to respond adequately to the embargo and its economic consequences.

The United States did consider the possibility of military action to secure the flow of oil from the Gulf. It was not until late 1974 that talk of the feasibility of an operation to seize oil fields surfaced within the administration. Defense Secretary Schlesinger, Secretary of State Kissinger, and Senator Jesse Helms were among those who publicly discussed the concept of military intervention by U.S. ground forces.[10] In 1975 the Congressional Research Service (CRS) published a controversial report entitled "Oilfields as Military Objectives, A Feasibility Study."[11] Although there is little evidence that an attempt to seize forcibly the oil fields was imminent, that Congress requested such a study indicated that the Department of Defense was considering some type of military operation in the Gulf itself. The CRS report concluded, however, that it would be extremely difficult to take control of the oil fields without destroying the pumping sites and refineries in the process.

As the options available in the energy and security realms appeared to be limited, the United States relied primarily on diplomatic initiatives to respond to the 1973 War and the embargo. After 1973, U.S. relations with Saudi Arabia and other states in the Gulf were to undergo radical changes. The U.S. govern-

7. President Nixon did take steps to encourage research in alternative energy and to reduce consumption of certain types of fuel.

8. From 1975 to 1979, prices rose from $10.46 to $13.34 per barrel. With inflation, this change represents a 4% decline. Robert Stobaugh and Daniel Yergin, "Energy—An Emergency Telescoped," *Foreign Affairs*, Annual Review (vol. 58, no. 3), 564.

9. For a good study of U.S. import policy, see Edward Sheffer, *The Oil Import Program of the United States: An Evaluation* (New York: Praeger, 1968).

10. See, for example, Henry Kissinger, *Business Week Magazine*, 13 January 1975, 66–76, or Jesse Helms, "Misjudgments in the Middle East," *Congressional Record*, 23 January 1975, 1103–1105.

11. Congressional Research Service, *Oilfields as Military Objectives, A Feasibility Study*, (Washington, DC: GPO, 1975).

ment was well aware that the Arab world had gained a great deal of economic leverage over the West; America therefore had to seek new ways to restore its own sources of influence in the Middle East. Yet, a significant problem had to be overcome: The embargo had undermined traditional assumptions about the nature of North–South relations. The decline of European colonialism had reduced the structural dependency of Third World countries on the industrialized world. By the 1970s, principles of self-determination and economic autonomy had, at least nominally, taken hold. Yet, the industrialized West continued to use its preponderance of economic and military power to shape its ties with less developed states. Rulers in the Middle East had indeed attempted to assert their political and economic autonomy; successive efforts to nationalize oil companies were clear examples. Yet, the oil embargo was a challenge on a different order of magnitude. A coordinated act on the part of Arab oil-producing states illuminated the vulnerability of the West's economy and bred a collective sense of impotence within the industrialized world. The military power of the United States appeared paradoxically ineffective, nor could the economic strength of the West be readily used to counter the embargo.

The impact of the war on the political climate in the Arab world offered the United States its first new source of influence. The crucial role of the United States in the war itself was evident to both combatants. The Israelis were indebted to the Americans for the airlift without which they could well have suffered a crushing defeat.[12] Likewise, when the Israelis were poised to destroy the Egyptian Third Army in the Sinai, it was America's diplomatic pressure that restrained them.[13] Arab leaders recognized well before 1973 the exclusive potential of the United States to influence Israeli policy. In March of 1970, President Sadat informed General Secretary Brezhnev and Prime Minister Kosygin, "I've told the Americans that if they can put pressure on the Israelis to play their part I'm ready to establish diplomatic relations with the US"[14] Two years later, Sadat in fact elected to expel the Soviets from Egypt and turned to the United States for military aid. The superiority of U.S. weaponry and Washington's multilateral negotiating position were clear advantages over alignment with the Soviet Union. Kissinger aptly described this predicament: "The Arabs may despise us, or hate us, or loathe us, but they have learned that, if they want a settlement, they have to come to us. No one else can deliver. Three times they have relied on Russian equipment, and three times they have lost it."[15]

---

12. Abraham Ben Zvi, "Regionalism and Globalism: The Problems of American Relations Toward the Middle East, 1950–1976," *International Problems* (Fall 1976), 112.

13. Henry Kissinger, *Years of Upheaval*, 573–574.

14. Sadat, cited in Mohammed Heikal, *Sphinx and Commissar—The Rise and Fall of Soviet Influence in the Arab World* (London: Collins, 1978), 222.

15. Kissinger, *Years of Upheaval*, 578.

A change in the structure of diplomatic contact between the United States and Arab regimes also enhanced Washington's influence in the Gulf. The long term presence of British, French, and American oil companies in the Gulf served to obviate the need for diplomatic contact between Washington and producer states. As discussed previously, successive U.S. administrations supported the presence of oil companies as a means of exercising political influence. The lack of governmental contacts was also a clear indication of the low strategic priority assigned to some of the the smaller Gulf states. The oil companies essentially served as interlocuters: In the months preceding the oil embargo, the Saudis relied heavily on Aramco executives to warn the U.S. government of potential oil sanctions.[16]

As foreign control of oil companies in the Middle East dissipated after the October War, so did the role of these companies as intermediaries between Gulf states and the U.S. government. Yet, there is little doubt that even if this traditional channel of communication had not broken down, the United States would have strengthened diplomatic contacts in the Gulf. For obvious reasons, Washington wanted to cultivate as many channels of influence as possible. The results of this approach were evident: In 1974 Bahrain, Qatar, the United Arab Emirates, and Oman all individually received American ambassadors.

The establishment of formal ties with these Gulf states and the strengthening of the diplomatic dialogue with others indeed increased American contact with leaders in the Persian Gulf. Yet, there were also certain socioeconomic changes within the regional states themselves that, in the long term, have had a more profound impact upon their relations with external powers. The impetus for these changes was the massive influx of revenues that resulted from rapidly rising oil prices. The sudden increases in national reserves meant that the producing countries had vast resources with which to buy weaponry—a situation that complemented well Nixon's twin pillar policy. The proliferation of arms transfers stimulated by oil revenues went far beyond facilitating Washington's preferred means of securing political leverage. The extensive building of air bases and military facilities that was funded by petrodollars after 1973 has significantly altered the strategic environment in the region.[17] Local states have vastly improved their military capability and the feasibility of foreign intervention has been enhanced considerably. Were the United States to undertake a major military operation in the Gulf, for example, U.S. forces would need access to these facilities.

Though the British maintained a military presence in the Gulf for decades

16. Numerous examples of letters sent between Arab governments and oil company executives can be found in U.S. Congress, Senate, *Multinational Corporations*.

17. Accompanying these sales were the construction or improvement of facilities, airfields, and ports. This infrastructure was as important as the weaponry itself.

before their withdrawal, they depended on a quite limited communications and logistics infrastructure. Throughout the 1950s and 1960s, the United States maintained the ability to intervene with sea-based and airborne forces. Yet, it was only the Soviets, because of their proximity to the region, that could credibly threaten to introduce substantial ground forces. As already mentioned, the United States did not perceive a Soviet move toward the Gulf as at all likely. Yet, the presence of Soviet troops only several hundred miles away gave them an important strategic advantage and meant that regional states could not ignore the rhetoric or behavior of their northern neighbor. Only after the communications and logistics infrastructure funded by petrodollars had been built could the United States consider challenging Soviet will with its own presence in the Gulf. The United States could not project considerable power to Southwest Asia or conduct operations there without a military infrastructure capable of receiving and supporting U.S. forces and equipment.[18]

The skeletal military infrastructure existing in Saudi Arabia and the lower Gulf was reflective of the generally low level of economic development throughout the region. Some of the oil revenues were used to stimulate internal investment and economic growth, yet, because of low absorption capacities and limited manpower, many states turned to foreign countries for investment opportunities. The West, because of its free foreign exchange system, became a depository for billions of dollars in Arab investment. The United States and Europe were also able to provide the technical assistance that these countries sought in order to develop their own economies. It was not only the oil-producing states that benefited; Gulf regimes provided large amounts of financial assistance to other less well-endowed Arab countries. Thus, while the embargo gave the Arabs a trump card over the West (the deprivation of oil), it also led to an unprecedented degree of economic interdependence among both producer and consumer states. To the producing nations, a thriving Western economy meant high oil consumption and demand, support for high oil prices, and a secure repository for the investment of revenues. For consuming nations, access to sufficient oil supplies at reasonable prices was crucial to the strength of their economies. Arab and Western economic interests converged after 1973 in a way that could only reinforce the position of the United States in the Arab world.[19]

Concomitant with Arab aspirations to emerge as a dominant force in the international economy was a shift among Gulf states toward more pragmatic and conservative policies aimed at legitimizing the government in a traditional Western framework. This did not mean the importation of Western models of

18. This point of intangible presence arose repeatedly during interviews with officials in Washington. The concept is elaborated upon later in this chapter.

19. This point was developed by Dr. Robert Mabro, discussion at St. Antony's College, Oxford, January 1983.

democratic pluralism. Yet, it did stimulate an attempt to cultivate a standard of living and the modern military and economic institutions associated with the West. One of the few areas of ideological compatibility between the Arabs and the Soviets before the 1970s had been the nationalization and independence movements advocated by leaders such as Nasser. As oil revenues mounted, these "leftist" strains were submerged in more conservative approaches to national development.[20] States in the Arab Gulf were attracted by the prospect of joining the community of "modern" industrialized nations. To do so required not only influence in the international economy, but also the recognition and respect of those states already part of the community. In order to earn such recognition, Arab states sought to modify their traditional image of being politically and economically underdeveloped.[21]

The Soviet Reaction

Before turning to the details of U.S. policy after 1973, one final issue necessitates discussion: the reaction of the Soviet Union to the October War. Despite the erosion of Sadat's relationship with the Soviets in 1972 and 1973, Soviet weapons and personnel were involved in Egypt's attack on Israel. Such support was not surprising given the escalating nature of the superpower rivalry in the Middle East. What was unprecedented, however, was the Soviet decision to make preparations to intervene with their own forces. Intelligence reports indicated that the full complement of the Soviet airborne infrantry—50,000 troops—was mobilized for deployment to the Middle East.[22] Not only had the Soviets never before sent ground troops in significant numbers to the Middle East, they also had never exhibited the capability or willingness to airlift significant forces well beyond the Soviet periphery. The United States responded by placing its forces on alert and issuing a stern warning to the Kremlin not to intervene. A makeshift ceasefire negotiated by both the Americans and the Soviets prevented either superpower from direct involvement in the war.

As the negotiating strength of the United States became apparent during the ensuing disengagement talks, so did the declining position of the Soviet Union in the region as a whole. Egypt was both weaned from and alienated by align-

20. Adeed Dawisha, "The Soviet Union in the Arab World: The Limits to Superpower Influence," in Adeed Dawisha and Karen Dawisha, eds., *The Soviet Union in the Middle East: Policies and Perspectives* (London: Heinemann for the Royal Institute of International Affairs, 1982), 21.
21. Any discussion of the social and political impact of the oil embargo would be incomplete without mention of the destabilizing effect of modernization on the region. This constitutes a separate issue, however, that is peripheral to the present discussion. The following chapter will look more closely at the effect of rapid modernization on the stability of the Shah's regime.
22. MccGwire, *Soviet Naval Influence*, 286.

ment with Moscow: Sadat recognized America's influence over Israel and was no longer willing to respond to the Kremlin's demands for military access and political obeisance. Although Sadat did not abrogate the Soviet–Egyptian Friendship Treaty until 1976, the Kremlin's leverage in Egypt declined steadily after the October War. In strategic terms, the Soviets had lost both their most important surrogate in the Middle East and their primary naval facilities in the Mediterranean. In political terms, the Kremlin was deprived of the influence throughout the Arab world that it had wielded by association with Egypt.

The Soviet Union responded to the loss of its main client through three specific initiatives. First, the Soviets attempted to repair the political damage by polarizing the split within the Arab world between radical and moderate states. They did so by increasing their rhetorical and military support for the PLO. They recognized the national rights of the Palestinians in 1973 and called for the establishment of a Palestinian state in 1974. Second, the Soviet Union attempted to compensate for its expulsion from Egypt by strengthening its alliances with Syria, Iraq, and South Yemen. Syria and South Yemen were of crucial importance because of their port facilities at Latakia and Aden, respectively. Finally, the Soviets reacted to their lack of diplomatic success in the Middle East by focusing their attention on other regions where competition with the United States was less formidable and less volatile. These included areas contiguous to the Gulf such as the horn of Africa—the Soviet–Somalia Friendship Treaty was signed in 1974—as well as more distant regions such as central Africa and Southeast Asia. The deployment of Poseidon missiles (which could be launched from the Indian Ocean) as well as American attempts to secure access to the island of Diego Garcia heightened Soviet concerns about securing access to ports along the coast of South Asia and East Africa. On the whole, the Kremlin seemed willing to accept its weakened position in the Middle East and to rely on cementing its political ties with Syria and Iraq while focusing its attention on other regions.

Despite this trend in Soviet policy, the containment of Soviet influence continued to shape America's initiatives in the Middle East. The emerging pattern of Soviet behavior suggested that the Kremlin, if it were to attempt to destabilize the region, would do so through largely political, not military means. To ensure the stability of the area and to close the gap between radical and moderate regimes became, in American eyes, the most effective ways of countering Soviet influence. Progress on the Arab–Israeli issue would deprive the Soviets of their proclaimed cause célèbre for involvement in the region, suppress regional conflict, and enhance America's own influence in the Middle East.

The years between 1967 and 1973 also showed that the United States had to maintain an aggressive and dynamic stance in Southwest Asia. The area had been molded into a single strategic theater. The strands linking the Arab–Israeli conflict, the flow of oil, and superpower rivalry were becoming increasingly intertwined. Though the Soviets were retreating from the region, the pattern of their behavior had been one of great flexibility. They found a willing partner in Egypt only after the Baghdad Pact and Western behavior had alienated Nasser. Their support for the PLO and Arab confrontational states emerged only after the political benefits became apparent. In the words of one analyst, in the Middle East, "[o]pportunism, not ideology, impels Soviet policy."[23] The behavior of the Arab states was equally unpredictable and volatile. The 1967 War, the British withdrawal, and the October War all threw the Middle East into disarray. Following each upheaval came an episode of regional competition in which Egypt, Syria, Jordan, and the Gulf states all attempted to enhance their influence within the Arab world. Thus, although the United States by the mid-1970s was in a position of strength in the Middle East, it could not afford to relax its diplomatic initiatives toward the region.

U.S. Security Policy, 1973–1979

Despite the initial panic surrounding the 1973 war and the oil embargo, the Ford administration by mid-1974 was optimistic about its role in the Middle East and the prospects for diplomatic progress in the Arab–Israeli conflict. After decades of stiff-lipped confrontation, the United States had succeeded in luring both sides to the conference table. The bilateral contact and consequent disengagement agreements were themselves sufficient causes for optimism. For the economic and political reasons already enumerated, there was an unprecedented convergence of interest between the Arab world and the United States. Of equal concern to policy planners in Washington was the restriction of Moscow's strategic access to and political leverage in the region. During the preceding two decades, U.S. policy in the Middle East was concerned primarily with the Soviet threat and Moscow's attempts to destabilize the region. The softened perceptions of Soviet intentions and the controlled superpower competition that emerged with the era of détente, combined with Moscow's loss of influence in the region after 1973, allowed the United States to focus more attention on intraregional political problems in the Middle East.[24]

Middle East policy in the Ford and Carter administrations was dominated by efforts to achieve political progress on the Arab–Israeli front. During the turmoil caused by the Watergate scandal and President Nixon's resignation, Kissinger continued his "shuttle diplomacy" in order to maintain a tenuous peace between Israel and Egypt. It was not until the Carter administration,

23. Alvin Rubinstein, "The Soviet Union and the Arabian Peninsula," *The World Today*, (November 1979), 448.
24. Yair Evron, "'Great Powers' Military Intervention in the Middle East," in Leitenberg, *Intervention*, 21–23, 32–33.

however, that such efforts aimed at long term solutions rather than temporary and piecemeal measures to prevent hostilities. Drawing upon a talented staff of specialists largely from the Brookings Institution, Carter devoted unprecedented emphasis to forging a comprehensive peace plan for the Middle East. That the administration was willing to revive the Geneva peace talks—again involving the Soviets in the negotiating process—was testimony to Carter's commitment to reaching a settlement of the Arab–Israeli question. Carter's willingness to involve the Soviets unwittingly proved to be a crucial event furthering the negotiation process. President Sadat, fearful of Soviet involvement, preempted Moscow's participation by unilaterally deciding to visit Jerusalem in November, 1977. This event showed clearly the potential for direct and fruitful contact between the Israelis and the Egyptians and stimulated Carter's attempt to conclude a formal peace treaty between the two countries. Yet, it also illuminated the extent to which American involvement was somewhat peripheral; concrete initiatives toward peace would have to come from the Arabs and Israelis themselves.

From the outset, Carter envisioned that the peace process, though Israel and Egypt were the principal participants, would elicit the support of a wide range of Arab states. The United States attempted to construct a moderate negotiating coalition composed of Egypt, Syria, and Saudi Arabia.[25] Sadat's participation was crucial—he had demonstrated his willingness to challenge even the moderate Arab consensus, and his country's military and political power made his involvement essential. The Saudis were to provide the link between Egypt and the Gulf states. Riyadh's importance lay in its economic influence in the Gulf and its emerging position as the leader pro tem of a moderate Arab coalition. The economic power of the Saudis was a result of their increasing influence over OPEC's production and pricing policies as well as the stimulant they provided to the region by hiring large numbers of workers from other Gulf states.[26] The Syrians were a long shot; since the 1950s, they had leaned toward the radical camp. If the political climate could coerce President Assad to join the moderates, it would strengthen the coalition considerably and restrict further Soviet leverage in the region.

Carter's optimism about wider Arab participation in the peace process was soon dashed. The Syrians neither participated in nor offered support for the peace negotiations. The Saudis, though not without equivocation, also refused to be implicated in Sadat's negotiations with the Israelis. Though this was perceived as a setback by all participants, Sadat, Begin, and Carter pressed

25. David Pollock, "Great Power Intervention in the Middle East: 1977–1978," in Leitenberg, *Intervention*, 313.

26. Jim Hoagland, "Saudi Arabia and the United States," *Survival* (March 1978), and Sharabi, "The Arab–Israeli Conflict," 17.

forward through 1978 and 1979. These efforts culminated in the signing of the Camp David Accords in September, 1978 and the Camp David Treaty in May the following year. There is no question that Camp David represented a significant victory for American policy. One need only glance at President Carter's memoirs to detect the extent of his political and personal investment in the Middle East peace process. Yet, because it did not receive more widespread support throughout the Middle East, the Camp David Treaty did not secure the comprehensive settlement that the administration had originally been seeking.

The emphasis of the Carter administration on political initiatives did not mean a neglect of the strategic considerations that emerged during the early 1970s. The Ford and Carter administrations, pursuing the basic guidelines set forth in the twin pillar policy, continued to sell arms to and rely on Iran as America's principal surrogate in the Gulf. They also devoted attention to strengthening America's naval presence in the Indian Ocean area. Since the late 1960s, the Soviets had increased the frequency of naval missions in the Indian Ocean and secured new points of access along the coast of East Africa. In response, the Ford administration requested and received funding to expand facilities on the British island of Diego Garcia in order to increase its capability to support U.S. operations in the Indian Ocean.[27] In the aftermath of the 1973 war, Bahrain was coming under pressure from its Arab neighbors to deny access rights to the American flotilla in the Gulf. Washington therefore sought an alternative site for home porting the MIDEASTFOR and for coordinating operations to protect, if necessary, the sea lanes for the transport of oil.

Concern about American naval superiority in the Indian Ocean also surfaced during the early Carter administration. In 1977, Presidential Review Memorandum 10 presented a reassessment of U.S. security interests on a global scale. Presidential Directive 18 resulted, calling for increased planning to take place on the projection of U.S. power to areas outside NATO. Although PD 18 commissioned the establishment of a quick strike force for operations in the periphery, its impact upon America's military posture in the Middle East was tempered by attitudes in both the State and Defense Departments.[28] The State Department feared that a more visible military presence in the region would elicit anti-American sentiment and put undue pressure on those regimes more closely aligned with Washington.[29] The State Department was also attempting to negotiate with the Soviets an agreement on the demilitarization of the Indian Ocean.

27. In 1966, the Americans secured access to Diego Garcia for fifty years by formal agreement with Britain. The Document was called "Availability of Certain Indian Ocean Islands for Defense Purposes." For the debate over funding for the project, see U.S. Congress, House, Foreign Affairs Committee, *Proposed Expansion of U.S. Military Facilities in the Indian Ocean* (Washington, DC: GPO, 1974).
28. *New York Times*, 24 January 1980, "How U.S. Strategy Toward the Persian Gulf Emerged."
29. Interview with General P.X. Kelley.

Efforts to expand facilities on Diego Garcia and to increase America's ability to project power to the Gulf obviously would have jeopardized these talks. The Defense Department resisted the establishment of a quick strike force because it would utilize existing U.S troops and therefore drain force levels available for Europe.[30] Furthermore, the individual services were not attracted to the types of missions identified for the force. In 1977, it appeared that a quick strike unit for the Middle East would deal primarily with domestic unrest, not larger and more conventional contingencies. As will be discussed in the following chapters, instructions to plan for these smaller scenarios proved insufficient to elicit a substantive response from the military bureaucracy.

While planning to project U.S. forces to the Gulf proceeded slowly, the Carter administration did take steps to improve American access to regional facilities. Funds were appropriated for the further expansion of Diego Garcia and the administration commenced negotiations to secure access to bases in Oman, Kenya, and Somalia to service vessels in the Indian Ocean.[31] The naval presence of the United States in the region, however, changed little between 1973 and 1979. A carrier task force continued to patrol the Indian Ocean for three to four months per year. Carter also decided to maintain the small flotilla for the Gulf itself—the MIDEASTFOR—at its previous size. The administration readily admitted that the capabilities of this squadron were quite limited and that its main function was to call at friendly ports throughout the region. A Department of Defense statement on Gulf policy summarized this well: "In this part of the world, the psychological significance of the U.S. military presence, and the web of military and economic ties with regional states carries far more importance than military installations. . . . The true locus of U.S. power—which can, if necessary be brought to bear in the region—lies at some distance principally at Guam and Subic Bay."[32] Again, the administration feared that a stronger and more visible presence would jeopardize its political goals.[33] And given the primacy of the Camp David process and the hope for widespread Arab support, this risk was not one worth taking.

While the strengthening of America's military presence was not itself a primary component of Carter's approach to Southwest Asia, the sale of American weaponry certainly was. The twin pillar policy firmly established arms transfers as a fixture of America's approach to the region. By the mid-1970s, sales to Iran, Saudi Arabia, and Israel constituted over one-half of America's global Foreign Military Sales (FMS) program.[34] The primary emphasis of the

30. *New York Times*, 24 January 1980, and military interviews.
31. Congressional Research Service, *United States Foreign Policy Objectives and Overseas Military Installations*, 93.
32. Ibid., 114, 118.
33. Ibid., 115.
34. U.S. Congress, House, International Relations Committee, *Conventional Arms Transfer Policy* (Washington, DC: GPO, 1978), 51.

twin pillar policy under Nixon had been to establish Iran as the predominant military power in the region; sales to other Gulf nations, including Saudi Arabia, were of less strategic importance. By the time of the Carter administration, the political importance of sales to the Saudis had risen substantially. Nevertheless, in qualitative and quantitative terms, sales to Saudi Arabia lagged far behind those to Iran.[35] The Shah had access to America's best equipment; the Saudis did not. Primary responsibility for policing the Gulf remained in Iranian hands. The Saudis indeed faced threats to their security and had legitimate reasons for building their military. Yet, in American eyes, sales to the Saudis were aimed more at buying political cooperation than structuring security arrangements in the Gulf. By design, but also by chance, the arms trade had served as a means of regaining some of the political leverage lost by the Western oil companies. The mutual benefit derived from the sales as well as the corps of technicians that accompanied any major transfer replaced the commercial ties and the foreign presence once provided by the oil companies. As one State Department official explained, the sale of arms "extends to the economic field, to the extension of technical assistance [sic], . . . to a common approach to the problems of the area."[36]

A second trend emerging after the October War was the increasing linkage between arms sales and Saudi oil policy. There was no question in Washington that political progress on the Arab–Israeli front was crucial to influencing Arab behavior. The embargo was imposed as a sanction against America's support for Israel; in explaining their decision to lift the embargo, the Arabs cited a favorable shift in American policy.[37] Yet, Washington needed a more flexible and immediate means to influence Arab attitudes and behavior and turned to the traditional tool of arms sales for this task. Though repeatedly denied by administration officials, it was clear by the second half of the 1970s that the United States was selling weaponry in order to influence oil production and pricing policy. By providing Saudi Arabia with the weapons they wanted, the United

35. In 1973–1974, for example, principal U.S. sales to the Saudis included 30 F-5Es, 20 F-5Bs, and 4 Hercules transport planes. Sales to Iran included 108 F-4s, 141 F-5Es, 4 surveillance aircraft, 6 tankers, and a number of helicopters and other smaller aircraft. In 1976–1977, the Saudis received a wide range of air defense equipment, the Iranians 160 F-16s. In 1978, when the Saudis received their first advanced aircraft (the F-15), the Shah arranged to purchase the highly sophisticated AWACS surveillance aircraft. The AWACS were not offered to the Saudis until 1981. Sources: Stockholm International Peace Research Institute, *World Armaments and Disarmament* (Cambridge, MA: MIT Press, 1974) and the International Institute for Strategic Studies, *The Military Balance* (London, IISS, annual).

36. U.S. Congress, House, *The Persian Gulf, 1974*, 90.

37. On 18 March 1974, OPEC ministers made the following statement: "It appeared to the Ministers that the American official policy as evidenced lately by the recent political events assumed a new dimension . . . [that will] lead America to assume a position which is more compatible with what is right and just toward the Arab occupied territories and the legitimate rights of the Palestinian people." *Keesing's Contemporary Archives*, 1974, 26617.

States hoped to convince the Saudis to maintain production levels that would ensure sufficient supplies and reasonable prices. There was indeed debate within Washington over the wisdom behind this strategy. Some argued that domestic economic concerns had a far greater impact on Saudi oil policy than did the Kingdom's relationship with the United States. To sell arms as a means of influencing production levels, they argued, was futile. No one doubted, however, that weapons transfers would solidify America's relationship with the Saudis. Whether such influence would extend to oil policies remained to be seen.

In 1974, a congressman, discussing the question of arms sales to Gulf states in hearings on the issue, suggested that "there is some value in developing a reciprocity of vital interest. . . . Perhaps it makes sense for you to be in a position to supply to them something they feel they need. . . ."[38] Initially, however, the nature of such reciprocity was unclear. This lack of clarity was in part a result of the yet unsettled structure of the oil market. With the participants in OPEC bickering among themselves over the leadership and policy of the organization, it was difficult for Washington to know how and where to apply its pressure. In the months following the initial oil shock in 1973, both the structure of OPEC and American understanding of the oil market congealed considerably. The Saudis gradually emerged as the most influential member of the organization. Their vast reserves, high income, and large budget surpluses provided the flexibility to vary production and price without straining the national economy. The Saudis could by no means control single-handedly the oil market. Yet, they could present a significant obstacle to any nation attempting to influence OPEC policy without Saudi approval. Under these circumstances, it is not surprising to find a substantial increase in the quantity of American military sales to Saudi Arabia after 1973. From 1973 to 1975, the annual figures for the value of U.S. Foreign Military Sales delivered to the Saudis were (in current dollars) $86.2, $226.5, and $300.4 million.[39] From 1973 to 1978, the annual figures for total Saudi arms imports were (in 1979 dollars): $124, $482, $323, $542, $1017, and $1194 million, respectively.[40] The quality of U.S. weaponry sold to the Saudis also increased markedly. The United States sold Saudi Arabia sophisticated air defense weaponry, including, in 1978, forty-five F-15s.

American willingness to provide the Saudis with sophisticated weaponry was by no means the sole determinant of Saudi oil policy. The ruling family wanted to maintain high prices to support the growing budget, but did not want to drive prices so high that consuming countries would seek alternative energy sources. The Saudis also wanted to regulate production to preserve their reserves for the

38. U.S. Congress, House, *The Persian Gulf, 1974*, 24.

39. Anne Hessing Cahn, "United States Arms to the Middle East 1967–76: A Critical Examination," in Leitenberg, *Intervention*, 129.

40. U.S. Arms Control and Disarmament Agency, *World Military Expenditures and Arms Transfers 1971–1980*, ACDA publication no. 115 (Washington, DC: ACDA, March 1983), 107.

future.[41] Nevertheless, it is clear that the United States saw Saudi control of production levels as a quid pro quo for arms sales. In discussing weapons transfer policy, one staff member of the Senate Foreign Relations Committee referred to the link between arms and petroleum as "beyond question."[42]

American dependence upon the Saudis emerged for reasons other than the Kingdom's influence within OPEC. With the assassination of King Faisal in March, 1975, Saudi Arabia was to play a greater role in shaping a moderate Arab consensus. As mentioned, President Carter counted on Saudi support for the Camp David process and was even willing to offer arms to Riyadh as an incentive for participation. As will be revealed in the following chapters, this was to be the first of many instances in which the United States was to overestimate both the willingness and the ability of the Saudis to extend themselves beyond the central position of the moderate coalition. Within certain bounds, Riyadh acted as a powerful political force in the Gulf. Beyond those bounds, however, the Saudis were rarely willing to venture.

Thus, by the late 1970s, the Carter administration was attempting to complement its political initiatives in the Middle East with selective and carefully structured arms deals. Although these sales did serve to enhance American leverage in the region, they paradoxically undermined U.S. influence in an important respect. The United States sold arms to specific countries to strengthen its political ties with the recipient and/or to enable that country to fulfill strategic missions compatible with U.S. interests. The problem was that many of the recipient states were themselves regional rivals: Saudi Arabia and Iran, Egypt and Israel, for example. As a result, an American sale to one party would usually elicit demands from other regional states claiming that they needed new weaponry to offset the recent infusion of arms into the area. This led to a self-perpetuating spiral. The United States overextended its reach; it expected arms sales to secure what eventually became contradictory objectives. The recipient states, by playing off these contradictory objectives, were able to manipulate the conduct of U.S. arms sales policy.

Several examples will illustrate this point. The Shah was receiving sophisticated weaponry to enable him to police the Gulf. In return, the United States expected Iran to protect America's strategic interests in the region. At the same time, however, Iran's regional aspirations and military predominance exacerbated the Saudis' sense of strategic vulnerability. The Saudis sought American equipment to counter the Iranian buildup, to address the threat from the Yemenis, and to improve domestic security arrangements. In Washington, the expected quid pro quo was Saudi control of OPEC's pricing and production

41. Quandt, *Saudi Oil Policy*, 28–35.
42. Seth Tillman, *The United States in the Middle East—Interests and Obstacles* (Bloomington, IN: Indiana University Press, 1982), 106. For further discussion of the link between oil and arms sales, see Nadav Safran, *Saudi Arabia: The Ceaseless Quest for Security* (Cambridge, MA: Harvard University Press, 1985), 411.

structure as well as their support for the Camp David peace process. Sales to
Egypt were likewise intended to induce Sadat's flexibility in the peace negotiations.[43] The Egyptians, meanwhile, were concerned about responding to possible aggression from the Sudan, Libya, or Ethiopia. Finally, the United States
continued to supply weaponry to the Israelis to enable them to maintain their
regional military superiority. To offset the growing capability of their Arab
neighbors, the Israelis requested, in increasing quantities, America's most sophisticated weaponry. Yet, the provision of arms to the Israelis, while it may
have strengthened deterrence and augmented U.S. bargaining leverage in the
region, was also to elicit Arab resentment and may have hindered the peace
negotiations. A clear pattern emerged: The objectives of U.S. sales to one party
undermined the objectives of U.S. sales to another party.

The friction among these seemingly contradictory aims of U.S. arms transfer
policy became evident in the course of sales negotiations in 1978. In 1976, the
Ford administration had made a verbal commitment to provide F-15 aircraft to
Saudi Arabia. In the words of one official, there was no written agreement, but
the United States had a "moral presumption" to offer Riyadh these highly
sophisticated aircraft.[44] Carter feared that a rejection of the deal would jeopardize both Saudi involvement in Camp David and Riyadh's willingness to control
oil prices.[45] In 1978, under pressure from Riyadh, the Carter administration
agreed to the sale and negotiated with both the Saudis and Congress over the
number of F-15s to be included in the arms package. Simultaneously, the administration was considering an Egyptian request for fifty F-5s. The administration
assumed its compliance would soften Sadat's negotiating position. Henry
Kissinger, in testimony before Congress, elaborated upon the political importance of this deal: "the sale of planes to Egypt . . . will only have a marginal
impact on the military balance in the Middle East. But it will have a profound
symbolic impact on Egypt's perception of its relationship with us and of the
perception of other Arab countries of their relationship to us."[46] The Israelis
vociferously opposed the sales to both the Egyptians and the Saudis. The United
States had not yet sold F-15s to any Arab state, and the Israelis feared that such a
move would pose a serious threat to their air superiority in the region. The F-5
was a much less sophisticated aircraft and would not significantly improve
Egypt's ability to penetrate Israeli air defenses. Yet, pro-Israel supporters in
Congress argued that the sale was politically unwise. It was too early to determine whether Sadat's peace initiatives were sincere. If they were not, the sale
would serve no purpose and only increase Sadat's ability to manipulate U.S.

43. U.S. Congress, House, International Relations Committee, *Proposed Aircraft Sales to Israel,
Egypt and Saudi Arabia* (Washington, DC: GPO, 1978), 73–76.
44. Ibid., 178.
45. Ibid., 3–5. The Saudis had fought against oil price rises several times after 1973.
46. Ibid., 149.

policy.[47] The Israelis also insisted that they be allowed to purchase an increased number of F-15s to offset the proposed sales to Egypt and Saudi Arabia.

The United States had, as it were, played its high cards too quickly. The F-15 was considered by many to be the most versatile and sophisticated weapon in America's conventional arsenal. The Saudis, Egyptians, and Israelis all knew the extent of Carter's political investment in the Middle East and how each could easily foil his plans for the region by withholding cooperation. By escalating the incentive for cooperation, the United States diminished its own leverage in the region. The more sophisticated the weaponry offered by the administration, the more stringent the demands of the recipient states. In order to gain political favor, the United States had to meet these demands by steadily increasing the quality and quantity of arms sold to regional powers. Furthermore, what began as three distinct sales was transformed by the behavior of the recipients into a single arms package. The Saudis, Egyptians, and Israelis each exerted pressure on the United States by comparing what was offered to them with that offered to the others. The administration was also concerned that if the United States did not sell the F-15, the French would provide the Saudis with the Mirage F-1. This would undercut the American arms industry and give Washington less control over the capabilities and potential uses of the weaponry provided. In the end, the administration resolved the dilemma by placing restrictions on the attack capability of the F-15s provided to Saudi Arabia, approving the sale of F-5s to Egypt, and increasing the number of F-15s sold to Israel. The episode illuminated, however, the contradictions inherent in U.S. arms sales policy as well as the decreasing ability of this instrument to influence the behavior of states in the region.[48]

America's role as a weapons supplier to the Middle East was further complicated by two developments in U.S. arms transfer policy: the International Security Assistance and Arms Export Control Act of 1976 and the President's Conventional Arms Transfer Policy of 1977. As arms sales to the Middle East increased after the October War, congressional interest in the export of weapons mounted. This was only one aspect of a widespread reassertion of congressional power in the realm of foreign affairs that began with the War Powers Act in 1973. This strengthening of Congress's role in the formation of foreign policy was stimulated by the Vietnam War, by the revelation of covert operations and bombings in Southeast Asia, and by the Watergate scandal. In terms of Middle East policy, Congress grew increasingly concerned with the long term effect of arms sales on regional stability. Criticism of the twin pillar policy focused on the potential for the flow of weapons to the Gulf to incite local rivalries and stimu-

---

47. Ibid., 107.
48. The reasons for the decreasing effectiveness of this policy instrument will be discussed in the following chapter.

late an arms race throughout the Middle East, from which the Soviets were likely to benefit.[49] In order to gain some degree of control over the sales process, Congress first passed the Arms Export Control Act in 1974 and revised it in 1976. The Act required that any sale of weapons of a value exceeding $25 million had to be approved by Congress. Successive administrations have sidestepped this provision by dividing arms deals into small packages whose value falls below the $25 million ceiling. This loophole, however, is impractical for transfers involving aircraft. Thus, most sales to the Middle East fell within the reach of Congress's expanding power.

On the first level of analysis, the Arms Export Control Act did not severely limit the administration's freedom of action; in the 1970s, Congress played a role in shaping the size and content of deals to the Middle East, but did not reject any sale proposed by the White House. What the Act did do, however, was integrate more fully the conduct of foreign policy with domestic political considerations. The rise of congressional leverage over arms deals meant that the Arab and Israeli lobbies stepped up their activities both on Capitol Hill and in the wider political arena. The discussion in the Senate over the sale of AWACS to Saudi Arabia in 1981 became more a battle between pressure groups than a debate over foreign policy.[50] Despite the approval of the sale, the Saudis as well as the Israelis expressed concern that U.S. foreign policy was neither predictable nor designed to serve the interests of the country. Lobby groups had indeed influenced decisions on arms sales before the mid-1970s. But congressional participation in the decision-making process gave pressure groups and private interests a new and readily accessible source of leverage.

President Carter's directive on conventional arms transfer policy revealed his own reservations about America's role as an arms merchant. In May, 1977, Carter concluded that arms transfers would be viewed as "an exceptional foreign policy implement, to be used only in instances where it can be clearly demonstrated that the transfer contributes to our national security interests."[51] The controls to be placed on arms sales included the following: a limit on the dollar volume, a restriction on the transfer of advanced weapons, a ban on coproduction, and linkage between sales policy and a recipient's record on human rights. There were two primary motivations for this change in policy. First, Carter

49. Edward Kennedy, "The Persian Gulf: Arms Race or Arms Control?" *Foreign Affairs* (October 1975), 26–33.

50. For details of the lobbying campaign, see Judith Levenfeld, *Arguments, Appeals and Arm-Twisting: Foreign Policy Lobbying and the 1981 Saudi Arms Sale*, unpublished Senior Honors Thesis, Government Department, Harvard University, 1983. Also see Steve Emerson, "The Aramco Connection," *The New Republic* (10 May 1982), and the "Petrodollar Connection," *The New Republic* (17 February 1982). Chapter 6 presents a more detailed analysis of the AWACS deal.

51. Congressional Research Service, *Changing Perspectives on U.S. Arms Transfer Policy* (Washington, DC: GPO, 1981), 122.

Table 3
ARMS TRANSFER AGREEMENTS WITH THE THIRD WORLD, BY SUPPLIER (IN MILLIONS OF CURRENT U.S. DOLLARS)ᵃ

	1973	1974	1975	1976	1977	1978	1979	1980
Total:	10,452	21,677	21,639	21,398	28,457	25,371	28,865	41,169
Non-communist	6,742	14,777	17,299	13,713	17,957	21,521	18,665	25,069
Of which:								
United Statesᵇ	4,412	10,097	10,989	9,813	9,957	10,311	9,965	9,659
France	500	2,100	2,320	1,035	3,170	2,725	4,310	7,935
United Kingdom	1,000	760	1,320	600	1,400	3,570	1,260	830
West Germany	140	670	750	730	1,220	2,310	890	870
Italy	290	430	1,040	220	980	1,330	340	2,680
Other free world	400	720	880	1,315	1,230	1,275	1,900	3,095
Communist	3,710	6,900	4,340	7,685	10,500	3,850	10,200	16,100
Of which: USSR	3,320	5,970	3,680	6,520	9,610	2,910	8,800	14,920
Dollar inflation index (1973 = 100)	100	107	117	131	136	146	158	174

ᵃUnited States data are for fiscal year given (and cover the period from July 1, 1972 through September 30, 1980). Foreign data are for the calendar year given. Statistics shown for foreign countries are based upon estimated selling prices. All prices given include the values of weapons, spare parts, construction, all associated services, military assistance, and training programs. United States commercial sales contract values are excluded, as are values of the Military Assistance Service Funded account (MASF) which provided grant funding for South Vietnam, Laos, Philippines, Thailand, and South Korea. MASF for FY1973 was $7,320,000,000, for FY1974 $840,000,000, for FY1975 $544,000,000. Related grant transfers to South Korea and Thailand, also excluded, were $11,000,000 in FY1979 and $151,000,000 in FY1980. All data are current as of January 1, 1981 and reflect termination of all sales contracts *other than* Iran. The value of prior Iranian contracts cancelled primarily by the Khomeini regime are as follows: FY1973 ($38,000,000); FY1974 ($390,000,000); FY1975 ($1,157,000,000); FY1976 and transitional quarter ($236,000,000); FY1977 ($2,953,000,000); FY1978 ($1,673,000,000); FY1979 ($6,000,000); FY1980 ($0). Third World category excludes Warsaw Pact nations, NATO nations, Europe, Japan, Australia, and New Zealand.
ᵇExcludes $3,271,000,000 from U.S. total for 1976, which represents the transitional quarter (FY 19T).
Source: Reproduced from Congressional Research Service, *Changing Perspectives on U.S. Arms Transfer Policy,* 13.

sympathized with the argument that unrestrained sales were leading to regional competition rather than stability.[52] Although a temporary balance of power might deter aggression, the long term effect of sales to the Gulf had been to militarize the region. Second, he felt that the United States, as the largest arms seller, had to take chief responsibility for reducing the "spiraling arms traffic."[53]

This directive was by no means intended to bring to a halt all transfers. But between 1977 and 1980, the value of U.S. arms agreements with the Third World declined in real terms, while the sales of other countries, such as the Soviet Union, increased markedly (see Table 3). President Carter also personally intervened to ensure that his new directive was implemented. In 1977, Carter's aides recommended that ten AWACS—as requested by the Shah—be sold to Iran. Carter, specifically to let the Shah know that the days of carte blanche purchases were over, decided to reduce the number of aircraft in the air defense package from ten to seven.[54]

There were two important ramifications of Carter's arms sales directive and the Arms Export Control Act. First, they led to a certain degree of anxiety among Gulf regimes as to the reliability of their major arms supplier.[55] Even if the administration were prepared to recommend a sale, Congress could well prevent its consummation. Second, pro-American states in the Gulf lost confidence in the consistency and orientation of U.S. policy. How could they depend upon an ally that was prone to fundamental changes in policy at least every four years?[56] Furthermore, it appeared that the United States was interested in reducing its military role in the Gulf. The Carter administration was seeking an agreement on the demilitarization of the Indian Ocean and had made a commitment to reduce arms sales to the region. The promulgation of these policies, as well as the tangible cutbacks in sales, led the moderate Arabs to question the economic and military interdependence that had been developing with the United States since the October War.

Conclusions

Following the 1973 War, the United States faced a new set of particularly puzzling security problems in the Middle East. For the first time in the postwar era,

52. Ibid., 122–123.
53. Ibid.
54. Gary Sick, *All Fall Down—America's Tragic Encounter with Iran* (New York: Random House, 1985), 26.
55. Safran asserts that the Saudis were uneasy about Carter's policy of restraint and felt reassured about the U.S. strategic commitment to the Kingdom by the sale of F-15s in 1978. See Safran, *Saudi Arabia*, 299–300. The Shah was also concerned about Carter's arms sales policy and its impact on U.S.–Iranian relations. See Sick, *All Fall Down*, 24–27.
56. This complaint about U.S. foreign policy has been expressed by many governments. See Abdul Mansur, "The American Threat to Saudi Arabia," in *Armed Forces Journal* (September 1980), 47.

Western access to oil reserves in the Persian Gulf was jeopardized. Arab Gulf states succeeded in withholding oil shipments to the West, drastically increasing oil prices, and influencing U.S. policy toward the Arab–Israeli conflict. Despite this new threat to U.S. interests, there was little change between 1973 and 1979 either in U.S. security policy toward Southwest Asia or in assessments of the military capability needed to implement that policy. Why was this the case?

First, it is important to recognize that the new challenge to U.S. interests came not from the Soviet Union, but from political developments within the Arab world. In fact, during the 1970s, the level of concern within the United States about direct and indirect Soviet advances into Southwest Asia remained relatively low. The Soviets' ouster from Egypt and the relative isolation of Syria and Iraq within the Arab world allowed the Ford and Carter administrations to perceive a marked decline in Moscow's leverage in the region. Adroit diplomacy initiated under Kissinger was also central to establishing the United States as the key external actor in the Arab–Israeli dispute. Furthermore, détente fostered a political environment which made possible a hiatus in the escalating nature of superpower rivalry in the Middle East. As Chapter 2 showed, shifts in U.S. security policy toward the region were primarily reactions to changing American perceptions of the Soviet threat. That concern within Washington about Moscow's intentions in the Middle East remained low during the 1970s is an important factor explaining the absence of U.S. military initiatives toward the region.

While U.S. assessments of the Soviet threat to the Gulf suggested little need for a shift in military policy, the intraregional situation was far less clear. After all, it was the Gulf states themselves that had attempted to deny the Western states access to their oil reserves. Although there was consideration of an attempt to take the oil fields by force, the military options for securing access proved to be extremely elusive. Even if the political will to seize the oil fields had existed, the vulnerability of pumping stations, refineries, and shipping sites made virtually all scenarios for intervention appear counterproductive. Nor did it seem likely that the United States would need to intervene in a local conflict. Despite the British withdrawal, relations among the Gulf states remained remarkably tranquil. Were a conflict in the region to threaten either the flow of oil or the stability of a pro-Western regime, the Shah had both the capability and the will to respond. Within the context of implementing both containment and an intraregional security policy, then, American planners saw no need to increase the allocation of military resources to the Gulf area.

The United States did strengthen its military posture in the Indian Ocean during the 1970s, though this was largely a response to the growing presence of the Soviet fleet rather than a means of preparing for military operations in the Gulf itself. The Ford and Carter administrations expanded U.S. facilities on Diego Garcia and sought naval access in Oman and along the eastern coast of Africa. Planners were concerned with preserving American naval superiority in

the Indian Ocean in order to protect sea lines of communication. These preparations for access, largely because of limited resources, were not accompanied by
any significant increase in on-station naval or ground forces in the Indian Ocean
area. If America's military presence in the region were to be expanded, responsibility would have fallen largely upon the Navy. Yet, the Pacific Command had
no desire to divert resources from the Pacific nor did the Atlantic Command
want to reduce the number of vessels available for the Mediterranean and
Atlantic. Presidential Directive 18 (1977) did direct the Pentagon to strengthen
American force projection capabilities. Yet, the Carter administration also identified re-equipping NATO as its top military priority. The Long Term Defense
Plan (LTDP) adopted in 1978 ensured that defense spending was to focus on
Europe, not Southwest Asia.

American security policy was based upon certain political assumptions as well
as upon these strategic considerations. Although the United States experienced
a relative decline in its power—that is, in broad terms, its ability to secure
desired outcomes—in the Middle East, the key variable was of a political and
economic nature, not a military one. The military balance in the region did not
change as such, but the power derived from America's military might was nega-
ted by the growing economic power of the oil-producing states. The United
States after 1973 needed to elicit the cooperation of Arab states to secure its
interests. Hard currency was no longer sufficient to purchase Arab oil; the Gulf
states could deliver their own demands to Washington for arms or political
pressure on Israel. Washington, forced to broaden its means of influence in the
region, placed increasing emphasis on arms sales, cultivated growing economic
interdependence with the producing states, and played a more active role in the
Arab–Israeli peace process.

Increased reliance on arms sales not only constituted an attempt to enhance
U.S. leverage in the Gulf, but it also reflected the constraints imposed upon
security policy by domestic politics. The legacy of Vietnam continued to play an
important role in shaping the public debate over foreign policy. Any administration advocating intervention in the Middle East would have faced strong popular and congressional opposition. Congress had imposed structural changes to
increase its control over military issues; the War Powers Act and the Arms
Export Control Act were cases in point. The Vietnam War also led to the
fragmentation of the consensus that had existed on America's global strategy,
particularly with respect to regional security problems. The Nixon Doctrine did
not reduce the scope of America's commitments in the periphery, but it did
change the means that would be used to honor those commitments. The lessons
of Vietnam, in combination with the rise of détente, challenged assumptions
about both the nature of Soviet intentions and the strategy of containment upon
which U.S. policy in the periphery was based. Were the Soviets intent on
fomenting communist takeovers in the Third World? Did the fall of South

Vietnam substantially damage U.S. interests in Southeast Asia and lead to a shift in the regional balance of power that had global implications? These questions emerged in the 1970s and led to a rethinking both of regional strategy and of the suitability of containment as the core principle behind U.S. policy in the Third World. Within this context, any effort to increase America's military presence in the periphery entailed a clear political liability. This consideration set certain limits upon the formulation of America's security policy toward Southwest Asia.

The final political assumption upon which U.S. security policy was based focused on the nature of and the stability of regional alignments. Through most of the 1970s, the United States believed that the Shah's regime was virtually unchallengeable. As we will see in the following chapter, even after the signs of popular discontent were clearly visible in 1978, Washington was slow to confront the fact that the Shah could well fall from power. While America's strategic calculations for the Gulf were based upon the stability of Iran, the emergence of a moderate Arab coalition after 1973 confirmed U.S. optimism about its military and political strategy for the Middle East as a whole. Sadat's bold initiatives in the peace process and Saudi willingness to play a more prominent role in regional politics and to undertake a closer and more visible relationship with the United States led to a self-perpetuating and advantageous cycle. The formation of a moderate Arab coalition encouraged American diplomatic efforts on the Arab–Israeli front, while simultaneously limiting Soviet influence in the region. The decline of Soviet leverage allowed the United States to devote more attention to regional issues, thereby strengthening the conservative coalition. At least temporarily, Israeli security, access to oil, and containment of the Soviets appeared to be complementary, not contradictory objectives.

The suitability of U.S. security policy toward the Gulf depended upon the relevance of these political assumptions about both regional politics and Soviet intentions. Until 1979, there was a close correspondence between America's military strategy for the Gulf and the political realities of the region. When the Iranian revolution and the Soviet invasion of Afghanistan challenged these assumptions, however, the United States was left with a security policy for Southwest Asia that was deemed at once obsolete and inadequate to protect U.S. interests in the Gulf.

Chapter Four

IRAN, AFGHANISTAN, AND
THE EVOLUTION OF
THE CARTER DOCTRINE

In the beginning of 1978, confidence in Washington about America's political leverage and strategic position in the Middle East was running high. The real price of oil had declined since 1975; despite Soviet gains in Ethiopia, détente had reduced East–West tension in the region as a whole; the Saudis were increasing their control over price levels within OPEC; the Shah had assumed responsibility for maintaining regional stability; and a peace treaty between Egypt and Israel was looking increasingly likely. By the end of 1979, American confidence about its ability to influence events in the Middle East had been shattered. Within a period of twelve months, the Shah had fallen from power, the Soviets had invaded Afghanistan, oil prices had risen 150%, and President Sadat of Egypt had been ostracized from the Arab world, casting a lonely shadow on his participation in Camp David. From a regional perspective, Washington's principal surrogate for over a decade, Iran, would no longer assume responsibility for maintaining stability in the Gulf. From a global perspective, the Soviet invasion of Afghanistan led to the final collapse of détente and the crumbling of the overall framework in which U.S. policy had been formed throughout the 1970s.

The events of 1979 affected the policies of the Carter administration toward the Middle East in two ways. First, Carter felt pressed to redress the immediate political and strategic losses incurred as a direct result of the revolution in Iran and the Soviet invasion of Afghanistan. Second, these events profoundly altered the lens through which the administration and Congress interpreted developments in the international arena. As the line of argument in the previous chapters showed, global perceptions and fundamental assumptions about Soviet behavior have been crucial to the formation of an approach to the Gulf. This chapter will attempt to show both how the United States reacted to the immediate implications of the crises in Southwest Asia and how the long term changes in global perceptions associated with these events have reshaped U.S. policy.

The format of this chapter is as follows. First, the strategic and political impact of the Iranian revolution and the invasion of Afghanistan on the regional states will be examined. Second, the study will question how the collapse of détente affected thinking in the Carter administration about Soviet intentions in the Third World and the relative military capabilities of the Soviet Union and the United States to project power over long distances. Third, changes in the perception of the relationship between Western access to oil and American security policy will be examined. Finally, the chapter will address how these various concerns were reflected in the formation of the Carter Doctrine.

The Revolution in Iran

The revolution in Iran was a gradual process; the Shah's power had been deteriorating for months before he finally left the country in January, 1979. This slow demise was torturous to observe from Washington, for the Carter administration appeared both unable and unwilling to assist the Shah in reversing the tide of popular discontent. President Carter initially stood solidly behind the Shah: "The key to stability was the monarch himself, supported by the military."[1] Top officials initially felt that if the Shah could establish a coalition government, much of the opposition might be placated. Yet, there was also fear in Washington and Tehran that any move toward liberalization might quicken the fall of the government.[2] Many in the State Department urged that the Shah step down, thereby providing the United States a better chance of cultivating favorable relations with a new leadership.[3] After the Shah eventually left Iran, the Carter administration did in fact offer support for the temporary leaders—Bakhtiar and Bazargan.[4] Yet, Carter discouraged both the Shah and his successors from using military force to impose order on the country. He feared that the involvement of the military would potentially lead to a lengthy and bloody civil war. In short, the Carter administration offered only ineffectual advice: It left the Shah in limbo, caught between liberalizing the government and suppressing his opposition.

It would be misleading to suggest that the Shah, if he had taken the proper measures, could have prevented the demise of his regime. The opposition, which was large and representative of a broad cross section of Iranian society,

1. Jimmy Carter, *Keeping Faith: Memoirs of a President* (New York: Bantam Books, 1982), 441.
2. Zbigniew Brzezinski, *Power and Principle: Memoirs of the National Security Adviser 1977–1981* (London: Weidenfeld and Nicolson, 1983), 359–365.
3. Ibid., 368.
4. Carter, *Memoirs*, 447–457.

included the intelligentsia, religious leaders opposed to secular modernization, the left (Tudeh and other smaller parties), and the traditional economic elite whose position had been eroded by industrial development. The Shah's government was highly centralized and lacked effective local organs. His high-paced modernization program led to inflation and neglect of the agricultural sector. His close and visible ties to the West stimulated anticolonial sentiment as well as tension over religious and cultural values.[5] It is thus doubtful whether the Shah, even with far-reaching reforms or pervasive repression, would have been able to contain the forces that fueled the revolution.

It is also clear that the United States was implicated in his demise. Washington had not only invested a great deal in the stability and power of Iran, it had also helped to shape and carry out the Shah's military and economic modernization programs. The twin pillar policy was based upon the supposition that the United States needed to cultivate a modern and powerful ally in the Gulf region to protect Western interests. This surrogate strategy was not only designed to avoid the circumstances which would require the overseas deployment of U.S. forces, it was also an attempt to demonstrate political sensitivity by allowing regional states to run their own affairs while offering military aid and technical assistance. The problem was that the rapid modernization and industrialization that accompanied this approach were also key forces contributing to the erosion of domestic support for the Shah. In this sense, the revolution represented much more than the loss of an important surrogate; it was a clear repudiation of the key political assumptions upon which the United States had based its Gulf policy for over a decade.

By 1978, the Shah's forces played a pervasive strategic role in the Persian Gulf. The large, well-trained, and sophisticated military machine in Iran enabled the Shah to offer assistance to regional states facing internal threats (such as Oman during the Dhofar rebellion), to deter interstate aggression in the Gulf area, and to protect the oil traffic in Gulf waters. The mountains in the north of Iran also offered prime sites from which U.S. surveillance stations could monitor military developments within the Soviet Union. When the government collapsed, not only did the Iranians abandon their willingness to fulfill these roles, they also lost the technical capability to do so. Without American mechanics and spare parts, much of the military hardware became useless.[6] Nor were there other states in the region to which the United States could turn to replace Iran.

5. For a concise review of the factors leading to the revolution, see George Lenczowski, "The Arc of Crisis: Its Central Sector," *Foreign Affairs* (Spring 1979). For more thorough analysis see Shaul Bakhash, *The Reign of Ayatollahs: Iran and the Islamic Revolution* (New York: Basic Books, 1984); Ervand Abrahamian, Iran Between Two Revolutions (Princeton, NJ: Princeton University Press, 1982); and Nikki Keddie, *Roots of Revolution: An Interpretive History of Modern Iran* (New Haven, CT: Yale University Press, 1981).

6. It should be noted that in the Gulf War, the Iranians have been able to maintain much more of their military hardware than analysts originally expected.

The Saudis were the logical choice, yet they simply did not have the military infrastructure or technical expertise to develop a defense system approaching that of the Shah. Furthermore, the ruling family feared building a military that would be large enough to pose a threat to the authority of the regime.[7] Nor was the climate in the United States conducive to building another "pillar" to defend U.S. interests. Iran, the country that had once assumed responsibility for maintaining the status quo in the Gulf, was suddenly the nation threatening to bring the most radical changes to the Middle East.

If President Carter had doubts about the efficacy of arms sales when he first came to office, the chaos in Iran only confirmed his reservations. The Shah's massive military buildup had led to high inflation rates in the country and was eventually to establish the army as a separate repository of power. This made the administration sensitive to the hesitancy of other Gulf countries to build large and modern military infrastructures.[8] What is more, sophisticated American weaponry had fallen into the hands of a leadership that was holding U.S. diplomats hostage in Tehran. Not only was this situation painfully ironic, but it also meant increasing opportunities for the Soviets to gain access to the West's most advanced weaponry. Arms sales were faring no better in the lower Gulf. While the turmoil in Iran was mounting, the United States was attempting to sort through its concurrent commitments to sell aircraft to Saudi Arabia, Egypt, and Israel (see Chapter 3, page 60). After submitting to pressure from the three potential recipients (and their powerful lobbies in Washington), Carter agreed to a joint package supplying planes to the three nations. Many in the administration and in Congress felt that the sale of F-15s to Saudi Arabia would secure Saudi participation in the Camp David talks. When the Saudis failed to live up to these expectations, officials became even more wary of having dispersed U.S. weaponry for no apparent gain.[9]

There were also broader criticisms to be leveled at the practice of seeking influence through arms. Before states such as Iran, Saudi Arabia, and Kuwait had accumulated large budget surpluses, they depended largely upon military grants as their main source of weaponry. After 1973, however, the oil-producing states could afford to purchase foreign weaponry, thereby reducing the leverage that the suppliers were able to wield over the recipients. An item that arrives through a commercial transaction usually entails fewer obligations than one that is gratis. Furthermore, if the United States was reluctant to provide certain weapons, the French were more than willing to increase their sales to the region. The militarization of the Gulf that followed from the twin pillar policy also gradually reduced the political influence that had accompanied American sales. The emergence of regional states with autonomous military capability increased

7. See Thomas McNaugher, *Arms and Oil, U.S. Military Strategy and the Persian Gulf* (Washington, DC: Brookings Institution, 1985), 139–143.
8. Interview with Tom Locher.
9. Tillman, *U.S. in the Middle East*, 107.

the extent to which Gulf regimes could meet their defense needs without the involvement of the major supplying countries. In order to maintain influence over its clients in the Gulf, the United States steadily increased the sophistication of the weaponry that it offered for sale. As the level of technology contained in each transaction increased, the scope for further leverage through arms sales decreased; there simply was not an unlimited number of rungs on the ladder. Recipient nations began to determine the terms of the sale rather than the United States. This trend was exacerbated in 1978–1979 when the second oil shock made the United States even more dependent upon Saudi political cooperation and their willingness to control oil production levels. These considerations, when combined with the chaos in Iran, raised serious questions about the extent to which the United States could rely upon arms sales to defend its vital interests in the Middle East.

The revolution in Iran thus had considerable impact upon U.S. perceptions of America's strategic vulnerability in the Gulf. Iran was no longer willing or able to assume military responsibility for protecting Western interests, nor was there another state within the region capable of replacing the Shah's role. Furthermore, the atmosphere in Washington was hardly conducive to appointing and arming a new surrogate. Two immediate strategic concerns emerged. First, the United States needed to enhance its own military capability in the Gulf in order to assume responsibility for the regional missions previously devolved to the Shah. A MIDEASTFOR capable of providing a symbolic presence was no longer sufficient. Second, the United States had to respond to the new threat posed to Gulf stability by a revolutionary Iran. This involved strengthening the internal security of neighboring states as well as their ability to cope with Iranian aggression.

To achieve both of these objectives—enhancing U.S. strategic access and bolstering the defense capabilities of local states—the United States was reliant upon the cooperation of regional actors. Such cooperation was dependent upon the impact of events in Iran upon the political atmosphere in the Middle East. And the regional implications of the revolution were indeed profound. To begin, the fall of the Shah jeopardized the ongoing Arab–Israeli peace negotiations. Because Israel had been receiving 60% of its oil supplies from the Shah, the chaos in Iran jeopardized the Israeli position in the continuing peace negotiations. Before Prime Minister Begin agreed to transfer sovereignty of the Sinai to Egypt, he exacted guarantees from Carter that the United States would remedy any shortfall in Israeli energy supplies.[10] It is also clear that Begin became more intransigent in his general approach to the negotiations with Egypt after the fall of the Shah. One possible reason could be that he feared the

10. Sharham Chubin, "Repercussions of the Crisis in Iran," in Treverton, *Crisis Management*, 110.

emergence of more radical political sentiment in the Arab world. Yet, Begin also realized the increased strategic importance of Israel to the United States in light of the collapse of Iran's military power and attempted to use this factor to his advantage in negotiations with Washington.[11] Without access to facilities in Iran, Israeli bases would serve as important staging grounds if the United States were to undertake an operation in the Gulf area. The rising tide of Islamic fundamentalism also meant that Arab states had to watch carefully domestic sentiments toward the Palestinian question. In combination with Begin's intransigence, this political trend made progress on the Arab–Israeli front much more difficult.

Within the Arab Gulf, there were two primary responses to the revolution and to the rise of the new regime under Khomeni. There was considerable fear that waves of popular discontent, stimulated by events in Iran, could spread throughout the region. Religious fundamentalism of the type that helped to topple the Shah could well have galvanized revolutionary sentiment in other states. Yet, the course of events in Iran posed more than a threat by example; Khomeni made explicit his intentions to overthrow the secular regimes surrounding him. The outbreak of the Iran–Iraq War in 1980 confirmed the worst fears of regional leaders that Iran was sufficiently strong to sustain a war with the most powerful Arab state in the Gulf. Within this framework, it was natural for America's allies in the Gulf, particularly the Saudis and Omanis, to seek U.S. weaponry and, if necessary, to turn to America's security umbrella. The United States could offer the limited military support necessary to suppress a coup, as well as the aircraft and weaponry needed to deter Iranian attacks on the cities or oil fields of neighboring states. In essence, it was strategic insecurity that was pushing the Gulf states into a closer relationship with the United States.

The other impulse which swept through the Gulf in 1979 hindered, rather than enhanced, cooperation with the United States. America was clearly implicated in the fall of the Shah; his close ties with Washington were well known as was the existence of a large American military and professional presence in Iran. The revolution illuminated the weaknesses in Washington's approach as well as the dangers inherent in close cooperation with the United States. The fall of the Shah and Egypt's expulsion from the Arab League undermined the moderate, pro-American coalition. The increasingly important role of Syria and Iraq in shaping political currents in the Arab world made cooperation with the United States even less attractive for Gulf states. Furthermore, Kuwait, though fearful of Khomeni's intentions, put pressure on both the Saudis and the Omanis to limit their ties to the United States. In light of these developments, could America's security umbrella provide stability in the Gulf or was it becoming an increasing political liability? If Islamic orthodoxy were incompatible with close

11. Ibid., 107.

military ties to the United States, which would best ensure the future stability of the Saudi regime?[12]

This fear of involvement with the United States conflicted with the more immediate concern for security. It is difficult to assess which of these two impulses carried the most weight. By the middle of 1980, however, it was clear that the Soviet invasion of Afghanistan and the Iran–Iraq war had heightened fears of a major military confrontation involving many, if not all, of the Gulf states. This intensified the willingness of the Saudis to turn to American military aid.[13]

Yet, even without the Iran–Iraq War and the Soviet presence in Afghanistan, there were several limitations upon the extent to which the Iranian revolution could have triggered a widespread resurgence of Islamic orthodoxy in the Arab world. Islamic fundamentalism was indeed a powerful political force. The threat of spreading orthodoxy impaired whatever degree of pan-Arab support for the Camp David initiatives that might have emerged. The seizure of the Grand Mosque of Mecca in November 1979 heightened fears within Saudi Arabia about a religiously motivated coup. Similarly, Sadat and Mubarak after him watched carefully the growing size and influence of the Moslem Brotherhood in Egypt.

Despite the role that Islamic fundamentalism played in shaping events in Iran, deep-rooted tension between the Persians and the Arabs limited the extent to which orthodox elements in the Arab Gulf identified the revolution as an event of religious significance that was to be emulated. Furthermore, while the Moslem population of Iran was largely Shiite, that of the lower Gulf was predominantly Sunni. Not only was there a history of tension between the two sects, but the ideological perspective of Sunni teaching was less oriented toward radical change than that of Shiites.[14] The religious leaders of the Sunni communities in countries such as Saudi Arabia and Egypt were also less excluded from political life than were the Shiite clergy under the Shah's rule. Thus, in the Arab Gulf the governing elite was generally more aware of the attitudes and sentiments prevalent in the religious sector and the clergy more satisfied with its own power and influence. Islamic fundamentalism was indeed a growing force in the Arab world after 1978. Yet, it was not sufficiently strong to prevent the Saudis from seeking security through military cooperation with the United States.

The final topic to be discussed in this section concerns the impact of the revolution upon domestic political considerations in the United States. The fall of the Shah, the seizure of the U.S. embassy, and the failure of the mission to

12. Tillman, U.S. in the Middle East, 108–109.
13. Brzezinski, Power and Principle, 450.
14. Rouhollah Ramazani, "Security in the Persian Gulf," Foreign Affairs (Spring 1979), 829.

rescue the hostages stimulated within both official and public circles a reevaluation of American diplomatic and military power. This reassessment did not focus
only on America's position in the Persian Gulf. As will be discussed shortly, it
extended to a wide-ranging analysis of both the impact of détente on U.S.
security policy and the stability of the balance of power between the United
States and the Soviet Union. While the dissipation of American power was a
topic of general discussion, particular criticism was directed at the Carter administration. On almost a daily basis, critics charged that the President's foreign
policy was both muddled and ineffectual. With the election looming in 1980,
Carter was under a great deal of pressure to make a decisive move in the foreign
policy arena that would both restore America's image as a responsible global
power and indicate that the President had regained control of his foundering
administration. In Carter's own words, "[t]he public was . . . becoming more
restive with each passing week because of our seeming impotence in dealing with
international crises."[15] These considerations were to color both the nature and
the presentation of Carter's new policy toward the Gulf.

The Soviet Invasion of Afghanistan

If there were any doubts in Washington about the depth of the turmoil in
Southwest Asia in 1979, they disappeared within hours on December 26 when
the Soviets moved into Afghanistan. Throughout the year, the Carter administration had carefully watched the buildup of troops in the southern republics
as well as the growing Soviet presence in Kabul itself.[16] Nevertheless, the actual
invasion caused virtual panic in Washington, as did the continuous deployment
of Soviet troops in Afghanistan during the weeks that followed. The growing
size of the Soviet commitment indicated that this was not a surgical coup
orchestrated by external forces, but an expansionist move aimed at occupying
and subordinating the country. The Soviets had exhibited both the will and the
ability to project force outside the Soviet bloc and had increased their air
capabilities in the Gulf region by basing strike aircraft in Afghanistan.[17] If war
were to break out, this would complicate the maintenance of American air
superiority in the Gulf area. From the perspective of the Gulf states, four Soviet
divisions had moved several hundred miles closer to their borders. Although a
thrust toward the oil fields would most probably come through Iran, the proximity of Soviet troops in Afghanistan intensified the Kremlin's intangible pres-

15. Carter, *Memoirs*, 489.
16. Brzezinski, *Power and Principle*, 426.
17. SU-24 Fencers based in Shindand could reach targets in the Persian Gulf. See McNaugher,
Arms and Oil, 28.

ence in the area and increased concern about fortifying early detection and air defense systems.

The American response to these strategic changes was hindered by a lack of consensus about Soviet motives. Soon after the invasion, four differing explanations of Soviet behavior emerged in academic and official literature. The first postulated that the Soviets were gradually making their way toward the Gulf and the Indian Ocean, both to gain control of the oil supplies and to secure access to a warmwater port. Intelligence reports indicating that the Soviets had formed plans to invade Iran lent support to this position.[18] Others argued that the resurgence of Islamic fundamentalism in Iran had stimulated fears in Moscow that popular uprisings might spread to Moslem communities in Afghanistan and even to the southern republics of the Soviet Union where much of the population is Moslem and speaks Persian.[19] The third prevalent opinion focused on events in Afghanistan itself. Although a Marxist coup had installed a pro-Soviet regime in Kabul in 1978, the dialogue between the Kremlin and President Hafizullah Amin deteriorated steadily during 1979. Rather than risk a major split with Kabul, the proponents of this view argued, the Soviets removed Amin by force and replaced him with a puppet government under Babrak Kamal. Finally, some argued that the invasion of Afghanistan was a reflection more of internal politics in the Soviet Union than of concern over events in the northern tier. A major split is known to have occurred between the KGB and the Soviet military over the wisdom of the Afghan operation, and it is possible that the military used this as an opportunity to assert its preeminence in the policymaking hierarchy.[20]

Although it is likely that a combination of these factors contributed to the Kremlin's decision to invade, with the advantage of hindsight, it appears that the third assessment was the most accurate. If the Soviets had had designs on gaining access to Gulf waters, the commitment of a sizable contingent of troops to Afghanistan would constitute a diversion of important assets, not a prudent first phase of the operation. If the stability of the southern republics had been the main concern, internal security operations in Moslem areas would probably have been more effective. It was because of its proximity to the Soviet Union and its strategic importance that the Kremlin was unwilling to allow Afghanistan to drift from the Soviet camp. Its political initiatives toward Amin

18. Interview with Harold Saunders.

19. Jiri Valenta, "From Prague to Kabul, the Soviet Style of Invasion," *International Security* (Fall, 1980), 118.

20. These last two interpretations were voiced repeatedly by officials in Washington during interviews with the author. See also U.S. Congress, Senate, Foreign Relations Committee, *U.S. Security Interests and Policies in Southwest Asia* (Washington, DC: GPO, 1980), 10; and U.K. House of Commons, *Afghanistan: The Soviet Invasion and Its Consequences for British Policy*, Fifth Report from the Foreign Affairs Committee (London: HMSO, 1980), ix.

had failed, and Moscow, in keeping with the Brezhnev Doctrine, decided to intervene. One can also surmise that in making this decision, the Kremlin underestimated both the potential resistance in Afghanistan itself and the harshness of the reaction in the West. Not only were East–West relations severely damaged by the move, but Soviet troops remain in Afghanistan with no apparent resolution in sight. Afghan rebels continue both to hamper Soviet military operations and to prevent the normalization of the country under Soviet political domination.

In the chaotic weeks immediately following the invasion, however, this assessment found little support; fear of a Soviet move toward the Gulf was at its peak. Senator Frank Church, Chairman of the Senate Foreign Relations Committee, described the political climate during this period as "momentary hysteria."[21] Robert Komer, Under Secretary of Defense for Policy, referred to the invasion as President Carter's "second rebirth," the first being his religious awakening and the second, the abandonment of his naive view of the Soviets.[22] Even after the panic receded, however, concern and anger over the Soviet invasion ran high in Washington. In the words of one prominent analyst, "it is quite possible that whatever their original intentions may have been, this does open up the danger of a wider range of actions by the Soviet Union."[23] The immediate reaction of the Carter administration was to call for universal condemnation of the invasion and to impose political and economic sanctions against Moscow. Of more long term significance, however, was that détente, the lens through which American security policy had been formed throughout the 1970s, had been shattered. This was to change radically U.S. perceptions of the Soviet threat to the Middle East and throw support behind a more aggressive American stance in Southwest Asia.

The Collapse of Détente and Assessments of the Military Balance

Late in 1978, the SALT II agreement, after years of negotiation between Washington and Moscow, came before the U.S. Senate for ratification. The debate that ensued stimulated for the first time since the Vietnam War a congressional and public reassessment of the global balance between the superpowers. The debate reached its peak during the height of the crisis in Iran and ended suddenly after the Soviet invasion, when President Carter withdrew the Treaty from congressional consideration. This by no means curtailed the thorough analysis of America's global strategic posture that had been triggered by SALT

21. Interview with Frank Church.
22. Interview with Robert Komer.
23. Marshall Shulman, cited in U.S. Congress, House, Foreign Affairs Committee, *East–West Relations in the Aftermath of the Soviet Invasion of Afghanistan* (Washington, DC: GPO, 1980), 36.

II. As the events in Southwest Asia unraveled, technical experts as well as those relying on more emotive arguments were able to reach a common conclusion: Détente and America's isolationist response to the Vietnam War had provided the Soviet Union an opportunity to gain ground in the nuclear and conventional balance of forces and to increase their influence in the Third World. The deployment of the SS-20 MIRVed ballistic missile and the production of large numbers of Backfire Bombers in 1977 contributed to the widespread perception that the United States had lost considerable ground in the arms race. Joseph Sisco, Under Secretary of State for Near Eastern and South Asian Affairs, described this trend as "the sustained and unabated increase in Soviet military strength over the last decade, replacing our nuclear superiority with nuclear parity."[24] Though the contents of the SALT II agreement dealt only with nuclear weapons, the context in which the debate occurred—the dual crises in Southwest Asia—focused attention on conventional capabilities as well. Even in Congress, the discussions of SALT II required, according to Senator Howard Baker, "a broad gauge Senate debate" covering the gamut of U.S. relations with the Soviet Union.[25]

   One of the focal points of this broad gauge review was the increasing involvement of the Soviet Union in areas outside the Eastern bloc. Analysts considered both the recent history of Soviet intervention in the Third World as well as increasing Soviet capabilities to project force beyond the periphery of the homeland. The list of communist-led coups during the latter half of the decade was extensive: Vietnam in 1975, Angola in 1975–1976, Ethiopia in 1977, South Yemen and Afghanistan in 1978, and Cambodia in 1979. There were unsuccessful leftist coups in the Sudan in 1976–1977 and in Somalia in 1978. The Soviets also increased their points of access in and around the African continent by securing basing rights in Mauritius, Ethiopia, and Guinea-Bissau. This intensification of military activities in the Third World was complemented by continuing rhetorical support for national liberation movements in developing countries. Even those who did not see such trends in terms of a Soviet drive toward domination of the Third World recognized that the growth of Soviet power and involvement abroad could have a destabilizing effect on the global balance of power. Donald Zagoria expressed this concern well:

> In sum, the forcible extension of pro-Soviet Communism backed by Soviet power to several new areas of the world poses serious new strategic problems for a variety of middle powers, many of whom look to the United States for leadership and support. . . . The danger is [not hegemony, but] that the spread of Communism and Soviet power will upset tenuous regional balances of power, lead to intensified

---

24. U.S. Congress, Senate, *U.S. Security Interests*, 47.
25. *International Herald Tribune*, 8 January 1980, "Baker Cites Senate Doubts on SALT II."

regional instability and make even more difficult the settlement of regional clashes that could lead to war.[26]

Analysts supported their concern about increasing Soviet involvement in the Third World by pointing to the alarming growth of Soviet power projection capabilities. In the late 1970s and early 1980s, a spate of books and articles appeared that attempted to reinterpret Soviet military doctrine in light of their growing arsenal of airlift and sealift assets.[27] The remarkable aspect of this literature and its conclusions was that much of the evidence was based on statements and trends that were by no means of recent origin. In other words, the preoccupation with the global role of the Soviet military was as much a reflection of the atmosphere within the United States as of Soviet behavior over the past two decades. It was as early as 1963 that Admiral Gorshkov described the new role of the Soviet Navy: "In the last war, naval operations took place mainly near the shore and were confined, for the most part, to operative and tactical cooperation with the army. Today . . . we must be prepared to reply to them [the aggressors] with crushing blows on naval and land objectives over the entire area of the world's seas."[28]

Yet, it was not until the mid-1970s that Western analysts began to relate the growth of Soviet conventional forces to Moscow's emboldened role in the Third World. During the 1960s and 1970s, Soviet power projection capabilities did indeed consistently improve. With their seven divisions of airborne infantry and specially designed light equipment, the Soviets could match, if not surpass, American abilities to intervene with airborne troops.[29] The development of a new strategic lift aircraft (An-22) and the ease with which the Kremlin could commandeer civilian planes contributed to high assessments of Soviet lift capabilities. The speed with which troops were airlifted to Afghanistan in 1979–1980 confirmed this growth in capability. The Soviet navy exhibited similar expansion, though not on an order of magnitude that threatened American naval superiority. It was the direction more than the result of naval developments that concerned American planners. The Soviet Amphibious Infantry was strengthened and Kiev class aircraft carriers, new destroyers, and landing ships were commissioned.[30] For the first time, the Soviets conducted convoy maneu-

26. Donald Zagoria, "Into the Breach, New Soviet Alliances in the Third World," *Foreign Affairs* (Spring 1979), 740.

27. See, for example, MccGwire, *Soviet Naval Influence*, and Christoph Bertram, *Prospect of Soviet Power in the 1980s* (London: Macmillan, 1980).

28. Admiral Gorshkov cited in Michael MccGwire et al., eds., *Soviet Naval Policy, Objectives and Constraints* (New York: Praeger, 1975), 251.

29. James L. Moulton, "The Capability of Long-Range Intervention," in MccGwire, *Soviet Naval Influence*, 240.

30. Charles G. Pritchard, "Soviet Amphibious Force Projection," in *ibid.*, 246–269.

vers in 1975 to improve their logistical support for long distance operations. Between 1968 and 1978, calls by Soviet ships at foreign ports increased some 300%.[31] Secretary of Defense Weinberger, in his Posture Statement for 1982, summed up the prevalent perception in the United States of these developments: "The Soviets are acquiring forces for, and operational experience in, the projection of power and influence at great distances from the Soviet Union."[32]

While the collapse of détente led to a harsh reevaluation of Soviet capabilities, it also sparked, not surprisingly, a sober reassessment of American ability to project force overseas. And in the aftermath of America's post-Vietnam "retreat from power," many in the government were dissatisfied with the conclusions. There were two principal areas of concern: the relative decline in the superiority of American sea power after Vietnam and the vast reduction of America's network of overseas bases that occurred during the 1960s and 1970s. American involvement in Southeast Asia required a vast supply line; there was a continuous flow of tankers and cargo ships to and from the area of hostilities. After the withdrawal of American troops in the early 1970s, there was a rapid decline in both military sealift and in the tonnage of merchant marine vessels that would be available for military uses.[33] In the context of the Nixon Doctrine and the atmosphere of isolationism in Washington, maritime mobility was one of the areas hardest hit by cuts in the defense budget after 1973. There was also concern about the proliferation in the Third World of missiles and other sea-denial capabilities.[34] As the Falklands War showed in 1982, precision-guided missiles can vastly reduce the advantages of naval superiority. Finally, there was a debate within the defense community as to whether America's traditional reliance on large powerful aircraft carriers should be changed in light of developments in Soviet naval strategy. Some argued that larger numbers of smaller, more flexible carriers would better contain the growth of Soviet sea projection capabilities.[35]

Concomitant with a reassessment of maritime assets was a reconsideration of America's overseas basing system. Whether deploying troops by air or sea, a

31. U.K. Ministry of Defence, *Statement on the Defence Estimates 1980* (London: HMSO, 1980), vol. 1, 39.

32. U.S. Congress, Senate, Armed Services Committe, *Department of Defense Authorization for Appropriation for Fiscal Year 1983*, Pt. 1, Posture Statement (Washington, DC: GPO, 1982), 177.

33. Congressional Research Service, *Soviet Policy and United States Response in the Third World* (Washington, DC: GPO, 1981), 237–238.

34. Geoffrey Kemp, "Maritime Access and Maritime Power: The Past, the Persian Gulf, and the Future," in Alvin Cottrell et al., *Sea Power and Strategy in the Indian Ocean* (Beverly Hills, CA: Sage, 1981), 46–47.

35. See Robert Komer, "Maritime Strategy vs. Coalition Defense," *Foreign Affairs* (Summer 1982); and Stansfield Turner and George Thibault, "Preparing for the Unexpected: The Need for a New Military Strategy," *Foreign Affairs* (Fall 1982).

prerequisite of any long-distance operation is a network of both en route bases and ports and facilities in the theater of destination. The proliferation of U.S. facilities overseas occurred after 1945, when the B-47 strategic bomber required either forward basing or refueling en route to reach the Soviet Union. The procurement of both the longer range B-52 bomber and intercontinental missiles obviated the need for these facilities, and the basing network became more oriented toward "showing the flag" in foreign countries, as well as supporting U.S. sea operations, reconnaissance, and satellite communications. As early as the mid-1950s, however, this network began to deteriorate. From 1953 to 1977, the number of U.S. overseas bases declined from 150 to 30.[36] During the same period, there was a slow but steady increase in Soviet bases outside Europe.

The deterioration of the U.S. network was partly a reflection of the diminishing need for these facilities, but was also an indication of political opposition within the host countries. Anticolonial sentiment put pressure on inherently weak governments in developing countries to deny access to foreign powers. Regional conflicts, such as that between Greece and Turkey, forced the United States to choose sides, thereby alienating countries that had previously been willing to offer valuable basing sites. And the gradual distribution of political and military power to outlying regions meant that countries such as the Philippines and Spain could make greater demands on the United States in return for access to military facilities. Again, the events in Southwest Asia in 1979 and the collapse of détente led analysts to pay increasing attention to these issues and to interpret them in the context of a Soviet Union that was steadily growing more powerful and more aggressive.

Oil and Security Policy

The final issue that will be discussed before turning to the actual policy response of the Carter administration concerns certain assumptions about access to oil that emerged in the late 1970s. The rise in oil prices of over 150% that occurred in 1978–1979 was a clear indication that the steps taken since 1973 to avert another oil crisis had not been effective. The United States, the West Europeans, and Japan had instituted collective and individual measures to preempt a repetition of the oil shortage that followed the 1973 embargo. The International Energy Agency (IEA), the European Economic Community (EEC), and individual governments introduced numerous programs to control the storage, distribution, and consumption of imported oil. Yet, when exports of Iranian oil,

---

36. Alvin Cottrell and Thomas Moorer, *U.S. Overseas Bases: Problems of Projecting American Military Power Abroad,* The Washington Papers, vol. 5, Georgetown Center for Strategic and International Studies (Beverly Hills, CA: Sage, 1977), 8.

interrupted by strikes and turmoil, dropped from 5 million to 1 million barrels per day in late 1978, all these measures proved powerless to cope with diminishing supplies and rising prices.

There were three principal reasons why the West was unable to forge an adequate response to the oil crisis in 1978–1979. First, as in 1973, there was very little coordination among importing states. Because the real price of oil fell in the late 1970s, oil companies did not build reserve stockpiles. When Iranian production dropped, firms competed to secure dwindling supplies. This increased demand and sent prices skyrocketing. Second, by the late 1970s, the world's major oil companies had lost the control of the allocation process that they had once held.[37] This resulted from the nationalization of oil interests in the producing countries as well as the proliferation of smaller independent companies in the West. Finally, the Saudis failed to play the moderating role within OPEC that they had since 1975. Rather than increase production to offset the loss of Iranian crude, the Saudis cut their own production by 500,000 barrels per day for the first quarter of 1979 and then again by 1 million barrels per day for the second quarter.[38] After courting Riyadh with arms sales and political initiatives on the Arab–Israeli front, Washington was baffled and angered by this behavior. What motivations were behind Saudi policy? Did the Saudis want to see prices rise to supplement their income or were they making known their dissatisfaction with U.S. policy? That they in fact raised production immediately after the administration approved an arms sale package in July suggested a partial answer. Yet, there was still a great deal of confusion within Washington over what aspect of their relationship with the Saudis had gone awry.

There is insufficient evidence to draw a direct link between the frustration and political strain caused by this episode and Washington's decision to increase its military capabilities in the Gulf. Yet, it is not unreasonable to assert that the failure of economic and political initiatives to secure adequate oil supplies led to increased consideration of the military option. In 1973, the United States sent a carrier task force to the Indian Ocean, where it remained until the end of the embargo. It was after the oil shock of 1973–1974 that the U.S. government first considered a military operation to seize the oil fields. By 1979, Carter realized that his preoccupation with oil prices had led to the neglect of steps to secure adequate supplies; the West was left in a very vulnerable position. This is not meant to suggest that the Carter administration actively considered a military response to the oil crisis of 1978–1979. Yet, in combination with the fall of the Shah and the Soviet invasion of Afghanistan, the failure of economic and political initiatives to maintain stable oil prices and supplies, at the least, increased the willingness of the administration, the Congress, and the American public to support an increase in U.S. military power in the Persian Gulf.

37. Badger, "Oil Supply," 134.
38. Quandt, *Saudi Oil Policy*, 17.

The Evolution of Policy

In the early days of the Iranian crisis, the Carter administration remained firmly committed to avoiding the introduction of U.S. forces into Southwest Asia. The administration reasoned that external intervention would only weaken the Shah's already tenuous political position. Moreover, it would have been extremely difficult for President Carter to gain congressional and public support for intervention in Iran, especially when the engagement of U.S. troops could well have led to a prolonged and bloody conflict.

As it became apparent that the Shah would be unable to maintain control, however, opinion in Washington began to shift. Growing concern focused not on the use of force in Iran per se, but on how the strategic situation in Southwest Asia would look after the Shah had fallen from power. When it was evident that the revolution would produce a country that was less supportive of, if not inimical to, American interests, the Carter administration was forced to consider how to assume responsibility for at least some of the potential military missions previously fulfilled by the Shah's forces.

It was not until November 2, 1978—almost ten months after the outbreak of domestic unrest in Iran—that the Special Coordination Committee (SCC) undertook the first high-level review of U.S. Iranian policy.[39] The administration's neglect of the Shah's precarious position was in part a result of Washington's preoccupation with the Arab–Israeli negotiations. Yet, Gary Sick, Carter's National Security Council (NSC) staff member responsible for Iran, also argues that officials seemed paralyzed by the limited policy options available.[40] Given the ingrained assumptions in Washington about the stability of the Shah and the importance of his regime to U.S. interests, no one seemed prepared to address the full implications of the mounting revolutionary momentum in Iran. Furthermore, the utility of introducing military force was by no means evident. On the contrary, given the mass-based nature of the movement, it was difficult to see how the use of U.S. forces could have produced a different outcome. Coercive methods would have been most effective if introduced before the discontent had spread. But at that point, no one could have foreseen that the sporadic public disturbances would eventually burgeon into a full-scale revolution. The administration was learning painfully that internal upheaval presents a breed of security threat that does not lend itself to military solutions.

About one month after the November meeting of the SCC, officials in the NSC and the Pentagon began to take concrete steps to address the growing security problems resulting from the chaos in Iran. Brzezinski sought public support for a more aggressive stance and warned that the "political chaos could well be filled by elements hostile to our values and sympathetic to our adver-

39. Sick, *All Fall Down*, 67.
40. Ibid., 66–67.

saries." At the same time, Secretary of Defense Brown instructed his staff to undertake contingency planning for military operations in the Gulf area.[41] It is important to note that this was not the first time that such a request had been made. Presidential Directive 18 had not only directed that planning for Southwest Asia take place, it had also commissioned the establishment of a rapid action force for non-NATO contingencies.[42] These instructions had had little impact upon the military bureaucracy, however, except that the Pentagon's Office of Program Analysis and Evaluation (PA&E) carried out a review of contingency plannning for Southwest Asia.[43]

Before 1977, the services had done virtually no planning for operations in the Middle East. The European Command had drawn up contingency plans for the region, but the Joint Chiefs had found them inadequate and failed to approve them.[44] Beginning in 1977, PA&E carried out analyses of a number of potential conflicts in the region, some involving a confrontation with Soviet forces and others focusing on hostilities with regional states. These studies were hampered, however, by a dearth of information about and interest in military operations in the Gulf area. Intelligence sources could not provide reliable analyses of the region simply because they did not have the relevant information on hand and did not perceive a need to collect it.[45] Nor were the individual services willing to devote manpower to planning for the Middle East, an area where no single command or service had mission responsibility. This neglect of the strategic situation in the Gulf tempered the impact of PD-18 on the bureaucratic machinery that was to implement it and was also to hinder Brown's attempts to generate contingency plans for the region in 1978–1979.

As the Shah's position worsened, there was mounting pressure within the administration to reconsider the vulnerability of America's strategic interests in the Gulf. Yet, there remained considerable division within the administration over the wisdom of increasing America's military presence. In the NSC, while Brzezinski favored a "new security framework" for Southwest Asia, others, such as Deputy Director David Aaron, were more skeptical of military options. In the Pentagon, while Brown supported efforts to increase American capabilities in the Gulf, his views were generally not well received among the Joint Chiefs and within the individual services. Secretary Vance and the State Department as a

41. See Kennedy School of Government, Case Program, "Shaping the National Military Command Structure: Command Responsibilities for the Persian Gulf," Case C95–85–628 (Cambridge, MA: Harvard University, 1985), 8–9.

42. Interview with Lt. General William Odom.

43. Interviews with Defense Department officials.

44. Kennedy School of Government, "Command Structure," 9.

45. Interviews revealed that PA&E had designated Southwest Asia as an area requiring attention even before PD-18. PD-18 thus gave impetus to the planning review for the region, but planners still lacked adequate intelligence information.

whole did not favor a new strategy for the Gulf, largely because the agency feared a political backlash within the Arab world. Because of the sensitivity of the issue in Washington, much of the planning for the RDF was done rather quietly, with a few individuals in the NSC and the Secretary of Defense relying on specific personnel in the Pentagon, rather than on the appropriate offices, to complete military analyses.[46]

While these bureaucratic struggles ensued, several visible developments indicated that U.S. policy toward the Gulf was in a state of flux. The first overt military action was taken in January, 1979 when the United States sent twelve F-15s to Saudi Arabia, primarily as a show of support. This was followed in March by a similar visit of AWACS. These events were meant to reassure the Saudis of America's commitment to their security and to ameliorate the impact of the impending Egypt–Israel Peace Treaty that was signed in late March.[47] These moves were far from extraordinary; for years the United States had been paying such visits to states in the Middle East.

In February, however, the administration made clear that these gestures were part of a significant shift in U.S. policy. Following a tour of the area by Secretary Brown, a quite revealing pronouncement from a Defense Department official asserted that: "We have made a policy decision about a more active role in the area. We told these countries things that they had not heard for a long time— namely, that the United States is deeply interested in the Middle East, we are very worried about what the Soviets are doing, we intend to be involved. That's a line that no American has taken with them since Vietnam."[48] Two other official statements during these same weeks are of significance in understanding the evolution of the RDF. First, in a news conference in February, Secretary Brown declared that the "U.S. is prepared to defend its vital interests with whatever means are appropriate, including military force where necessary."[49] This is essentially the same terminology that formed the core of the Carter Doctrine—about one year later—supposedly in response to the Soviet invasion of Afghanistan. Second, there were several vague references from officials concerning efforts to construct a "collective security" system in the Gulf with the tangible support of the United States.[50] At the time, these allusions seemed little more than wishful thinking. Yet, as will soon become evident, the concept of a cooperative security system was an integral part of the evolving policy.

Despite these public pronouncements, however, planning for operations in Southwest Asia continued to proceed very slowly in the Pentagon. The mea-

46. Interviews with General P. X. Kelley and Lt. General William Odom.
47. *International Herald Tribune*, 20 February 1979, "Brown Said to Urge Boost of U.S. Forces."
48. Defense Department official cited in ibid.
49. Secretary of Defense Brown on CBS News, *Face the Nation*, 25 February 1979.
50. *New York Times*, 13 March 1979, "Yemen War Tests New Carter Policy."

sures considered included prepositioning military hardware, holding exercises with regional states, and supplementing U.S. naval and air deployments in the Gulf area.[51] In April, Secretary Brown made another attempt to bring the concept of a rapid strike unit to fruition by instructing the Joint Chiefs of Staff (JCS) to study possible command arrangements for the force. When this failed to produce results, Brown in June sent a formal request to the Chiefs asking that they prepare a paper recommending a command structure for the Gulf area by September 1.[52] The reply came on August 29, and the Chiefs equivocated between devolving responsibility for Southwest Asia to the Readiness Command (REDCOM) and establishing an independent task force to fulfill the rapid deployment mission.[53]

On October 22, Brown sent a memo to the JCS instructing them to establish by March 1, 1980 an independent joint task force which would be charged with handling security arrangements in Southwest Asia.[54] What forces would constitute the force, what its relationship with other commands would be, and what operational strategy it would adopt were all left unresolved. Equally unclear was whether this request would produce tangible results. Would the military bureaucracy, as it had done for years, continue to resist the creation of a regional strike force? Or was civilian pressure sufficiently intense to jolt the Pentagon into action?

The taking of American hostages in Tehran on November 4 played a significant role in shaping the answers to these questions. Early attempts to plan a rescue mission produced little more than frustration and revealed the inadequacy of America's capability to project force to the region. Of equal importance was the fact that the hostage crisis necessitated daily meetings of the top officials from the NSC, State Department, and Defense Department. These meetings provided both an appropriate forum for the discussion of general strategic issues in the Gulf and an opportunity for those who favored a strengthened American posture to present their conception of Gulf security to the more reluctant actors. As they had done earlier, Brzezinski and the NSC staff were careful to present their security framework in a somewhat veiled manner, thereby hoping to avoid eliciting harsh reactions from those in the Pentagon and State Department opposed to the RDF concept. By revealing their plans in a piecemeal fashion, they were attempting to garner gradually widespread support for their strategic initiatives toward Southwest Asia.[55]

By December, plans for a new policy toward the Gulf had congealed con-

51. Brzezinski, *Power and Principle*, 447.
52. Kennedy School of Government, "Command Structure," 17.
53. Ibid., 22.
54. Ibid., 24.
55. This negotiating strategy was described by William Odom, Brzezinski's chief military assistant. He related that this approach invoked much ire among State Department officials when they realized the full scope of the initiatives that the NSC was pursuing.

siderably among key actors. In an NSC meeting on December 4, President Carter instructed the State and Defense Departments to begin seeking military access arrangements with states in the Gulf area. Ten days later on December 14, Secretary Brown held a press conference at which he officially announced that the United States would establish the Rapid Deployment Force in March of the following year.

Within two weeks of this announcement, the Soviets invaded Afghanistan. And, as will soon become evident, this event was crucial in determining both how quickly Brown's directive was carried out and what operational strategy was to be designed for the RDF. Many in Washington who were staunchly opposed to the concept throughout 1979 became firm proponents of the RDF after the invasion. Furthermore, events in Afghanistan led President Carter to focus on America's need to respond to Soviet aggression as the theme of his State of the Union address. On January 23, 1980, he articulated what was to become the "Carter Doctrine": "Any attempt by any outside force to gain control of the Persian Gulf region will be regarded as an assault on the vital interests of the United States of America and such an assault will be repelled by any means necessary, including military force."[56] This clear and dramatic policy pronouncement was a further step gathering bureaucratic, congressional, and public support for the RDF.

Given this brief chronology of the events leading up to the establishment of the RDF and the promulgation of the Carter Doctrine, what factors appear to have been most prominent in shaping the evolution of policy? It is clear that even before the turmoil in Iran, some members within the administration wanted to enhance America's ability to project power to the periphery. These calls for bolstering America's rapid deployment capability, however, fell upon deaf ears. Even after Secretary Brown, in February 1979, made a public statement affirming American willingness to use force to defend U.S. interests in the Gulf, arrangements for the RDF proceeded slowly. Why was the RDF not established until March of the following year? Why was it so difficult for the administration to garner bureaucratic support for a regional strike force? Was the RDF established because of unyielding pressure from the White House or did events in Southwest Asia sufficiently alter political and strategic perspectives in Washington? These questions will be addressed by looking at the bureaucratic dynamics behind the formation of policy.

Détente and the post-Vietnam withdrawal were central to setting the tone of the Carter administration's foreign policy. The former led to the investment of considerable effort in formal arms negotiations with the Soviets and in generally improving the state of superpower relations. The latter led to a strategic withdrawal from peripheral areas and intensified the focus on Europe, already stimulated by détente. These perspectives were reflected in diplomatic initiatives:

56. State of the Union Address cited in Brzezinski, *Power and Principle,* 426.

SALT II, the negotiations on the demilitarization of the Indian Ocean, and the
U.S. restriction on conventional arms sales were cases in point. The State
Department grew committed not only to these specific measures, but also to
cultivating a political climate which would further its efforts to conclude successfully arms control agreements. The State Department naturally resisted steps
which would jeopardize this climate.

Given these efforts to negotiate with the Soviets an agreement on the Indian
Ocean (and the personal investment of specific individuals in the process), it is
easy to see why the State Department was staunchly opposed to initiatives to
strengthen America's military presence in the region. A more aggressive U.S.
policy toward the Gulf not only would undermine an agreement on the Indian
Ocean, but it also would challenge the State Department's broader goals with
respect to U.S.–Soviet relations. It is also important to note that State Department officials complained that they were excluded from decisions about the
RDF, claiming that the NSC staff deliberately avoided consultation in order to
circumvent State Department opposition.[57] The State Department thus saw the
RDF as a challenge to both its general negotiating strategy and its authority as
the principal agency responsible for forming foreign policy.

Within the Pentagon, service interests and the military command structure
are essential to understanding the organizational dynamics behind the development of the RDF. The services, as they had done in the past, resisted devoting
resources to establish a permanent regional strike force for two principal reasons.
First, Europe was the focal point of strategic planning and resource allocation.
The defense of NATO territory was considered to be the top priority of the
military, and each service wanted to protect its role in the European theater.
Second, the services wanted to avoid involvement in domestically unpopular,
unconventional wars, such as that fought in Southeast Asia. Confronting
guerilla warfare in the inhospitable climate and terrain of Southwest Asia was
not a mission particularly appealing to the military establishment.

During 1979, each service also had its own reasons for resisting the proposal
to establish a strike force. The Marine Corps, because of the mixture of sea and
ground forces that might be needed in the Gulf, seemed particularly well suited
to adopt the Southwest Asia mission. The problem was that the Marines feared
that by becoming the RDF, they would exclude themselves from playing any role
in Europe.[58] Because the Marine Corps was comprised of only three main
divisions, the Gulf mission could well require all its manpower. The Navy,

57. See Brzezinski, *Power and Principle*, 427–428. For the view of a State Department official in
the Carter administration see David Newsom, "America Engulfed," *Foreign Policy* (Summer 1981).
Newsom asserts that the Carter Doctrine "grew out of last minute pressures for a presidential speech.
There have been no congressional hearings and little public debate. As far as is known, neither the
current [Reagan] administration nor the previous one has ever conducted a detailed study of the
implications of the policy or its alternatives" (p. 17).
58. See Kennedy School of Government, "Command Structure," 19–20.

though primarily responsible for operations in the Gulf area until 1980, was uncomfortable with the demanding ground scenario postulated by planners. The Navy was willing to focus on protecting the tanker routes and keeping open the Straits of Hormuz, but was less forthcoming about sending carriers into the Gulf itself to protect territory and oil fields. Because of the vulnerability of vessels in Gulf waters, such missions, the Navy argued, would require at least three carriers: two inside the Persian Gulf and one in the Gulf of Oman. The Navy claimed that this would divert too many resources from other areas.[59] The Army was interested in adding missions to the scope of its responsibility if this meant an increase in its budget. But the Army feared that it would be forced to allocate resources for light airborne divisions rather than the preferred heavier units that would be of more use in Europe. Finally, the Air Force saw its potential mission in Southwest Asia primarily as one of providing lift. Given a limited budget, the Air Force preferred to procure tactical fighters rather than lift aircraft. In short, the services were well aware that the RDF was likely to be constructed of existing forces. This meant that by adopting responsibility for Southwest Asia, they would be diverting resources from preferred missions to uphold a questionable commitment that could well involve them in an unconventional and undesirable war in the periphery.

The military command structure placed a further obstacle in the path of the RDF. To review briefly command arrangements for the Middle East, the Kennedy administration in 1961 established the Strike Command (STRICOM) to handle the deployment of troops and the conduct of operations in areas not covered by existing commands. In the wake of the Vietnam War, STRICOM was dissolved in 1971 and the task of coordinating overseas deployment was assigned to the newly formed Readiness Command (REDCOM). STRICOM's regional responsibilities were incorporated into the areas covered by the other unified commands. The Middle East mission was divided among the European Command (EUCOM) and the Pacific Command (PACOM). EUCOM covered the land mass from the eastern Mediterranean states to Iran, including the Persian Gulf. PACOM was assigned Pakistan, Afghanistan, and the Indian Ocean.

This division of labor complicated military planning for the Middle East. REDCOM, because it was concerned solely with lift and deployment, received little budgetary attention, especially in the aftermath of Vietnam. Both EUCOM and PACOM treated the Middle East as of peripheral importance: their primary interests lay elsewhere. In organizational terms, this meant that there was no single bureaucratic entity within the command structure that stood to benefit from strengthening America's capability in the Middle East. There was no locus of authority within the military establishment to give impetus to plan-

---

59. Interview with Geoff Kemp. The Navy was also quite averse to the very idea of sending carriers into the Gulf.

ning for Southwest Asia. In the words of one Pentagon analyst, "[t]here was no organization or command like EUCOM or PACOM in the position to lobby and compete for scarce resources to be devoted to improving our capability to deal with that part of the world."[60] Moreover, this arrangement meant that the creation of the RDF would cause strife within the Pentagon, simply because three separate unified commands (REDCOM, PACOM, and EUCOM) would compete for control over the force.

PACOM suggested that its territorial responsibility be expanded westward to include the Gulf littoral states and the Gulf itself. EUCOM countered that its area of responsibility should be expanded eastward to include Pakistan, Afghanistan, and the access routes to the Gulf in the Indian Ocean. REDCOM claimed that, as the command designated to handle rapid deployment operations, the mission in Southwest Asia should fall under its auspices. The proposals from PACOM and EUCOM were essentially unfeasible: To assign full responsibility for the Gulf to one command at the exclusion of the other would have caused a considerable political battle within the military. Yet, there was a more prominent organizational problem that made all three proposals unattractive. If detailed planning and procurement for operations in the Middle East were to take place, an organization had to be created whose sole responsibility was focused on the region. To assign the mission in Southwest Asia to an existing command would not have created sufficient bureaucratic momentum to implement the administration's new policy. As had happened in the past, the designated command would have treated its operational responsibility in the Middle East as a secondary commitment.

Chiefly for this reason, Secretary Brown instructed that a new joint task force—the Rapid Deployment Joint Task Force (RDJTF)—be created. The RDJTF was to be subordinate to REDCOM, yet could communicate directly with the JCS through a liasion office in the Pentagon. At the admission of many, this was a suboptimal solution, but was done to set the process in motion while minimizing political costs. There was much support within the administration for the creation of a separate unified command for the Middle East.[61] That this would have been a costly move became clear during the Reagan administration, when the RDJTF was transformed into the Central Command (CENTCOM). General Warner, the commander of REDCOM, resigned when the decision to establish CENTCOM was made. This revealed that the subject of command arrangements for the Middle East was a very sensitive issue within the military bureaucracy. The political limitations that emerged from these sensitivities proved to delay and to complicate efforts to establish a quick strike force for the Middle East.

60. Chris Shoemaker cited in Kennedy School of Government, "Command Structure," 13.
61. Robert Komer and Lt. General Odom, both key actors in establishing the RDJTF, stressed that a unified command was not created largely because of the potential political fallout.

How did the Carter administration eventually circumvent these obstacles? Did the positions of the State Department and the Pentagon shift and, if so, why? Why did the Carter administration succeed in establishing a rapid strike force when numerous attempts to do so since 1945 had failed?

It is clear that the White House resorted to persistent pressure to ensure that the State and Defense Departments responded to its directives. Early requests for planning papers simply went unanswered or were delayed considerably. Yet, in light of the worsening strategic situation in the Gulf and the need for a decisive shift in foreign policy for domestic consumption, the administration grew firmly committed to following through its plans to strengthen America's military posture in the Gulf. The role of civilian intervention was paramount. While the JCS was mired in command arrangements and service rivalry, actors such as Brzezinski in the NSC and Robert Komer in the office of the Secretary of Defense played key roles in both devising a new strategy for the Gulf and ensuring that it would be executed by a reluctant bureaucracy. It was the persistence of certain individuals that brought the concept of the RDF to life and prevented it from becoming a stillborn entity.

Organizational as well as individual perspectives, however, were affected by the course of events in 1979. The turmoil in Iran and the hostage crisis raised the possibility of sending U.S. forces to the Gulf. Requests for contingency plans illuminated to the military how inadequate U.S. planning and capabilities were. Yet, the single most important event shaping organizational attitudes was the Soviet invasion of Afghanistan. Although the decision to establish the RDF had been taken before this event, the invasion played a crucial role in reducing bureaucratic resistance to the RDF and in shaping an operational strategy for the force.

The Soviet invasion fundamentally altered the orientation of the administration's foreign policy. The attitudes that had given impetus to SALT II, the negotiations on the Indian Ocean, and the efforts to restrict conventional arms sales quickly faded. This meant that there was less opposition throughout Washington to the overt strengthening of America's capability to intervene in the Middle East.[62] Furthermore, the invasion led to the promulgation of the Carter Doctrine. The formal statement of policy gave credibility to the RDF and was intended to indicate clearly to the public, Congress, the State Department, and the Pentagon that a significant shift in America's approach to the Gulf had taken place. This clarification of America's military commitment to the Middle East was important in setting the bureaucratic machinery in motion and in securing the appropriations necessary to support the administration's procurement recommendations.[63]

62. Brzezinski, *Power and Principle*, 430.
63. Ibid., 446.

The Soviet move also allowed the administration both to focus public attention on the need to deter Soviet aggression and to publicize the RDF as a force
designed specifically to fulfill that mission. This made the Carter Doctrine easier
to sell to the American public and more palatable to Gulf regimes. To emphasize
this point, President Carter explicitly asserted that the United States would use
force to repel any attempt by *outside* forces to gain control of the Persian Gulf.
This attempt to placate the fears of Gulf leaders about the goals of the RDF eased
the State Department's concern about making a public declaration of U.S.
intentions to intervene in the Middle East if necessary. In more private surroundings, U.S. officials did not preclude the possibility of intervening in circumstances other than those involving the Soviet Union. When pressed on
whether the United States would defend Saudi Arabia against Iran, for example,
Robert Komer, Under Secretary of Defense for Policy, admitted that "our decision would depend on many variables."[64] Yet, David Newsom, Under Secretary
of State for Political Affairs, was careful to point out that the RDF would work
with, not against, Gulf regimes: "[W]e are seeking . . . to obtain a degree of
cooperation which will give us the capacity to support our friends in the area. It
is a strategy which is based on their continued independence and sovereignty
and our willingness to cooperate with them on a basis that fully respects that
sovereignty."[65]

Finally, the Soviet invasion ensured that the Carter Doctrine would go
beyond the planning stage and that efforts would be made to make the implementation of America's new policy both feasible and credible. The military had
repeatedly resisted attempts to establish a regional strike force since 1945. Even
between 1977 and 1979, when the Pentagon's Office of Program Analysis and
Evaluation was carrying out studies of Soviet and U.S. power projection
capabilities in the Gulf region, planning for contingencies in Southwest Asia
received little attention. The services showed more interest in the regional
mission by mid-1979—well before the Soviet invasion of Afghanistan—when
the military guidance called for planning to focus on a Soviet contingency in
Iran. The decision to focus on a Soviet contingency rather than on a broad
range of scenarios was made for two reasons. First, there was growing concern
that the Soviets might take advantage of the chaos in Iran to invade the
northern portion of the country. Second, the focus on a Soviet contingency was
meant to stimulate a more substantive response from the Pentagon.[66] This was a
scenario that was sufficiently demanding to elicit from the military the shifts in
resource allocation that the administration had been seeking. To address lower
level internal threats as the basis for planning had simply provided insufficient

64. Robert Komer cited in U.S. Congress, House, *U.S. Interests in the Gulf 1980*, 81.
65. David Newsom, cited in U.S. Congress, Senate, *U.S. Security Interests*, 85.
66. Personal communication with Robert Komer, 29 July 1985.

momentum to effect these desired changes in procurement and strategy. Even with this new incentive, however, it was not until the Soviet invasion of Afghanistan that the procurement and planning process gained significant bureaucratic momentum. After December, few obstacles hindering the formation of a new military strategy for the Gulf remained. The State Department was no longer preoccupied with salvaging détente, and the Pentagon and intelligence community now viewed a Soviet thrust toward the Persian Gulf as a feasible scenario that required immediate attention.

The key point is that the Soviet invasion of Afghanistan—and the consequent collapse of détente—ensured sufficient bureaucratic momentum and the public support essential to transform the Carter Doctrine from a political gesture into a substantive change in U.S. security policy. Before the Soviet move, official and public support for a reassertion of U.S. military power in the Gulf was hindered by numerous uncertainties. Under what circumstances would the use of U.S. force be useful in resolving intraregional conflict? Could troops be used to protect the flow of oil? Would an increase in foreign military presence not exacerbate existing political problems? The Soviet invasion, because it raised the spectre of a superpower confrontation in Southwest Asia, paradoxically simplified the policy dilemma. The task of confronting the Soviets in Iran was by no means easy, but the prospect served to reduce uncertainty. Politicians and planners alike could focus their attention on a specific, demanding, and well-defined scenario.[67]

Despite the atmosphere of panic that pervaded Washington following the Soviet invasion, the Carter administration knew well that the most serious threat came not from the Soviets directly, but from their ability to gain political and military access should the region fall into chaos. History had shown that the greatest threat to U.S. interests was the potential radicalization of the Gulf and the consequent erosion of the West's political leverage in the region.[68] This was both the most likely and the most comprehensive challenge to the U.S. goals of stemming Soviet encroachment, securing oil flows, and effecting a solution to the Arab–Israeli conflict.

The essential paradox was that American efforts to deter the Soviets by increasing U.S. military capability in the Gulf could well intensify this more likely threat. Furthermore, exclusive focus on the Soviet Union seemed necessary to elicit a substantive response from the military bureaucracy. To establish a force that could deter the Soviets and restore America's credibility and image in

67. This analysis corresponds well with John Steinbruner's cybernetic theory of decision-making. In his model, decision-makers opt for the solution which best reduces uncertainty. This notion will be elaborated upon in Chapter 9. See John Steinbruner, *The Cybernetic Theory of Decision: New Dimensions of Political Analysis* (Princeton, NJ: Princeton University Press, 1974).

68. Komer in U.S. Congress, Senate, Armed Services Committee, *Department of Defense Authorization for Appropriations for Fiscal Year 1981*, Pt. 1 (Washington, DC: GPO, 1980), 145.

the Arab world—without presenting the United States as a colonial, expansio-nist power—was the enormity of the challenge facing planners. For the Carter Doctrine to achieve its goals, the administration had to integrate global and regional considerations and to find the delicate balance between meeting mili-tary requirements and honoring political exigencies.

This focus on the military implications of the Carter Doctrine is not meant to minimize the broad political objectives of the new policy. The administration was particularly concerned with restoring American influence in the Gulf re-gion, both to secure the cooperation of regional states and to check Moscow's growing leverage. Without Iran, symbolic presence was not real presence. As long as the Soviets were 700 miles from the Gulf while the Americans were 7000, no degree of political maneuvering could successfully counter Soviet influence.[69] In the words of Shahram Chubin, "[t]he Soviet Union has staying power; it requires no presence (it is present). . . ."[70] It was Soviet will that the United States had to challenge as much as Soviet power. And as long as Washington did not meet that challenge, the Soviets commanded a certain authority, albeit symbolic, throughout the region. The American response had to be more than vocal; only through concrete steps to increase its military capabilities in the region could the Carter Doctrine achieve its dual purpose of deterring Soviet aggression and restoring America's image and political leverage in the Middle East. The political strategy that would accompany the establish-ment of the RDF was in rudimentary form in 1980. Yet, testimony before Congress revealed the broad aims that this shift in policy was to achieve: "This would be a meaningful signal to the U.S.S.R., it will encourage and bulwark our friends in the area; it will reinforce the central role of the United States in resolving the Arab–Israeli dispute; including the Palestinian question; and it offers the best hope that further Soviet advances toward the Straits of Hormuz can be deterred."[71] Whether these goals were simply examples of wishful think-ing and how they were to be attained are the topics of the following chapters.

Conclusions

There is no question that the implications of the Iranian revolution and the Soviet invasion of Afghanistan warranted a thorough reassessment of U.S. strategy in the Persian Gulf. The fall of the Shah led to the loss of America's principal ally in the Gulf and was a clear repudiation of the twin pillar policy.

69. Jonathan Alford, "Soviet–American Rivalry in the Middle East: The Military Dimension," in Dawisha, *The Soviet Union*, 135.
70. Shahram Chubin, "U.S. Security Interests in the Gulf in the 1980s," *Daedalus* (Fall 1980), 47.
71. Joseph Sisco, cited in U.S. Congress, Senate, *U.S. Security Interests*, 48–49.

The Soviet invasion of Afghanistan moved Soviet troops closer to the Gulf and heightened America's sense of impotence and strategic vulnerability in the region. For over three decades, the United States had maintained a very limited military capability in the Middle East. Suddenly, this capability appeared alarmingly insufficient to cope with the intensifying external and intraregional threats to American interests. What were the key considerations determining how the United States was to restructure its military posture in the region? How successful was Washington in incorporating global and regional considerations into its new security policy for Southwest Asia?

Within a regional context, a reassessment of America's military capability in the Gulf had to address the strategic implications of the Iranian revolution. Iran during the 1970s was the dominant military power in the Gulf. The Shah's desire to be the guardian of stability in the region coincided with American interests. A strong pro-Western Iran served to solidify the position of conservative states within the Arab Gulf. And the Iranian military took responsibility for patrolling the Gulf and coming to the assistance of regimes faced with internal threats. Was it possible for the United States to assume responsibility for these missions? America could by no means hope to replace the political role played by the Shah; the conservative bloc had been dealt an irreparable blow. Furthermore, U.S. troops were far more of a political liability in the Gulf than were those of the Shah. In strictly military terms, however, the United States had sufficient existing capabilities to replace the Shah's guardian role in the Gulf. The MIDEASTFOR was already on station; if strengthened, this force could have patrolled the Gulf and the northern Indian Ocean and assumed responsibility for smaller contingencies on the peninsula. The more demanding military problem emerged from the prospect of fighting Iranian or Iraqi forces or Soviet forces lured southward by the chaos in Iran. For these contingencies, the United States would need armored ground divisions and tactical air support. It was this type of large-scale operation that the U.S. military, as of 1979, was unprepared to undertake. While confrontation with the Soviets represented the most demanding scenario, given the emerging radicalism in Iran and its consequent destabilizing effect on the region, it was Iranian or Iraqi aggression that posed the most likely threats both to the security of lower Gulf states and to the flow of oil. This concern with intraregional contingencies was reflected in early planning for the RDF, and the changes in military posture associated with the Carter Doctrine enhanced America's ability to intervene in conflicts involving local actors. But by the second half of 1979 and certainly after the Soviet invasion of Afghanistan, the key focus of U.S. military planning was on the Soviet threat.

In comparison with the Iranian revolution, the Soviet invasion of Afghanistan, in an objective sense, had less profound strategic implications for the United States. The Soviets increased their ability to project air power to the Gulf by using airfields in Afghanistan as forward bases. The Soviets were in the process of modernizing their forces in the southern republics in the late 1970s, but these troops remained at a relatively low state of readiness. The Soviets also had exhibited a growing willingness and capability to project power over long distances. Yet, the move into Afghanistan did not reveal any quantum leap in capability that had previously been hidden from U.S. intelligence sources. Despite these factors, the Carter Doctrine and the RDF were crafted to deter a direct Soviet invasion of Iran by ground forces. The shift in U.S. policy must therefore be understood more as a result of a perceived change in Soviet intentions than as a response to growing Soviet capabilities. The United States began to interpret Soviet behavior and Soviet capabilities in a new light.

Thus, the key question is whether events in Afghanistan made a Soviet move toward the Gulf appear either more likely or more feasible. The political and military costs of the war in Afghanistan, if anything, reduced the likelihood of a simultaneous invasion of Iran. Nor did a large Soviet military presence along the border with Iran suddenly appear in 1980. It is also clear that, from a Soviet perspective, the fall of the Shah made a thrust into Iran neither easier nor more attractive. Despite the loss of some military capability, the Iranians still could have mustered a significant resistance. What is more, the initial Soviet reaction to the revolution was favorable; the most powerful state in the northern tier had clearly broken from its traditional Western tilt. A Soviet invasion of Iran thus appeared less likely after 1979 than it had in previous years. Strategic considerations alone are inadequate to explain the nature of America's response to the crises in Southwest Asia.

The most important consequences for U.S. policy of events in Iran and Afghanistan lay not in their immediate implications for Gulf security, but in their impact on broader strategic and political perspectives in Washington. It is clear that some officials in the Carter administration, even well before the fall of the Shah, were concerned about America's strategic vulnerability in peripheral areas in general, and in the Persian Gulf in particular. Yet, within the context of détente and the post-Vietnam climate, proposals to bolster U.S. force projection capabilities received little bureaucratic or public support. The events of 1979 fundamentally altered this political context. In the wake of the Soviet invasion of Afghanistan, a reassertion of American power was no longer a political liability. On the contrary, President Carter was seeking a visible and forceful shift in foreign policy to restore the public confidence in his administration which was eroding throughout the Iranian crisis. Carter needed a dramatic change in policy that reflected a reassessment of America's global posture. An increase in the size of the MIDEASTFOR or a quiet effort to increase lift capabilities would not have achieved this objective.

It is also clear that the policymaking process itself left a discernible imprint on the orientation of the Carter Doctrine and the concept of the RDF. Civilian intervention in military planning played an essential role in creating a new strategy for the Persian Gulf. The decision to establish the RDF was essentially imposed upon a reluctant Pentagon by the White House. It was the persistence of certain individuals—such as Zbigniew Brzezinski, and William Odom in the NSC and Robert Komer in the Office of the Secretary of Defense—that ensured that planning for the RDF would come to fruition.

The presentation of the strategic problem in the Gulf was crucial to overcoming bureaucratic opposition to the proposed shift in America's Gulf policy. Focus on intraregional conflicts, though they posed the most likely threats to U.S. interests, did not elicit the substantive response from the Pentagon that the administration had been seeking. Concentration on the Soviet threat, however, did set the necessary planning and procurement processes in motion. While Washington responded very sluggishly to events in Iran, it reacted sharply and quickly to the Soviet move into Afghanistan. The bureaucracy was selectively responsive; it was far more sensitive to the global implications of shifts in Soviet behavior than to the impact of the Iranian revolution on political and strategic considerations in the region. The invasion of Afghanistan, by making the prospect of a Soviet move toward the Gulf a more urgent and a more credible problem, served as a convenient stimulus to the bureaucratic machinery. By ruining hopes of maintaining détente or securing progress on arms control, the invasion also served to reduce the State Department's opposition to the RDF. In general, there was a broad shift in organizational attitudes toward supporting a strengthened U.S. posture in the Gulf. Exactly why the United States seems to have exaggerated the Soviet threat, however, will be examined in more detail in the final chapter.

This focus on strategic and bureaucratic concerns is not to suggest that the administration's decision to alter its military posture in Southwest Asia was not based on certain assumptions about shifting political trends within the Persian Gulf. Carter's ineffectual response to the crisis in Iran had raised doubts about the willingness and ability of the United States to come to the aid of its allies. The Carter administration therefore wanted to reassure the Saudis and other pro-Western regimes that it would stand behind its commitment to defend them. To demonstrate such resolve, the Carter Doctrine had to be backed by a tangible change in America's security posture in the region. The administration perceived this objective as compatible with the high degree of political uncertainty within the region. Confronted with threats from Khomeni, Islamic fundamentalism, and Soviet aggression, it seemed reasonable to expect states in the Gulf to rely increasingly on America's security umbrella. As we will see, these expectations ultimately proved to be accurate, yet only for the short term. The Carter administration had failed to take into account other aspects of Gulf politics which were to make close ties to the United States considerably less attractive.

In its broadest strategic context, the Carter Doctrine marked not only a change in security policy toward the Gulf, but also a reassessment of America's regional priorities and global military commitments. Southwest Asia had joined

Europe and Northeast Asia as one of America's central strategic zones. Not only were military personnel and materials assigned to Southwest Asia, but such changes were made at the expense of the potential strength of U.S. power in other theaters. The number of troops actually deployed in Europe did not decline; however, divisions earmarked for the central front were also assigned to the Rapid Deployment Joint Task Force. Furthermore, the United States insisted with vehemence that NATO as a collective unit assume responsibility for defending Western interests in the Middle East. Even Japan became involved in the consideration of the deployment of U.S. troops to Southwest Asia.[72] With the Soviet invasion of Afghanistan coming on the heels of the fall of the Shah, Soviet influence in the Gulf became inextricably bound to the question of oil flows from the Gulf. It was this fusion of threats which thrust the Middle East into a position of new importance in U.S. global security policy.

The implications of the Iranian revolution went far beyond the loss of a strategic ally and a new need to devote military resources to the Gulf. The fall of the Shah constituted an outright rejection of the approach to regional security upon which America had depended throughout the 1970s. The forces that contributed to the Shah's power and his ability to serve as a reliable surrogate were the same forces that contributed to his demise. Carter's approach to the Soviets was equally unrewarding. By the late 1970s, it appeared to many in the administration that the Soviets had taken advantage of détente both to gain an edge in the strategic balance and to expand their leverage in the Third World. Again, American policy produced a result that contradicted its original objectives.

The Carter Doctrine was a reaction to this predicament. It marked a reassertion of American global power and was to reduce the country's reliance on surrogates to secure U.S. interests in the Third World. What the Carter Doctrine lacked, however, was a clear conception of how these objectives were to be achieved. The Carter Doctrine identified the Persian Gulf as a "strongpoint" and resurrected symmetrical containment as the policy most suitable for coping with the Soviet threat. Yet, could the United States, without a regional military presence, realistically expect to confront Soviet forces in an area contiguous to the Soviet Union? Were available resources sufficient to make this commitment a credible one? Was America's grand strategic entry into the Gulf compatible with the realities of regional politics? These dilemmas that the United States faced in the Persian Gulf were to become manifest between 1980 and 1982 during the formulation and implementation of a new strategy for Southwest Asia.

---

72. Masahiro Sasagawa, "Japan and the Middle East," in Steven Spiegel, ed., *The Middle East and the Western Alliance* (London: George Allen and Unwin, 1982), 42–43.

Chapter Five

THE RAPID DEPLOYMENT FORCE: PLANNING, STRATEGY, OPERATIONAL REQUIREMENTS

The task of deploying a large number of U.S. troops to Southwest Asia presented an unprecedented challenge to American military planners. The distances involved in transporting men and equipment from the United States were enormous; the theater lacked a sufficient military infrastructure; the climate in the region was extremely harsh; and any operation depended upon the elusive political cooperation of regional states. What is more, speed was imperative. Whether it was a Soviet invasion or a local coup, the earlier that U.S. forces could arrive, the better the chance of achieving their objectives. A long and slow logistics line such as that used to support operations in East Asia would be useful only in a protracted war. The United States needed air transport and sealift to follow—precisely those assets which had suffered most through the post-Vietnam cutbacks.

Though the Carter Doctrine incorporated both political and strategic objectives, its immediate goal was to establish a credible American military capability in the Middle East. This was the first step in realizing whatever long term strategy lay behind the policy decisions of the Carter administration. In the words of Robert Komer, "without a firm foundation in military potential, our political strategy would be barren."[1] The decision to augment America's military capability in Southwest Asia was one matter; how to do it was another.

There were three essential questions facing planners. First, what should the Rapid Deployment Force (RDF) be able to do? Around what scenarios should planning proceed? Second, what level and type of force capability would best fulfill the designated missions? And third, what was the most suitable means of implementing and preparing for the chosen strategy? It was clear that the devel-

---

1. Robert Komer, cited in U.S. Congress, House, *U.S. Interests in the Gulf 1980*, 66.

opment of a credible military capability required the cooperation of regional states. Which states and what type of cooperation were the crucial issues. The previous chapter established the political and strategic assumptions upon which the Carter Doctrine was based. This section examines the military requirements needed to implement U.S. policy. The goal of the next chapter is to investigate how and to what extent these two components were integrated.

Planning

The first step in designing both the structure of the RDF and its operational strategy was to define the missions the force would potentially fulfill. Should planning revolve around a Soviet contingency in Iran or should preparations be made to deal with intraregional conflicts as well? Initial planning for operations in Southwest Asia focused primarily on intraregional contingencies, such as Iraqi aggression in the lower Gulf, though Soviet intervention was also considered.[2] By the second half of 1979, however, even before the Soviet invasion of Afghanistan, contingency planning had shifted to concentrate almost exclusively on operations against the Soviets in Iran. Despite the objections of officials in the State Department and members of Congress, the military guidance (the document that sets priorities for sizing, force structure, and strategy) instructed planners to design an RDF based upon meeting a Soviet attack in Iran.[3] This singular concern with the Soviet threat is somewhat puzzling given the general awareness in the Defense Department of the more likely internal threats as well as the fact that the groundwork for the RDF was laid in 1979— before the invasion of Afghanistan. It is worth investigating in more depth why this bias prevailed in designing a strategy for the RDF. The following points represent possible, and by no means mutually exclusive, explanations.

The Pentagon defended its focus on a Soviet contingency by claiming, as it had many times in the past, that planning for the worst case is preparation for lesser contingencies as well.[4] There is, no doubt, some truth to this argument. A force designed to defeat, say, two divisions should be quite capable of defeating one division. This follows, however, only if other factors are held constant. And in the Gulf area, given the wide range of potential enemies, the variations in terrain and climate, and the political uncertainties that would determine access

2. Interviews with military officials.
3. Interviews in the State Department, Defense Department, and with congressional staff members all confirmed the exclusive focus of planning on a Soviet contingency. Members of Congress were most vociferous in criticizing the apparent neglect of more likely intraregional threats to U.S. interests.
4. Stansfield Turner, "Toward a New Defense Strategy," in *New York Times Magazine* (10 May 1981), 15–16.

and regional assistance, purely quantitative methods of assessment must be treated with skepticism. The commandos and special units that would be needed to interdict Soviet advances in the northern mountains of Iran would be of little use in defending Saudi Arabia against Iran's heavier divisions. Furthermore, because the level of military infrastructure in Southwest Asia varies greatly from one area to another, planning must be suited to specific regions. The logistical support, equipment, and maps needed to fight the Soviets in Iran would differ considerably from that required to defend the Arabian peninsula.

A second explanation of the focus on a Soviet contingency was that an invasion of Iran was not only the worst case, it was also the most demanding in terms of equipment and troop requirements. By basing procurement on this contingency, the Pentagon was seeking to maximize the budgetary allocation for Southwest Asia. The problem with this explanation is that the services did not stand to gain a large increase in their budgets because of the added mission in the Middle East. Most new expenditures were to be devoted to increasing lift, not procuring weapons or augmenting manpower. And lift assets have never been at the top of the services' procurement lists.

The most persuasive explanations for the focus of planners on a Soviet contingency in Iran concern several political and bureaucratic issues raised in Chapter 4. By directing public attention on Iran, the United States was able to allay fears among Gulf states that the purpose of the RDF was to interfere in internal Gulf affairs. This was a means of publicizing the Soviet threat, hopefully to the end of intensifying regional leaders' concerns about the Soviet Union. If the strategic perspectives of regional states corresponded with those of the United States, it would be easier for Washington to secure access to bases and facilities in the Gulf area. Although some planning for smaller contingencies was done on a more secretive basis, the scope of analysis was constrained by political considerations. During the initial phases of planning, operations to seize the oil fields were not discussed, for example, because of fear that such information would eventually be leaked to the press.[5]

It is also clear that competition among the services affected the orientation of contingency planning. The Navy and Marines favored emphasis on smaller non-Soviet contingencies that would require chiefly naval and amphibious operations. The Air Force and Army, on the other hand, argued that planning should proceed around a Soviet invasion, largely because the Iranian scenario required air strikes and ground combat troops as well as naval and amphibious support. Planning for a mission that involved all four services was understandably to meet less bureaucratic opposition than planning for a contingency that involved only two.

Finally, the Soviet move into Afghanistan was a key event ensuring that the

5. Military interviews.

RDF's strategy was to be based upon a major contingency in Iran. In 1980, there was an atmosphere of virtual panic surrounding the threat of a Soviet move into Iran. Intelligence reports in August indicated unusual maneuvers of Soviet troops along the border.[6] Washington was preoccupied with the possibility of a confrontation with the Soviets, and although this was not a desirable scenario for the Pentagon, it was the one with which the military and the national security apparatus as a whole were most familiar and to which they were most willing to respond.[7] As mentioned in Chapter 4, even before the invasion of Afghanistan, planners were instructed to focus on a Soviet contingency in part because a more demanding scenario would elicit a more substantive bureaucratic response. The Soviet invasion, in keeping with this logic, did stimulate bu-reaucratic momentum for the RDF. Yet, this exclusive focus on the Soviet threat also had a significant impact on the nature and orientation of the opera-tional strategy for the force that was to emerge in 1980–1981.

Strategy

The result of these budgetary, strategic, political, and organizational factors was that planners were instructed to design a strategy for the RDF that would enable the United States to deter and/or resist a Soviet invasion of Iran. The distances involved in transporting troops to Southwest Asia, the availability of lift and manpower, and the problems of securing regional access were the chief con-straints facing military planners. Before addressing the mechanics of force pro-jection, however, a more general strategic issue had to be confronted: Should the United States extend its nuclear umbrella to cover the Persian Gulf?

The option of extending an American nuclear guarantee to Southwest Asia had its inherent appeal. A nuclear strategy for the Persian Gulf would have obviated the need to assign another major conventional mission to the military. This was particularly attractive because any significant rise in military manpower seemed highly unlikely. Some military analysts also argued that the United States had no choice but to rely on a nuclear strategy. They pointed to the sheer volume and power of the ground forces the Soviets could send to the Gulf to conclude that the United States would have to rely on nuclear weapons either to deter or to repel the Soviets.[8] The argument rested upon the supposition that a

---

6. Brzezinski, *Power and Principle*, 451.

7. This explanation, which is based on arguments about cognitive processes, will be elaborated upon in the final chapter.

8. A Pentagon study—the Wolfowitz Report—supposedly came to this conclusion. See *New York Times*, 2 February 1980, "Study Says a Soviet Move in Iran Might Require Atom Arms," and *The Economist*, "Defending the Gulf: A Survey" (6 June 1981), 29.

conventional deterrent simply lacked credibility: The Soviets would be well aware of their overwhelming superiority in Iran.

The problem of credibility, however, cut both ways. Would the Soviets really believe that the United States would rapidly escalate to the use of nuclear weapons in Iran? Given the waning credibility of the U.S. nuclear guarantee to Europe, would the declaration of a similar guarantee to the Persian Gulf be meaningful? The strategic debate over Southwest Asia confronted the same questions of proportionality and credibility that the doctrine of massive retaliation faced in the late 1950s. Although the defense of the Persian Gulf was in 1980 considered to be of "vital interest" to the United States, Southwest Asia was still part of the "periphery" and was not at the top of America's list of strategic priorities. If America's options were restricted to the early use of nuclear weapons, the Soviets could well doubt the U.S. commitment and feel that they could move into northern Iran with impunity and without facing American resistance. Furthermore, the implementation of a nuclear strategy required little, if any, change in strategic posture or force deployment. Many argued that a visible shift in America's military presence in the Gulf would have more effect on the Soviets than a shift in U.S. declaratory policy. Analysts thus criticized the proposal to rely on nuclear deterrence in Iran as lacking sufficient credibility to influence Soviet decisions.[9]

Reliance on a nuclear strategy in Southwest Asia was also criticized by those seeking a solution that offered greater political and military flexibility. Did the United States want to be in a position in which its options for responding to a Soviet invasion of Iran were restricted to either no response or to the early first use of nuclear weapons? Even if a nuclear strategy enhanced deterrence, it would provide little room for maneuver if deterrence failed and the Soviets had begun to move into Iran. A Soviet willingness to attack would indicate a Soviet willingness to test America's nuclear guarantee. This would dilute the extent to which the United States could use the threat of nuclear retaliation as a bargaining chip to halt the Soviet advance. The Kremlin would have already made the decision to accept this risk.

This scenario thus quickly begs the crucial question: Would American officials, in fact, be willing to use nuclear weapons against the Soviets in Iran?

9. One could also argue that American reliance on a nuclear strategy in Southwest Asia could enhance deterrence with respect to the Soviets. Soviet fear of a nuclear response would increase simply because the United States would not have other military options. Similiar arguments have been made about the central front, suggesting that a very weak conventional posture for the West would make early use of nuclear weapons more likely and therefore increase deterrence. See, for example, Bernard Brodie, *Escalation and the Nuclear Option* (Princeton, NJ: Princeton University Press, 1966). This argument is weaker when applied to Southwest Asia, however, because the Soviets are likely to believe that the United States would be less willing to use nuclear weapons in the defense of Iran than in the defense of Europe.

Although there is no clear answer to this question in the public record, it is clear that high-level officials in the Carter administration were divided on this issue. Brzezinski recounts an illustrative discussion that he held in September, 1980 with Secretary of Defense Brown and Secretary of State Muskie:

> Muskie offered the judgment that Congress would not feel that a nuclear war was worth 11 percent of our oil, and Brown rather sharply responded by asking what would happen if the Soviets invaded Iran and we did nothing. Did Muskie really believe that our losses would be only a percentage of our oil supply? Muskie retorted that the American people might even accept the loss of Europe rather than risk nuclear war. I then joined in by asking Muskie if he accepted the proposition that the loss of the Persian Gulf might lead to the loss of Europe, and Muskie reluctantly agreed that that might be the case. In that case, I asked, isn't it vital that we deter the Soviets from moving into Iran?[10]

It was equivocation on this last issue that made a nuclear strategy for Iran appear particularly unsuitable. It was by no means safe to assume that the administration would risk a nuclear confrontation with the Soviets over the status of Iran or the flow of oil from the region. The United States depended on Gulf oil for only 7–9% of its energy supply; it was the economic vitality of Western Europe and Japan that would be threatened if the Soviets destroyed or gained control of the oil fields.[11] Granted, such a development would cause significant political and economic damage to the West as a whole, yet was the defense of Iran worth nuclear war?

In addition, there would be the difficult question of when to interject nuclear weapons: in the northern mountains (atomic demolition mines could be used in the passes), in the Zagros Mountains, or at the rim of the the oil fields? There was also the problem of what type of delivery system to employ. Although planners focused primarily on the use of theater nuclear weapons, they also considered the employment of strategic weapons to strike depots and command and control targets in the southern Soviet Union.[12] Yet even if low-yield battlefield weapons were used with accuracy, there would be a high risk that limited nuclear war would escalate to strategic nuclear exchanges. And if it did not, the tactical advantages of the battlefield use of nuclear weapons would still be, at best, ambiguous. U.S. forces would need to disperse to avoid being lucrative targets for Soviet nuclear attacks. This would complicate the task of defense.

10. Brzezinski, *Power and Principle*, 451–452.

11. U.S. Congress, Senate, *U.S. Security Interests*, 265–271. In 1980, Western Europe and Japan relied on Persian Gulf oil to meet approximately 50% and 75% of their energy needs, respectively.

12. Throughout most of the post-war period, U.S. war plans for responding to a potential Soviet move into Iran have included nuclear options. See Joshua Epstein, *Strategy and Force Planning: The Case of the Persian Gulf* (Washington, DC: Brookings Institution, 1987), 13–18.

One would have to assume that an exchange of nuclear weapons would also lead to the speedy elimination of whatever ground troops were involved in the conflict. This would provide a distinct advantage to the side that could most quickly provide reinforcements: the Soviets.[13] In short, the use of strategic or theater nuclear weapons would raise the risks of escalation to general war and provide questionable tactical advantages in terms of prosecuting the ground war in Iran. If in fact the American president were unwilling to risk a nuclear confrontation over Iran, America would be left with a strategy that was neither an effective deterrent nor a realistic means of defending the country's vital interests. These considerations led planners to develop a wider range of military options for responding to a Soviet move into Iran.

The decision to broaden America's options in Southwest Asia in many ways paralleled the emergence of "flexible response" during the Kennedy administration. Massive retaliation was neither a credible deterrent in Third World areas, nor did it provide, at least in doctrinal terms, the option of graduated commitment through conventional means. As a result, the Kennedy administration made efforts to expand America's force projection capabilities and emphasized training in counterinsurgency warfare to enable U.S. forces to cope with unconventional Third World contingencies. The principal difference in 1980 was that U.S. planners faced a confrontation with the Soviets in the periphery, not with regional armies or local insurgents. This made planning requirements much more demanding and raised the question of just how feasible it would be for U.S. forces to wage a conventional war with the Soviets in Southwest Asia.[14] With upwards of 24 Soviet divisions in the southern republics (and more in neighboring Afghanistan) and essentially no American ground troops in the region, the prospect of meeting a Soviet advance was, to say the least, daunting.

Several conclusions began to emerge from the debate over Persian Gulf strategy. It became apparent that the option of nuclear escalation was inappropriate as a first move for the United States. The risks involved were too high; this jeopardized the feasibility of implementing a declared strategy of immediate escalation and thus weakened its credibility. The United States needed a set of intermediate steps that would initially confine the conflict to the conventional level and to a single region. The goal of such a conventional strategy would be to slow, if not stop, a Soviet advance, thereby increasing the costs of the invasion

13. For an elaboration of these points, see Epstein, *Ibid.*, 18–23.

14. As the war in Vietnam showed, the United States vastly underestimated the force levels and fire power needed to defeat the opposition. Whether justified or not, the United States, at least at the outset, perceived the war in Vietnam as a lower level regional insurgency, requiring the precise application of force to defeat an inferior enemy. The capability of Vietcong and North Vietnamese forces proved far greater than expected, yet fell far short of what the Soviets could send to Southwest Asia. In Iran, U.S. forces would face a far superior enemy and the conflict could well, by American design, spread to other regions.

to the Soviet Union and giving the United States more leverage and time to press for a negotiated settlement. The strategic dilemma thus focused on how best to constrict the Soviet advance given the limitations on both the number of U.S. troops that could be sent to the region and the time that American forces would have to get to the Gulf before Iran was under Soviet control.

The details of a conventional ground strategy for the RDF began to take shape early in 1980. During 1979, planning for a Gulf contingency proceeded quietly in the NSC and in the Pentagon's Office of Program Analysis and Evaluation (PA&E). As mentioned earlier, the issue was a sensitive one because of opposition to the RDF from the State Department, the services, and the command chiefs. After President Carter's State of the Union address in January, however, it became apparent to all agencies in Washington that planning for the RDF was to proceed with quickened pace and that the new policy would have tangible implications for force structure and resource allocation. It was at this point that the individual services began to take keen interest in security arrangements for the Persian Gulf.

Even for individuals integrally involved in the planning process, it would be very difficult to assess the impact of service competition on the formation of an operational strategy for the RDF. The process involved a complicated interaction of personalities, political dynamics, economic concerns, and strategic considerations. What one can do with some degree of accuracy, however, is analyze the position of each service toward security arrangements in the Gulf and then assess the extent to which these respective positions were reflected in the strategy that eventually emerged for the RDF.

In very general terms, the services aligned into two camps: the Navy and Marines against the Air Force and the Army. Although responsibility for the Persian Gulf area had previously been split between the Atlantic and Pacific fleets, the Navy alone could perform only a limited role in the ground defense of Iran. Carriers could be used to protect the sea lines of communication and as bases for a limited number of strike aircraft. If large numbers of ground troops were to be sent to the area, however, the Navy's primary role would be to provide sealift. This was not the Navy's preferred mission because it entailed an increase in the allocation of resources to noncombat assets and meant that the Navy would spend much of its efforts transporting the troops and enhancing the combat role of other services.

For these reasons, the Navy supported a strategy that emphasized America's naval superiority in the region. Two options were put forth. First, several carrier task forces could be sent into and around the Gulf, providing the flexibility to protect both the oil fields and the passage of tankers through the Straits of Hormuz. The problem here was the vulnerability and lack of maneuverability of carriers in the Gulf. If the Soviets gained access to airbases in southern Iran, they would be able to send both fighters and strike aircraft into the airspace over the carriers. Furthermore, there was concern that airpower could not be used to repel an attack on the oil fields without destroying the refineries themselves. Tactical aircraft would certainly be useful in protecting the oil fields, but in support of, not in place of, ground combat troops.

The second option focused on the concept of horizontal escalation. There were two variations. In the first, once the Soviets moved into Iran, U.S. ships would begin to attack Soviet ships in waters away from the Soviet homeland, working from one region to the next. The strategy was based on the assumption the Kremlin would prefer to withdraw from Iran rather than to watch the gradual destruction of its navy. The fairly obvious shortcoming of this proposal was that such a conflict would likely escalate to general war as soon as American and Soviet fleets clashed in various peripheral waters. By first attempting to confront the Soviets within the Gulf area, there was at least some hope of confining the conflict to one theater. A second variant of horizontal escalation involved responding to a Soviet invasion of Iran by attacking a Soviet surrogate, say Cuba or Angola. Here the problem was one of correspondence: What Soviet leader would not gladly sacrifice Castro for control over the Gulf? Furthermore, if the United States already faced conventional inferiority in the Gulf, it would make little sense to divert resources to some other area of the periphery. As we will soon see, horizontal escalation was not precluded from the range of planning options devised to respond to a Soviet move into Southwest Asia. Yet, the first variant was seen to be too risky, and the second neither sufficiently effective nor strategically sound, to serve as America's first and primary move following a Soviet invasion. It is also the case that neither option would have involved a significant redeployment in peacetime and therefore would have done little to increase deterrence with respect to the Soviet Union.[15]

The Marine Corps, for different reasons, also favored a strategy that deemphasized armored ground combat in Iran. Yet, the Marines, because of their traditional role as the service responsible for amphibious insertion in the periphery, had to tread a thin line. They supported a strategy that required a limited number of ground troops, yet not one that would entail the projection of heavily armored divisions deep into Iran. The Marine Corps thus favored a demanding ground strategy along the Gulf littoral, yet was careful not to undermine its own role by devolving inadvertently increasing responsibility for the mission in Southwest Asia to the Army. Inasmuch as the Marines would be dependent upon the Navy for transport and support, these two services shared an interest in supporting a naval/amphibious strategy for the RDF.

The Army, though at first reluctant to devote resources to Southwest Asia,

15. For a more thorough discussion of horizontal escalation, see Joshua Epstein, "Horizontal Escalation: Sour Notes on a Recurrent Theme," in Robert Art and Kenneth Waltz, eds., *The Use of Force, International Politics and Foreign Policies*, 2nd ed. (Lanham, MD: University Press of America, 1983); and *Strategy and Force Planning*, 30–43.

for obvious reasons favored a strategy that emphasized the use of heavy combat divisions in Iran. Although the Army preferred to devote resources to armored rather than light divisions, the service did see the need for easily transportable airborne units. In 1979, Army Chief of Staff Bernard Rogers proposed the establishment of a "unilateral corps," a special conglomeration of light units that could be transported to the Gulf region by the Air Force.[16] The Army thus supported a strategy that revolved around fighting a demanding ground war in Iran. Such a contingency would call upon the Army's lighter units, the 82nd (Airborne) and the 101st (Air Assault), as well as its more heavily armored divisions.

The Air Force generally stood behind the Army's position largely because it would have been responsible for transporting light divisions to the Gulf. The Air Force, as the Navy, was not, however, satisfied with its potentially exclusive role as a transport service. As a result, the Air Force put forth a strategy that called for deep air strikes into northern Iran as well as air support for ground units. Because targets in the north were difficult to reach using only naval airpower, this emphasis on missions into central and northern Iran carved out a niche for the Air Force. The Air Force and the Army thus stood to benefit from a strategy which called for extensive operations in the interior. In a manner similar to the Navy and Marines, they aligned behind a strategy that augmented their roles in the RDF's composition and potential operations.

Before looking at the actual strategy that evolved, one further organizational factor is relevant. Late in 1979, the decision was taken to establish the RDJTF as a subordinate task force within REDCOM. At the same time, however, a Washington Liasion Office was established in the Pentagon which allowed the RDJTF headquarters in Florida to communicate directly with the JCS. As a result, bureaucratic squabbling over command responsibility continued. General Volney Warner, commander of REDCOM, complained that the "direct line" between the RDJTF and the JCS "by-passes the chain of command in which planning guidance should pass through me. . . ."[17] Furthermore, officials in both the NSC and the Pentagon continued to argue that the RDJTF be transformed into a unified command for the Persian Gulf region. The struggle over command arrangements hindered the formation of a coherent strategy for the RDF simply because it was not clear who would ultimately be responsible for planning or from where available units would be drawn. Moreover, because the RDJTF was subordinate to all other commands and somewhat of a pariah within REDCOM, it lacked the necessary bureaucratic authority to drive the planning and procurement process essential to the formation and implementation of a new military strategy for Southwest Asia.

16. Kennedy School of Government, "Command Structure," 20.
17. Ibid., 31.

The Zagros Strategy

The operational strategy for the RDF, dubbed the Zagros strategy, emerged from these organizational dynamics and from certain key strategic considerations. From the outset, it was clear that planners had to make a trade-off between firepower and the speed of deployment. Given severe constraints on lift, the heavier the troops, the longer the transport time to the Gulf. Furthermore, speed was essential. Timely arrival in Iran provided several advantages. The earlier U.S. troops could hamper the Soviet advance, the better the chances of convincing Moscow to limit its objectives. Once a significant number of Soviet troops had taken up secure positions in Iran, it would be more difficult for the United States both to carry out defensive operations and to persuade Moscow to withdraw. To rely exclusively on rapidly deployable mobile units had a clear shortcoming: Light divisions would be useful in mountain warfare, but would not fare well against heavily armored Soviet divisions in a more prolonged engagement. A choice emerged between erecting a forward defense in the northern mountains of Iran (using mobile troops) or attempting to partition Iran by placing heavier fortified troops in Khuzestan, just south of the Zagros Mountains. (See Map 2.)

For two principal reasons, planners chose to combine these options. First, a forward defense in the north would delay the Soviet advance and gain time for heavier divisions to establish themselves in the south. Early resistance might also convince the Soviets to halt the invasion or alter their objectives. Second, the United States could not openly adopt a partition strategy simply because it would send the wrong signal to the Soviets. It would essentially indicate that they could invade and seize northern Iran without confronting American forces.[18]

How was this forward defense to be carried out? Though the initial light units sent into Iran could not challenge heavy Soviet divisions, they would be able to capitalize on two potential advantages: the terrain in Iran that favors defensive positions and the problems of logistics and communications that would hamper a Soviet advance. The geography of Iran played an essential role in shaping a strategy for the RDF. Between the Soviet border and the oil-rich plains of Khuzestan are two mountain ranges. Depending on their rate of advance, the Soviets would confront the Qareh Dagh, Elburz, or Golul Dagh ranges as soon as they crossed the border. Then the Zagros mountains separate the central plain from the main objective of Khuzestan and its oil reserves. Along the few main roads upon which Soviet columns would advance in the mountains there are hundreds of choke points—bridges, precipices, or gaps that make passage dangerous.[19] If the RDF could block some of these vulnerable points, the Soviet

18. Military interview.
19. David Newsom, "America Engulfed," 18.

advance would be severely curtailed. In the words of one analyst: "In short, the Soviets would be operating in truly forbidding terrain, over northern Iran's limited and vulnerable transportation system—a system so constricted that at its narrowest points, the mere disabling of lead elements would bring whole columns to a standstill. . . ."[20]

The principal scenario around which planning for the RDF proceeded involved the early insertion of U.S. forces into the mountain passes in northern Iran. Under the Zagros strategy, special units would mine the road system in the mountains and attempt to disrupt Soviet columns. These commandos would be supported by air strikes flown from Diego Garcia, regional airfields, or American aircraft carriers in the eastern Mediterranean or Persian Gulf area.[21] The objective of these combined ground and air operations would be twofold: to make the Soviet advance so difficult and costly that the Kremlin might reconsider its initial decision to invade, and to provide time for the United States to transport heavier troops to southern Iran.

The initial units sent into Iran would consist of the Marines stationed in Diego Garcia and the lighter army divisions, such as the 82nd Airborne. Although most air transport capabilities would first be used to carry lighter troops, heavier divisions would follow using available airlift and sealift. According to the Zagros strategy, these heavily armored units would be placed in southern Iran and attempt to secure a forward base in Khuzestan from which American operations in Iran could be staged. Yet, these forces would also establish a final line of defense just south of the Zagros mountains. This line would provide a

20. Joshua Epstein, "Soviet Vulnerabilities in Iran and the RDF Deterrent," *International Security* (Fall 1981), 136.

21. B-52Hs based in Diego Garcia could carry out strikes in Iran without refueling. However, these bombers would be vulnerable to Soviet tactical aircraft and air defenses in northern Iran. They could more safely bomb areas in central Iran where they would be out of the range of Soviet aircraft based in Ashkhabad. It would be far preferable for the United States to fly sorties from bases in Saudi Arabia, Turkey, or southern Iran. While fighter aircraft could gain air superiority over Iran, strike aircraft could carry out the missions against the advancing Soviet columns. Access to regional bases, however, as will be discussed shortly, can by no means be assumed. The use of carrier-based airpower is more problematic. With one in-flight refueling, a carrier-based A-6 with a bomb load of about 6000 pounds has a range of approximately 950 miles. From carriers based in the eastern Mediterranean or the Gulf of Oman, the A-6s could reach targets in northern Iran. Depending on conditions and flight profile, such missions might require reduced bomb loads. If the United States were able to maintain air superiority in the Gulf itself and were willing to accept the increased risk of losing a carrier, aircraft carriers could be moved into Gulf waters, significantly reducing the distance from platform to target. Nevertheless, because the number of aircraft that can carry out strike missions from a carrier is limited (some must be held back to protect the carrier), the United States could carry out far more sorties if able to gain access to airfields in the region. For an excellent discussion of the operational component of tactical air missions in the Gulf area and the ranges of various aircraft, see McNaugher, *Arms and Oil*, 53–64.

territorial definition that had hitherto been nonexistent. If the Soviets were to advance as far south as Khuzestan, the imaginary border drawn by U.S. forces would serve two purposes. First, if the Soviets chose not to cross this line, Iran would be effectively partitioned between the superpowers. And since most of the oil fields would be under U.S. control, this was an outcome the Carter administration was ready to accept.[22] Second, if the Soviets succeeded in breaking through this line, the United States would then face the options of vertical escalation, horizontal escalation, or withdrawal.

The extent to which either the Carter or Reagan administration supported a strategy of horizontal escalation if the Soviets entered Khuzestan is unclear. This is partly because such plans have not been discussed publicly, but also because of differing opinions within both administrations as to whether the defense of the Persian Gulf warrants a potential nuclear confrontation between the superpowers. For deterrent purposes, the issue was left unresolved; it was important that the Soviets believe that the United States would be willing to escalate. In President Carter's own words, the Carter Doctrine "would have been backed by concerted action, not necessarily confined to any small invaded area or to tactics or terrain of the Soviets' choosing."[23] As discussed above, however, there were serious flaws with a strategy of horizontal escalation, and there was by no means a consensus on the issue within the administration.

The Reagan administration, at least on a public level, was even more committed to horizontal escalation. The Posture Statement for Fiscal Year 1983 asserted that "even if the enemy attacked at only one place, *we* might choose not to restrict ourselves to meeting aggression on its own immediate front."[24] One analyst described the implications of this policy for strategy in Southwest Asia: "our deterrent capability in the Persian Gulf is linked with our ability and willingness to shift or widen the war to other areas."[25] Again, rhetoric must be distinguished from doctrine and strategy. These statements were directed more at the Soviets than at the Pentagon's planning staff. Horizontal escalation was neither precluded from American military planning nor seen as a desirable option. For the reasons already mentioned, however, it was one of the least sensible options available to American planners.

The fact that both administrations kept open the possibility of horizontal escalation did not indicate that the Zagros strategy failed to provide planners with the wider range of military options that they had been seeking. The RDF's strategy created steps for the controlled escalation of military conflict and, in

22. Interview with Randy Beers.

23. Carter, *Memoirs*, 483.

24. U.S. Congress, House, Appropriations Committee, *Department of Defense Appropriations for 1983*, Pt. 1 (Washington, DC: GPO, 1982), 116.

25. *The Washington Post*, 17 July 1981, "Threat Against Cuba Possible."

this sense, enhanced deterrence at three distinct levels. First, the Zagros strategy was, in General Kelley's words, a "preemptive strategy."[26] As soon as Soviet troops began to move for the Iranian border, U.S. commandos would be sent into the northern mountains. American forces would be available to greet and harass the Soviet advance. This potential confrontation between American and Soviet troops was to prevent the Kremlin's first move. Second, once Soviet troops moved toward the Zagros, they would meet considerable resistance, particularly in the mountains themselves. Again, U.S. forces would attempt to block the passage of Soviet columns through the few roads in the Zagros, providing more time for heavier divisions to arrive and take up defensive positions in Khuzestan. If the advance was sufficiently difficult and injurious, they might turn back. Although the Soviets might be confident of an eventual victory in Iran, the continual harassment and temporary blockage of advancing columns could provide a deterrent after the commencement of hostilities. Finally, if and when the Soviets were to reach southern Iran, U.S. forces would be able to muster a considerable defense and the possibility that the United States might escalate horizontally or vertically could deter Soviet troops from attempting to cross the boundary created by American troops. The fact that U.S. forces had already expended considerable effort to hamper the Soviets would enhance the credibility of America's threat to use nuclear weapons or spread the conflict to neighboring regions. If this final line of defense failed to make the Soviet advance sufficiently costly, the administration would be confronted with the same strategic dilemma that it had originally tried to avoid (is the Persian Gulf worth a major nuclear confrontation?). Yet, at least several intermediate steps would have been taken to defuse the conflict before confronting the unenviable choice between retreat and escalation.

Given this sketch of the Zagros strategy, what can one conclude about the bureaucratic dynamics of the planning process? It is clear that the RDF's strategy marked a clear victory for the Army and the Air Force. The focus of planning on a major contingency in Iran favored these two services that might have been excluded from planning for smaller scenarios. The decision to erect a forward defense and to undertake operations deep into Iran—not just on the Persian Gulf littoral or around the oil fields—ensured the Army and Air Force a significant, if not dominating, role in planning and in potential operations in Southwest Asia. The Marine Corps and the Navy were by no means neglected. Marine units would, in fact, be the first to arrive in Iran, and a Marine general, P.X. Kelley, was appointed as the first commander of the RDJTF. The RDF's strategy was in part an indication of the need to elicit cross-service support by involving all four services in planning and execution. The participation of a wide range of forces was also, however, a reflection of the breadth of the military

26. Interview with General Kelley.

operations that would be required in Southwest Asia. While maritime operations were necessary to guard access routes, ground and air forces were essential to protect oil fields and to delay or halt a Soviet advance. Nevertheless, the general orientation of the Zagros strategy toward forward defense and fighting a ground war in Iran revealed the imprint of service interest on the formation of strategy.

Before turning to the operational requirements of the Zagros strategy, several conceptual weaknesses in U.S. planning should be mentioned. The feasibility of the strategy described above depends heavily upon American early warning capabilities. Without considerable advance notice of Soviet mobilization, American units deployed in Iran would serve as little more than a "throwaway" tripwire force. The light units that could arrive in the Gulf on short notice would lack sufficient firepower to confront heavy Soviet divisions already advancing deep into the country.

Given the low state of readiness of Soviet troops in the southern republics— only two to three divisions are combat ready—analysts have been fairly confident that Soviet mobilization could take up to three months and that these activities would be clearly detected by intelligence sources.[27] Detection itself, however, does not necessarily mean that U.S. forces would be adequately prepared to counter a Soviet move into Iran. As Richard Betts showed well in his study on surprise attack, intelligence failures rarely result from missed signs of mobilization, but from the misinterpretation of available information.[28] The Soviets could send more troops to Afghanistan under the guise of reinforcement and then enter Iran from the east rather than the north. They could also undertake a partial mobilization of troops along the border with Iran—under the guise of an exercise—and then stage the invasion with only a number of the available divisions in the south. In short, there are numerous ways in which the Soviets could attempt to foil America's early warning system. This does not render the Zagros strategy ineffective or unsuitable. It simply means that planners cannot be assured of receiving accurate and timely warning of a Soviet move into Iran.

The second conceptual problem concerns the tendency within both administrations to blur the distinction between deterrent and defensive strategies. The difference is, of course, a subtle one. The extent to which the Soviets are deterred from invading Iran is in part a function of their perception of the defensive capabilities of the United States in the region. Furthermore, there is considerable overlap in operational terms between deterrent and defensive strategies. Striking advancing Soviet columns in northern Iran both deters further

27. See Valenta, "From Prague to Kabul," 130; and McNaugher, *Arms and Oil,* 25–31.
28. See Richard Betts, *Surprise Attack: Lessons for Defense Planning* (Washington, DC: Brookings Institution, 1982).

Soviet operations and serves as a delaying tactic to allow U.S. forces to establish defensive positions in Khuzestan. Nevertheless, there was confusion in both the Carter and Reagan administration over the requirements of deterrence and, consequently, over the objectives of the RDF.

The Carter administration in its public statements was committed to the deterrent role of the RDF: The new policy will be a "meaningful signal to the U.S.S.R. . . . and it offers the best hope that further Soviet advances toward the Straits of Hormuz can be deterred."[29] Yet, there was clear equivocation over the requirements of deterrence. Robert Komer, one of the architects of the RDF in the Pentagon, seemed to link deterrence to America's ability to deprive the Soviets of their main strategic objective—the oil fields. Komer emphasized that "[w]e believe we could deter the Soviets if we had enough rapidly deployable strength to be able to bar them from seizing control of the bulk of the Persian Gulf."[30] The principal mission of the RDF was still to deter the Soviet Union, yet such deterrence required the ability to stop the Soviets through force, not simply to hamper the Soviet advance or to threaten escalation. The internal debate about the requirements of deterrence had bureaucratic as well as intellectual roots. A tripwire strategy involves the sacrifice of forces to trigger escalation, a scenario not well received by service planners. Why lose a division, analysts in the Pentagon queried, if the United States is going to escalate in any case. They argued that if the United States were to send troops to the Gulf, it should do so under the operational assumptions of erecting a defensive rather than a tripwire strategy.

Despite this debate in the Pentagon, planning for the RDF during the Carter administration was oriented toward constructing a credible deterrent force based upon constricting Soviet operations. Defeating the Soviets in Iran does not appear to have been considered a feasible option. Secretary of Defense Brown made this clear in an address before the Council on Foreign Relations: "What is important is the ability rapidly to move forces into the region with the numbers, mobility and fire power to preclude initial adversary forces from reaching vital points. It is not necessary for our initial units to be able to defeat the whole force an adversary might eventually have in place."[31]

During the Reagan administration, the requirements of deterrence changed considerably. The new administration affirmed its commitment to uphold the Carter Doctrine and took steps to double the number of troops assigned to the RDF. Augmenting the force was to strengthen deterrence and enhance the ability of the United States to confront the Soviets in Iran through conventional means, without needing to resort to horizontal or vertical escalation. This was

29. Joseph Sisco, cited in U.S. Congress, Senate, *U.S. Security Interests*, 48–49.
30. Robert Komer, cited in U.S. Congress, House, *U.S. Interests in the Gulf 1980*, 68.
31. Brown, cited in Kennedy School of Government, "Command Structure," 30.

made clear in Secretary Weinberger's 1984 Defense Budget Report to the House Appropriations Committee:

> But credible deterrence, either nuclear or conventional, requires that we have the ability, in case deterrence fails, to halt any attack and restore the peace on terms favorable to us and our allies. And we must accomplish that while trying to limit the scope, duration, and intensity of a conflict. . . . In seeking to limit the *intensity* of a conflict, we must be able to halt an attack and restore the peace by employing forces that do not require escalating the conflict to new dimensions of warfare. Since Soviet-bloc forces would probably enjoy numerical superiority in most theaters in which they might launch a conventional attack, we must be able to offset that advantage with qualitatively superior conventional forces.[32]

In the same report, Secretary Weinberger elaborated upon the prerequisites of deterrence: "For deterrence to be effective, we must be capable—and be seen as being capable—of responding promptly to aggression, with forces of sufficient size and strength to limit the extent of a conflict. . . ."[33]

These statements reveal a shift in the emphasis of America's Gulf strategy in two respects. First, deterrence no longer depended upon the prospect of meeting U.S. forces, but on Soviet perceptions of America's ability "to halt any attack." Increasing the size and proficiency of the RDF, by enhancing the ability of the United States to stop a Soviet advance, was to strengthen deterrence. Second, it was clear that the administration took seriously the prospect of defending the Gulf through conventional means by offsetting the Soviets' numerical advantage with America's qualitative superiority. This would obviate the need to rely on threats of escalation both to deter and to halt a Soviet advance. The prospect of strengthening deterrence by credibly threatening to defeat Soviet forces lay behind the Reagan administration's proposal to expand the RDF to $7\frac{1}{3}$ divisions.

These diverging views about the requirements of deterrence were closely related to a third conceptual weakness shared by both administrations: overly simplistic and pessimistic assessments of the regional balance of forces. Assessments of massive Soviet conventional superiority, based on traditional methods of force comparison, drove force planning during the Carter and Reagan administrations. According to this prevailing wisdom, the Soviets could send more than twenty divisions into Iran while the United States could send at best four divisions (roughly the original size of the RDF). There is little need for complicated analysis to predict the outcome of such a mismatch.[34] Such assessments

32. "Report of the Secretary of Defense Casper W. Weinberger to the Congress," U.S. Congress, House Appropriations Committee, *Department of Defense Appropriations for 1985*, Pt. 1 (Washington, DC: GPO, 1984), 33.

33. Ibid., p. 158.

34. For examples of analysis along these lines, see Epstein, *Strategy and Force Planning*, 7.

led the Carter administration to assume that conventional defense was unfeasible and that deterrence had to rest on a strategy of resisting and injuring Soviet troops. The Reagan administration reacted to the same assessments by undertaking steps to build toward a capability that would provide effective and credible conventional defense.

The problem is that divisional comparisons of this type are virtually meaningless. American and Soviet divisions are hardly comparable. They contain different numbers of troops, are organized and trained differently, and carry weaponry and armor of vastly different type and quality. Meaningful comparisons can be made only after such factors are taken into consideration. This can be done by converting divisions into Armored Divisional Equivalents (ADEs), units that are weighted to reflect mobility, survivability, and firepower. According to scoring methods used by the U.S. Army, an RDF of roughly six divisions (the number assigned to the force in 1986–1987 was about $6\frac{2}{3}$) is equivalent to about six ADEs. Each Soviet division is valued at 0.64 ADEs.[35] A divisional ratio of 20 : 6 is therefore equivalent to an ADE ratio of approximately 12.8 : 6. This is substantially below the ratio of 3 : 1, commonly assumed by American and Soviet defense planners to be the attacker–defender ratio which an offensive army must surpass to be confident of overcoming the defender.[36] While the 3 : 1 figure should be viewed only as a rough "rule of thumb," this analysis of the conventional balance in the Gulf does present a radically different picture—one that is far more realistic than that provided by simplistic divisional comparisons. When one considers the additional advantages that accrue to the defender because of the terrain in Khuzestan and the constraints on Soviet logistics, the balance looks even more favorable for the United States.[37]

It is unquestionably unwise—and potentially dangerous—to place too much confidence in the ability of any model to predict accurately the outcome of military engagements. The "fog of war" and the uncertainties it produces limit

35. This system has been developed by the U.S. Defense Department and scoring for different types of divisions has been standardized. The values assigned to U.S. and Soviet divisions in this analysis are taken from Epstein, *Strategy and Force Planning*, 70–71. These scores do not take air power into consideration. For further discussion of this scoring system see William Mako, *U.S. Ground Forces and the Defense of Central Europe* (Washington, DC: Brookings Institution, 1983).

36. Epstein, *Strategy and Force Planning*, 74.

37. Joshua Epstein calculates that because of constraints on logistics trucks, the Soviets could at best sustain an attacking force of about eleven divisions. This also assumes that the Soviets build up their force levels in central Iran before mounting an attack on Khuzestan. See *Strategy and Force Planning*, 112–116. Epstein also calculates that an RDF of even less than five full divisions could in fact defeat an eleven-division Soviet force as long as U.S. troops had sufficient time to establish defensive positions before the Soviet offensive. For dynamic simulations of different U.S.–Soviet engagements in Iran see pp. 80–89. Epstein's limitation of the Soviet force to eleven divisions seems somewhat specious. While a Soviet invasion of, say, twenty divisions would indeed divert logistics assets and manpower from other theaters, there is no reason to assume that Soviet willingness to invade Iran would not be accompanied by a willingness to divert resources from other areas. Though this scenario is unlikely, it is not more improbable than the invasion of Iran itself.

the degree to which force modeling can capture the dynamics of battle. Yet even this rough calculation, while it by no means indicates that a six-division RDF would be able to defend successfully against a Soviet move into Khuzestan, does suggest that the Soviets would not be able to undertake a thrust toward the oil fields with a high degree of confidence in attaining their objectives. This, in turn, suggests that the pessimism of the Carter administration was unfounded; the conventional defense of Khuzestan may well be feasible given sufficient warning time and lift capability. Furthermore, this assessment indicates that the Reagan administration's efforts to increase the size of the RDF to $7\frac{1}{3}$ divisions may well be unnecessary. In fact, there are several reasons why enlarging the RDF will not substantively strengthen deterrence at any level.

First, the initial level of deterrence (corresponding to interdicting Soviet columns in the northern mountains) would not be affected by additional troops. A larger RDF would not enhance resistance in northern Iran; it takes a relatively small number of commandos and air strikes to destroy choke points in the mountains. Second, while the addition of another one or two divisions would enable the RDF to mount a more effective defense in Khuzestan, a six-division force clearly erodes Soviet confidence about obtaining an easy victory, if victory at all. John Mearsheimer cogently argues that offensive powers that are denied the option of blitzkrieg—a quick and easy victory—often reconsider the costs and benefits of aggressive action when a longer war of attrition seems likely.[38] He shows that removing the option of blitzkrieg seems to be the core requirement of effective conventional deterrence. The six-division force thus far surpasses this core requirement, and may, in fact, be larger than is needed. An expanded RDF would neither ensure a U.S. victory nor enhance deterrence. If the Soviets were willing to engage in a risky and costly engagement with five or six U.S. divisions, it is difficult to see how confronting seven divisions would alter the initial calculus leading to the decision to attack. Third, deterrence also rests on maintaining the options of vertical or horizontal escalation. A larger RDF does not enhance this level of deterrence. Finally, it could also be argued that the larger RDF in fact *weakens* deterrence because strategies relying upon it lack credibility. The United States simply does not have sufficient manpower or lift to deploy such a force to the Gulf. As will be discussed shortly, a deployment on this scale would drain resources from Europe and employ more lift capability than the United States has or is planning to procure.[39] By basing planning on force levels that the RDF could not achieve, the United States would be undermining the credibility of its deterrent posture.

In sum, the debate about the optimal size of the RDF is integrally wedded to

38. John Mearsheimer, *Conventional Deterrence* (Ithaca, NY: Cornell University Press, 1983).

39. Thomas McNaugher calculates that in 1988, the United States will be able to deploy the RDF to the Gulf in the time desired by planners (thirty to forty days) only if "all lift assets are set in motion simultaneously and . . . [if] other contingencies do not rob CENTCOM of lift assets." The important point is that *all* available lift would have to be utilized. See *Arms and Oil*, 67–68.

differing views of the requirements of deterrence and to differing methods of assessing force balances. These two conceptual issues must be clarified within Washington before the debate about the size and force structure of the RDF can be resolved. Given that a six-division force denies the Soviets the option of blitzkrieg, and may well be able to defeat the force that the Soviets could send to ˙Khuzestan, it provides a credible deterrent and is sufficient to fulfill America's strategic objectives in Iran.

Operational Requirements

Much of the difficulty in designing a credible and operationally feasible strategy for the RDF came not from bureaucratic "muddling," conceptual weakness, or overly pessimistic or simplistic force comparisons but from severe resource constraints upon American capabilities in the Persian Gulf area. The three key parameters that would determine the strength and flexiblility of U.S. military capabilty in the Gulf were firepower, lift, and regional access. In all three areas, the shortcomings were enormous. How would a force that originally could send a few light divisions to the Gulf hope to cope with as many as thirty Soviet divisions supported by airpower based in Afghanistan and the Soviet Union?[40] Initially the size of the RDF was not determined in accordance with its potential mission. Rather, the divisions assigned to the force were essentially the same ones that were assigned to REDCOM—light, air mobile units that could be transported quickly. In the early stages of planning, the RDF was to be assigned only those troops not already committed to NATO or Northeast Asia.[41] It soon became apparent, however, that these units would be insufficient to carry out the designated missions and more troops were included in the RDF configuration. Furthermore, lift capabilities were woefully insufficient. The light units that could be transported by air would begin to arrive within days of notification. But America's heavier units would be transported by sea and it would take a minimum of three months for complete divisions to arrive in the Gulf.[42] Whether this second wave of troops would still be useful would depend upon the accurate and early detection of warning signals, the efficiency of Soviet mobilization, and the speed of the Soviet advance into Iran.

Another potential problem emerges from the fact that most of the units eventually assigned to the RDF were already earmarked for NATO use (see Table 4). As discussed above, the establishment of the RDJTF and CENTCOM

40. The maximum number of deployable troops was 200,000. See Jeffrey Record, *The Rapid Deployment Force and U.S. Military Intervention in the Persian Gulf* (Cambridge, MA: Institute for Foreign Policy Analysis, 1981), 53. I am assuming the Soviets had roughly twenty-nine divisions deployed in the southern Soviet Union and Afghanistan. See McNaugher, *Arms and Oil*, 25–26.
41. Kennedy School of Government, "Command Structure," 26.
42. Turner, "New Strategy," 50, 55.

Table 4
FORCES AVAILABLE TO THE RDJTF AS OF 1980

Unit	NATO earmarked?	Light/heavy
Army		
1 airborne division	No	L
1 air assault division	Yes	L
1 infantry division	Yes	L
1 mechanized division	Yes	H
1 armored brigade	No	H
1 cavalry brigade	Yes	L
2 infantry battalions	Yes	L
Marines		
1 amphibious force	?	L
Air Force		
12 tactical fighter squadrons	Yes	
2 tactical reconnaissance squadrons	Yes	
2 tactical airlift wings	No	
Navy		
3 carrier battle groups	Some	
1 surface action group	Some	
5 aerial patrol squadrons	Some	

Source: Jeffrey Record, *The Rapid Deployment Force,* 54.

created considerable strain among command chiefs over geographic and mission responsibility. A conflict in the Gulf would certainly intensify international tensions, and the European Command as well as European leaders would be loath to see troops earmarked for NATO sent to Southwest Asia. The problem of setting regional priorities and allocating troops accordingly would be exacerbated if the United States chose to respond to a Soviet move into Iran through horizontal escalation. United States forces would then be fighting on two fronts; this would increase the likelihood of hostilities in Europe and therefore accentuate the need to withhold troops for the central front mission.

Attempts to redress these deficiencies in lift and force levels were reflected in both strategy and procurement. If capabilities did not influence general policy, they did influence strategy. The Zagros strategy was designed to circumvent some of the strategic problems posed by America's numerical inferiority by relying on mobility and taking advantage of the terrain. The Carter administration's support for horizontal escalation revealed a belief that the conventional defense of Iran was neither credible nor feasible. As far as procurement was concerned, the purchase of additional sealift and airlift capabilities was a top priority of budgetary requests for the RDF. The administration requested and received funding for seven prepositioning ships, eight SL-7 high-speed container ships, and additional transport aircraft, including forty KC-10s and fifty C-5s.

These measures did not solve the lift problem, but they significantly improved America's ability to project force to the Persian Gulf.[43]

By 1988, the United States should be able to transport roughly five full divisions to the Gulf in about five weeks.[44] If one assumes a month of warning time due to Soviet mobilization, and a month of delay in each of the two mountain ranges, the United States has sufficient lift and time to transport all six divisions allocated to the RDF before the arrival of Soviet forces in Khuzestan.[45] This assumes, however, that all lift assets are utilized, a questionable assumption given the likelihood of rising tensions and mobilization in Europe.

Even with unlimited lift, however, the implementation of the Zagros strategy would require one final, yet elusive, element: regional access. The problem of gaining military access to the Gulf was, from the beginning, the greatest obstacle to enhancing America's capability in the region. One Marine Amphibious Brigade consisting of 3800 soldiers was designated as the first unit that would be sent to Iran to delay Soviet advances. The equipment and supplies for these men were prepositioned on ships at Diego Garcia, about 2000 miles from the Gulf (approximately a four-day sail). Yet, supplies for forces other than this small initial unit could not be placed on Diego Garcia. There were not facilities for storing such volumes, nor was the Pentagon willing to send large amounts of equipment to a remote island in the Indian Ocean where it would be inaccessible for contingencies in other areas.

Although troops could be flown into the Gulf relatively easily from virtually anywhere, the munitions and fuel that such forces would require were simply too voluminous to transport quickly from the United States. One of the greatest problems was supplying high-quality fuel for the tactical aircraft that would carry out the initial missions in the mountains and support the ground forces throughout the operation. To supply just one wing of F-15s for thirty days requires well over 10 million gallons; the original RDF configuration contained two fighter wings, while CENTCOM was assigned ten wings.[46] To airlift sufficient fuel to the region was unfeasible; the tankers would use more fuel than they could

43. By 1988 when delivery of these new lift assets should be completed, the United States will be able to send roughly four divisions to the Gulf in about four weeks. In 1983, it was able to send roughly two divisions in this same period of time. See Congressional Budget Office, *Rapid Deployment Forces*, 29–45. Also see McNaugher, *Arms and Oil*, 67–68.

44. McNaugher, *Arms and Oil*, 68.

45. Epstein calculates that a small force of only six engineering platoons could delay the task of traversing the mountain ranges by about a month. For a discussion of delay and warning time see *Strategy and Force Planning*, 56–63.

46. Fuel consumption was calculated on the basis of two sorties per day per F-15. Each sortie (to and from northern Iran) would require approximately 2500 gallons of jet fuel. A wing consists of seventy-two aircraft.

deliver. Sealift was the obvious alternative, but it would take between twenty-four and thirty-six days to deliver each load.[47] Because of these restrictions, it was necessary that adequate supplies be prepositioned within the theater itself and transported to the staging area from these stores. A similar problem existed for other types of equipment, supplies, and munitions.

A sizable American operation in the Gulf area required not only sites for prepositioning, but also airfields both for receiving troops and equipment and for staging strike missions. Regardless of where the fighting might be, tactical fighters had to be based at airfields that were no further than 400 to 500 miles from the area of conflict.[48] Some missions could be carried out from aircraft carriers in the Mediterranean or Persian Gulf, yet regional air bases would be essential to securing air superiority and carrying out the large number of sorties envisaged in contingency planning. What is more, large support teams had to accompany the airborne divisions and fighter wings. To deploy the 82nd Airborne Division—one of the smallest—would require some 11,000 support personnel.[49] An airfield had to have the facilities to house these personnel as well as the machinery to service the aircraft. Access to such facilities in war meant preparing them in peacetime.

Initial attempts to resolve these problems revolved around securing a forward base in the Gulf area. A formal American base would guarantee timely access and allow the United States both to tailor the facility to its needs and to preposition sufficient stocks. Yet, this proposal met opposition both in Washington and from the Gulf states that would potentially host such a base. As early as 1977, a congressional study pointed to the unreliability of bases in the Middle East and urged that the United States should therefore develop an independent lift capability.[50] The cost of constructing and stocking new facilities also dampened enthusiasm for the project. The most persuasive criticism of the basing scheme, however, was that it was opposed by the regional states themselves. In February of 1979, the Saudis adamantly rejected the possibility of the construction of an American base on their territory.[51] Other Arab countries, including Egypt, were equally reluctant to play host to a U.S. base. In 1981, six Gulf leaders signed a communique pledging to keep the region "free of international

---

47. Should the Suez Canal be closed to traffic, the journey around Africa would take approximately thirty-six days.

48. The F-15E, a fighter modified for long-range missions, will have a mission radius of about 750 miles. See McNaugher, *Arms and Oil*, 58.

49. Record, *The Rapid Deployment Force*, 64.

50. Anne Hessing Cahn, "U.S. Arms to the Middle East," 122.

51. *New York Times*, 27 February 1979, "Saudis Reject Idea of a U.S. Base." Interviews revealed that the proposal to base troops in Saudi Arabia found most support among Defense Department officials. See Safran, *Saudi Arabia*, 303.

rivalry, especially in regard to the presence of naval fleets and foreign bases."[52] Even before this statement, however, the United States quickly learned to keep its distance; in April of 1980, Robert Komer told the House Committee on Foreign Affairs that: "[G]iven the national system and the sensitivities of the nations in the area . . . it would not be politically wise for us to seek formal bases of the sort we had in the fifties where we were flying the American flag with thousands of troops . . . present."[53]

If military planners were to forego the option of a forward base, they had to seek other arrangements; the RDF simply could not function without "access to capable, regional facilities."[54] As will be discussed in Chapter 6, the United States did succeed in securing regional access and in convincing several Gulf states to overbuild their facilities and allow American prepositioning.[55] The problem was that not all Gulf states were equally suitable in terms of providing strategic access to the region.

A glance at Map 1 reveals that certain countries—namely Turkey and Saudi Arabia—had distinct advantages as staging grounds. They were in fact the only countries from which the full range of U.S. tactical aircraft could reach targets throughout Iran. Although supplies and fuel could be transported from other regional states to the staging ground, planners assumed that Dhahran in Saudi Arabia and/or bases in Turkey would be made available to the United States. There were plans for facing a contingency in Iran without the help of the Saudis or the Turks, but their cooperation was considered to be crucial to the RDF's capability in the region.[56] That neither Saudi Arabia nor Turkey has been willing to make formal access arrangements with the United States has therefore jeopardized the reliability and feasibility of the Zagros strategy.[57]

Conclusions

For the first time in the postwar era, the United States in 1980 faced a severe gap between the nature of its strategic commitment in Southwest Asia and its

52. Washington Post, 13 November 1981, "Gulf Arabs Set Framework for Economic, Military Cooperation."

53. Robert Komer, in U.S. Congress, House, U.S. Interests in the Gulf 1980, 76.

54. Ibid., 73.

55. Military interviews. Overbuilding refers to the practice of regional states constructing larger facilities than they need for their own use, thereby making it feasible for other forces to use the bases if necessary.

56. Interview with Randy Beers.

57. In 1985, it was reported that the Saudis had agreed in 1984 to grant access to U.S. forces if the Soviets moved toward the Gulf or if there were an intraregional crisis that the Saudis were incapable of handling on their own. Given the fluctuations in Saudi policy and their long-standing hesitancy to allow U.S. forces on their territory, one has reason to doubt the reliability of this agreement. See New York Times, 5 September 1985, "Saudis to Let U.S. Use Bases in Crisis."

military capabilities. The crux of the strategic dilemma focused on how to extend deterrence to the Persian Gulf. Given the initial imbalance between U.S. and Soviet conventional capabilities in the region, the formulation of a credible and feasible military strategy for the Gulf proved to be no easy task. A conventional deterrent seemed particularly difficult to erect. The United States had neither a permanent base in the area nor lift sufficient to project considerable force to the region. Although the United States by no means ruled out the possibility of using nuclear weapons in Southwest Asia, sole reliance on a nuclear deterrent simply lacked credibility. Nor did either the Carter or Reagan administration want to face immediate escalation as its only option for responding to a conventional Soviet attack. Horizontal escalation was also considered, but it faced serious logical flaws. If the United States were already devoting resources to establish a front in Iran, why would America want to place a further strain on its resources by opening simultaneously another front elsewhere? Furthermore, it would be very difficult to find a region to attack (short of the Soviet homeland) that would be valuable enough to the Soviets to make them reconsider their move into Iran.

Given the problems inherent in extending deterrence to the Persian Gulf, the emergence of a coherent conventional strategy for the RDF constitutes an impressive instance of innovation within the military establishment. Planners faced a daunting imbalance of forces with respect to the Soviets and faced serious constraints in manpower and lift. They attempted to circumvent these constraints, however, by making use of the light troops that could be sent to the region and by taking advantage of the terrain in Iran. Harassment in the northern mountains was to discourage the Soviets and to gain sufficient time to erect a fortified line of defense in the south.

The strategy designed for the RDF, though it by no means ensured that the United States could stop a Soviet invasion of Iran through conventional means, did provide a coherent and credible means of extending a U.S. deterrent to the region. America's strategy for the Persian Gulf was essentially a revised version of its approach to the defense of Europe. The main difference was that in Iran, unlike in Europe, the United States was willing to trade space for time. The Zagros strategy would allow the Soviets to occupy central Iran, yet, in doing so, would provide time for the buildup of U.S. force levels in Khuzestan. Conventional forces were to serve as a first level of deterrence and provide military options short of immediate escalation to the nuclear level. The same shortcomings in NATO strategy were apparent in America's approach to the Gulf, only on a more acute level. In Southwest Asia, the conventional balance was more inequitable than in Europe and the threat to escalate to the nuclear level, because of the lower stakes, much less credible. Nevertheless, the essential components of deterrence were in place; the Soviets faced the prospect of meeting U.S. forces and a high degree of uncertainty about their ability both to attain their objectives and to avoid escalation to the nuclear level.

The coherence of the RDF's strategy becomes even more impressive in light of the muddled process that produced it. The Zagros strategy was not the outcome of a rational process in which planners sought to find the most suitable means of fulfilling a specific military mission. Rather, the influence of bureaucratic forces was evident throughout. Exclusive focus on a Soviet contingency was in part a reflection of the need to orient organizational attention on the Persian Gulf. It is also clear that the services played a significant role in shaping strategy. The decision to undertake forward defense in addition to protecting the oil fields themselves reflected the pressure brought to bear by the Army and the Air Force. This is not to suggest that it would make better strategic sense to rely solely on Navy and Marine forces along the littoral itself. On the contrary, a declared strategy of forward defense prevents the Soviets from calculating that they could seize northern Iran with impunity and means that they would meet early resistance in an attempt to move toward the Gulf. In this specific instance, service rivalry seems to have produced an optimal outcome: It does make more sense to use all four services in the Gulf rather than just the Navy and Marines—the two traditionally responsible for the area. Competition for the mission in Southwest Asia, though it disturbed the planning process, also led to innovation in the formulation of strategy.

Criticism of the decision-making mechanism should be directed not at the outcome of the planning process, but at several of the key assumptions upon which the RDF's military strategy was based. Within the context of these key assumptions, the Zagros strategy made very good sense. The central question is whether these assumptions were accurate. The United States identified the extension of a credible deterrent to the Gulf area as its principal military goal in Southwest Asia. By defining the strategic challenge in the Gulf in these terms, the RDF's strategy revolved around responding to a Soviet invasion of Iran. Planning indeed should have been carried out on the basis of this scenario, but not to the exclusion of preparations for lesser contingencies. Even during the Reagan administration, when attention was focused more on intraregional problems, planning for the RDF continued to revolve around a confrontation with the Soviets. This was to neglect some of the lower level regional scenarios in which U.S. forces were more likely to become involved and to neglect the security concerns of local states.

The second uncertain assumption upon which planning was based was that the regional states would be willing to cooperate with the United States in the preparations for and the execution of America's new strategy for the Gulf. The feasibility of the Zagros strategy depended upon America's ability to gain strategic access to the region. Even after the RDF had been established and new airlift and sealift procured, the effectiveness of U.S. military power in the Gulf was contingent upon the political cooperation of regional actors. If the goals of the Carter Doctrine were to be realized, there had to be a clear link between military strategy and the political realities of the region. How the Carter and Reagan administrations attempted to establish this link is the topic of the next chapter.

Chapter Six

U.S. POWER IN THE GULF: MILITARY STRATEGY AND REGIONAL POLITICS

The task before the Carter and Reagan administrations was formidable, yet clear. The United States needed explicit military cooperation from countries alienated by America's position on the Arab–Israeli conflict and disappointed in Washington's ineffectual response to the chaos in Iran and the Soviet invasion of Afghanistan. Saudi Arabia and Oman were not averse to improving their military ties with the United States. Yet, the Saudis in particular did not want to be dependent upon America for their own security needs, nor were they willing to allow any extensive cooperation to be publicized for fear of popular opposition and backlash. The Kuwaitis, on the other hand, were opposed to explicit cooperation with Washington. They preferred to purchase arms from both the Soviets and the West and resisted the presence of any foreign power in the Gulf. And therein lay an inherent conflict between the Carter Doctrine and the political realities in the Gulf; for if the RDF were to provide the United States with a credible military capability—one that was sufficiently powerful and visible to deter the Soviets or local aggressors—it required regional access, if not a permanent presence.

Thus, the challenge facing the Carter and Reagan administrations was not how to build the RDF—that had already been decided—but how to construct a political framework within which the Gulf regimes would be receptive to American aims. The key was to provide those incentives, whether it be a quiet handshake or a major military exercise, that would strengthen cooperation on a broad scale between the United States and the Gulf states. There existed a middle ground between establishing a major U.S. base in the Gulf and continuing to tolerate glaring strategic vulnerability in the region. Finding that middle ground would make the difference between forming cooperative alliances and inciting anti-Western sentiment.

There were several principal variables at the core of U.S. policy toward Gulf security after 1979, and these issues form the focus of the ensuing discussion. First, there was great concern over how to publicize the change in policy. Should the RDF be presented as part of a global strategy, a regional strategy, or a reaction to vulnerablity in a specific theater? Second, it was clear from the outset that the undertaking as a whole had the potential to change profoundly relations between Washington and the states of the region. Negotiations on the RDF, regardless of their content, stimulated more contact at all governmental levels. How could the Gulf states be convinced that a U.S. military presence was, in fact, in their interest? Preparations for the force meant a potentially dangerous increase in the number of U.S. personnel in the area. Yet, improvements in host country facilities also augmented the military capabilities of those states. Could the RDF and its related preparations serve as an enzyme for broader political and strategic cooperation between the United States and Gulf states?

The third variable concerns the use of arms sales as a new type of policy instrument. The breadth of motivations for arms transfers to the Middle East has already been discussed at length (see Chapter 2). Yet, the Carter Doctrine stimulated a new concern: Should America sell sophisticated weaponry to Saudi Arabia so that such equipment would be available to U.S. forces in a regional contingency? This question played a crucial role in determining the merits of the AWACS sale to Saudi Arabia in 1981, a move that was to be of the utmost importance in the development of America's strategy for the Gulf.

Finally, there was the ever present stumbling block: the Arab–Israeli conflict. The two key interrelated issues were the role that Israel would play in the RDF strategy and the attitude of the Gulf states toward the Palestinian question. Israel was quite willing to grant the United States access to its military facilities. Furthermore, Israel's location and the sophistication of its military infrastructure and air defense system would provide the RDF with distinct advantages. The obvious question was whether these advantages were worth the risk of political alienation in the Gulf. Since the 1960s, Arab leaders had repeatedly asserted that their animosity toward the United States was a result of the persistence of the Palestinian problem and America's "unwavering" support for Israel. Yet, there has always been skepticism in Washington as to the sincerity of such concern for the Palestinians. Changing perceptions of this issue in the United States were reflected in the erratic approach of both the Carter and Reagan administrations to the peace negotiations. Just how central a role should the Palestinian question play in U.S. policy?

One final introductory remark concerns the overriding importance of Saudi Arabia in the policy of both administrations. In October of 1979, a Pentagon official affirmed that "Saudi Arabia remains the cornerstone for attaining U.S.

foreign objectives in the Arabian Peninsula."[1] In September of 1981, General P.X. Kelley, Commander of the RDF, asserted that the "strategic and geopolitical significance of Saudi Arabia is quite likely second to no other nation on the face of the earth in its importance to the future well-being of the free world."[2] It is important to bear this factor in mind when analyzing policy toward the region as a whole.

The Carter Administration—Laying the Foundation

Throughout the last two years of his term, President Carter was accused of leading a confused and muddled administration, especially with respect to policy in the Middle East. This impression was fostered by several domestic incidents as well as his failure to respond effectively to the crisis in Iran. The U.S. delegation to the U.N. was embarrassed by both a mistaken vote concerning Israel and the resignation of Ambassador Andrew Young for having met with a representative of the PLO. One of the main reasons for the apparent lack of leadership was the wide range of opinions within Washington over the appropriate response both to the Iranian revolution and to the failure of the moderate Arabs to support Camp David.

This indecision was reflected in the halting military moves taken by Carter early in 1979. As discussed in Chapter 4, President Carter feared that a show of force would worsen the situation in Iran.[3] By mid-March the United States had deployed only a small naval task force to increase its presence in the Indian Ocean. Carter also sent a group of F-15s to Riyadh in January, followed by a tour of AWACS in March. As the chaos intensified and the embassy in Tehran was eventually beseiged, however, the administration showed increasing concern. By November, two carrier task forces—the Midway and the Kitty Hawk—had been moved to the Indian Ocean. The RDF was receiving more widespread support in Washington and preparations for a potential U.S. deployment to the Gulf were gaining speed. In November, funding requests for the CX—a new strategic lift aircraft for the Air Force—and the maritime prepositioning ships were included in the Fiscal Year 1981 budget proposal. Within six months of the December announcement to establish the RDF, seven loaded supply ships were

1. *New York Times*, 25 October 1979, cited in Congressional Research Service, *Saudi Arabia and the United States—The New Context in an Evolving "Special Relationship"* (Washington, DC: GPO, 1981), 57.

2. General Kelley cited in U.S. Congress, Senate, Armed Services Committee, *Military and Technical Implications of the Proposed Sale to Saudi Arabia of Airborne Warning and Control Systems (AWACS) and F-15 Enhancements* (Washington, DC: GPO, 1981), 84.

3. Carter, *Memoirs*, 440–447. See also, *Daily Telegraph*, 3 January 1979, "Gulf Crisis Prompts U.S. 'Fire Force'."

stationed at Diego Garcia.[4] After the Soviet invasion of Afghanistan, other RDF programs proceeded with similar rapidity. The decision to establish a rapid strike force for the Middle East emerged slowly and met with considerable bureaucratic opposition. Yet, once the process had been put into motion, the Defense Department acted with remarkable efficiency.

How did Gulf regimes perceive the decision to establish the RDF and these visible developments that accompanied it? Was the sole mission of the RDF to deter the Soviets or would it be used to interfere in internal Arab affairs? Even if the Saudis approved of U.S. initiatives, could they afford to cooperate militarily and thus implicate themselves in what was seen as America's pro-Israel policy? The presentation of American intentions and their perception in the Gulf were as important as the policy objectives themselves.

As far as Washington was concerned, it was crucial that the Gulf states be acutely aware of the Soviet threat and perceive close ties with the United States to be the best deterrent available. The United States publicized that the RDF's main task was to confront the Soviets in Iran and emphasized that a conflict with the Soviets might rapidly escalate. Public pronouncements were complemented by private negotiations that attempted to convey the same message. United States Air Force intelligence was shared with several governments in the Gulf to impress upon them the urgency of the Soviet threat as well as the role that they could potentially play in helping to counter it.[5] The emphasis lay on cooperating with the United States rather than on bowing to American power.

This diplomatic approach played a crucial role in negotiations for access to bases within the region. The Carter administration focused upon Oman, Kenya, and Somalia to provide facilities and prepositioning sites in the theater. In April of 1980, Oman and Kenya signed agreements providing access in return for military aid; Somalia followed suit four months later. Each of these countries was attracted by the prospect of U.S. aid, yet each had distinct reasons for responding favorably to Washington's overtures. Oman hoped to increase its military strength and political leverage in the Gulf by receiving more sophisticated American weaponry.[6] Kenya sought political strength in the African world through alignment with America and was concerned about escalating tensions with the Sudan and Libya. Somalia had recently ended close ties with the Soviet Union and was in search of a new source of support for its battle with Ethiopia over the Ogaden.

Why the United States sought agreements with these countries is not quite as apparent. Oman, only some 600 miles from Dhahran, would be an excellent rear-staging ground for the RDF. Yet, Berbera and Mombassa are 1244 and 2080

---

4. Record, *The Rapid Deployment Force*, 47.
5. *London Times*, 10 October 1980, "U.S. Offers Air Information to Arab Allies."
6. Interview with General Kelley.

miles, respectively, from Dhahran. The time and cost of transporting materiel and fuel from these bases would be prohibitive. There were clearly other reasons for concentrating on these countries, foremost of which was that they were the only regimes in the area with whom an agreement could be reached fairly rapidly.[7] Even before the development of the RDF, negotiations had been under way with these three countries to secure ports at which U.S. vessels in the Indian Ocean could call. The United States could not risk lengthy negotiations on this issue. Once the decision to build the RDF had been made, it became important for Washington to stand behind the new policy in both word and action. And securing access agreements was a necessary signal to both the Soviets and regional states of American willingness to uphold the commitment contained in the Carter Doctrine. Oman, Kenya, and Somalia also offered a wide range of political orientations.[8] If one state decided to revoke the agreements, the other two could well continue to honor the right to access. America had faced just this situation when, after the United States used Oman as a staging ground for the hostage rescue mission, the Sultan Qaboos threatened to deny American forces access to his bases.

The approach taken by U.S. negotiators was to educate potential host states about their strategic vulnerablity and to illustrate how the United States could assist them in meeting their military needs. A State Department spokesman said in July of 1979 that "we shall pursue our consultations with governments there to find out which is the best way to work together to consolidate stability in that area."[9] The United States was no longer seeking surrogates in the Gulf nor attempting to shift the regional balance of power through arms sales. Rather, by offering states a certain degree of capability as well as assuring their security, officials hoped to lure regimes into closer cooperation with Washington. The military ties provided, in effect, the foundation and the motivation for increasing diplomatic contact as well as more convergence on political and strategic issues.

Despite these reassurances, the Saudis were hesitant to cooperate with the United States. They lacked confidence in Washington because of America's unpredictable political system and its recent setbacks in Iran and Afghanistan. Even if the President decided in favor of strong military action, the Saudis reasoned, Congress or a powerful interest group could prevent that action from being taken.[10] The Saudis were also puzzled by constant references in the American press to the instability of Saudi Arabia. They questioned, as other Arab states did, whether the ultimate aim of the United States was not to destabilize

7. Interview with Reginald Bartholemew.
8. Interview with Tom Locher.
9. *New York Times*, 6 July 1976, cited in Congressional Research Service, *Saudi Arabia*, 56.
10. Mansur, "The American Threat," 47.

Gulf regimes and use the RDF to seize the oil fields.[11] Furthermore, U.S.–Saudi relations had suffered considerably during 1979. The Camp David Treaty had politically split the Arab world and pushed the Saudis away from their more moderate orientation. Washington had been disappointed by the Saudis' failure to support the peace process and by their decision to decrease oil production during the first two quarters of 1979.

The Saudi reaction to the Carter Doctrine must also be viewed within the context of Gulf politics. The seizure of the Grand Mosque of Mecca in November of 1979, while stimulating concern about improving internal security arrangements, also made clear the potential risks of domestic opposition. Overt cooperation with the United States could well serve to exacerbate fundamentalist threats to the regime. In terms of external threats, both Iran and Iraq were opposed to Saudi involvement in the evolving U.S. security scheme. Iran objected to an increasing American presence in the region. Iraq was hoping to capitalize on the revolution in Iran to enhance its own leverage in the lower Gulf.[12] American offers of security assistance only impeded the willingness of the sheikdoms to look to Iraq for protection from Iran.

The initial reaction of the Saudi government to the Carter Doctrine was one of public condemnation, but private approval. Provided U.S. forces remained "over the horizon," the Saudis welcomed the American commitment to the Kingdom's security.[13] The United States, however, needed more than a blessing at arm's length; only actual cooperation could meet the requirements of the RDF. United States planners assumed that Dhahran would be available in a contingency. But a base without adequate fuel, equipment, and communication systems would be of little use to a sizable American force. General Kelley made this clear to the Senate Armed Services Committee: "If the United States is to deploy meaningful combat power to that part of the world under any scenario . . . it is absolutely essential that we have free and willing—and I emphasize those two words, free and willing—access to Saudi land bases, Saudi ports, Saudi host nation support, and a considerable labor pool from the Saudis."[14] Initially, Saudi Arabia was simply unwilling to accept such terms.[15] In time, the Saudis did shift their position, but not without exacting a high price from the United States.

In their negotiations over regional access for the RDF, officials stressed the potential benefits to both parties of increased cooperation between the Saudis and the United States. Exactly what incentives the Americans offered to the

11. Ibid.

12. Safran, *Saudi Arabia*, 360.

13. *New York Times*, 5 February 1980, "Americans Say Saudis Welcome U.S. Resolve to Defend Persian Gulf." See also Safran, *Saudi Arabia*, 359.

14. General Kelley, cited in U.S. Congress, Senate, *Military Implications*, 38–39.

15. Congressional Research Service, *Saudi Arabia*, 57.

Saudis did not become evident until the debate on the AWACS sale in 1981 made public much important information. Beginning in 1979, the United States carried on with Gulf regimes extensive negotiations focusing on the potential establishment of a regional defense system.[16] Though the details were by no means clear at the time, the Saudis were to take the lead in constructing a security network, and the United States was to provide the necessary military and technological assistance. Planning for the RDF was only one small component of America's evolving policy. Efforts were being made to improve local defense capabilities and to encourage security cooperation among Gulf regimes. As far as Washington was concerned, progress in these areas would allow regional states to assume more responsibility for local defense and would encourage closer cooperation between Gulf regimes and the United States. As the potential leaders of a security framework, the Saudis stood to improve their own defense capabilites while emerging as the dominant political force in a new alignment of Gulf states.

Events in 1979 and 1980 contributed to the intensity with which both the United States and Gulf regimes pursued efforts to improve security arrangements. In June of 1979, war again broke out between North and South Yemen. Although hostilities did not spread to the territories of neighboring states, Saudi Arabia, the United Arab Emirates, and Oman all paid close attention to the conflict. America's concerns were heightened by the fact that the Soviets, by 1979, were providing arms to both North and South Yemen.

While the impact of the Yemeni conflict on peninsular security was limited, the outbreak of the Iran–Iraq war in September, 1980 had potentially far greater implications. Despite reports that the capability of the Iranian military had eroded after the Shah's departure, Iran was able to hold the initial Iraqi offensive. What the lower Gulf states had previously seen as a tacit threat from a revolutionary Iran suddenly became an imminent danger. In September, 1980, the Iranians responded to an Iraqi raid on Tehran by threatening to bomb Saudi Arabia and Oman.[17] In November, Iranian planes attacked territory in northern Kuwait.[18] The Saudis reacted to the outbreak of the war by requesting immediate assistance from the United States. Within days, Carter sent four AWACS to Riyadh to deter Iranian attacks on Saudi oil fields. It was agreed that these aircraft would patrol Saudi airspace, but remain under the complete control of American personnel. This stipulation was of special significance because at the time the Saudis were pressuring the United States to sell them five AWACS as well as an enhancement package for the F-15s purchased in 1978. The United States also proposed the establishment of a joint U.S.–Saudi naval task force to

16. *Washington Post*, 1 November 1981, "Saudis' AWACS Just a Beginning of New Strategy."
17. Carter, *Memoirs*, 559.
18. Safran, *Saudi Arabia.*, 370.

protect navigation in the Gulf. The Saudis, not wanting to publicize their increasing reliance on the United States, promptly declined the offer.[19]

Saudi concern about the adverse implications of visible cooperation with the United States was by no means unfounded. Libya reacted to the deployment of U.S. AWACS by breaking diplomatic relations with Saudi Arabia. Syria also condemned Saudi willingness to participate in America's strategic design and reacted by signing a Friendship and Cooperation Treaty with the Soviet Union in October.[20] The Saudis called upon U.S. assistance because of an imminent threat to their security. Yet, it became quite clear that such reliance on Washington came not without its political costs. As we will see, such costs prevented these specific instances of military coordination between the Saudis and the Americans from being translated into more long term political and strategic cooperation.

Even before the outbreak of the Gulf War, Saudi Arabia and the United States had discussed the possibility of a major arms deal to improve Saudi air defense capabilities. In February, 1980, National Security Advisor Brzezinski met Crown Prince Fahd for extensive discussions on military matters. It was reported that they essentially agreed upon an arms package containing five AWACS and F-15 enhancement equipment.[21] However, it was not until June that the State Department officially announced the Saudi request for the arms deal. The Senate strongly opposed the sale, pointing to a commitment made by Secretary of Defense Brown in 1978. In a letter to the Senate Foreign Relations Committee dated May 9, Brown asserted that "the U.S. will not furnish such MERs (bomb ejection racks) . . . nor do we intend to sell any other systems or armaments that could increase the range or enhance the ground attack capability of the F-15s."[22] The main object of this limitation had been to prevent the Saudis from having the capability to challenge Israel's air defenses.

By 1980, however, the administration felt that strategic changes in the Gulf warranted a reassessment of this policy. Iran was no longer the protectorate of the Gulf. On the contrary, Khomeni's regime presented an immediate threat to the political and territorial security of Gulf states. According to Secretary of Defense Weinberger and other sources, the Carter administration was prepared to recommend the AWACS sale to Congress.[23] Carter sensed the congressional and public opposition to the deal, however, and decided to cancel the package to gain political support before the impending presidential election. Only eleven

19. Ibid., 367.

20. Ibid., 413.

21. *Washington Post*, 18 August 1980, in Congressional Research Service, *Saudi Arabia*, 59.

22. Harold Brown, cited in Nimrod Novik, "Weapons to Riyadh, U.S. Policy and Regional Security" (Tel Aviv: Tel Aviv Center for Strategic Studies, 1981), 8.

23. U.S. Congress, Senate, *Military Implications*, 63, and Congressional Research Service, *Saudi Arabia*, 59, 61.

days before the election, he announced that "we will not agree to provide offensive capabilities for the planes that might be used against Israel. . . ."[24] That this move was in fact motivated by domestic political concerns became clear after his defeat, when Carter offered to make a joint announcement with President-elect Reagan to recommend the deal to Congress. Reagan declined the offer, but sought congressional approval of the sale only two months after his inauguration.[25]

The Saudi reaction to Carter's handling of the deal reflected a clear awareness of what was at stake for the United States. Their ambassador to Washington asserted that "the Kingdom of Saudi Arabia would consider all other possible sources to obtain the necessary means to defend itself. Nobody has a monopoly on relations and friendship with the Kingdom of Saudi Arabia."[26] This could have been an idle threat, but it was reinforced by a much more serious move. Prince Fahd, in the course of negotiations during 1980, had agreed to fund a communications center that would serve as the headquarters for an integrated Gulf defense system. In late October he withdrew this offer.[27] The implications for the United States went far beyond financial considerations; this was a direct challenge to America's evolving strategy for the Gulf.

The Carter administration had faced a dilemma: Its strategic objectives in the Gulf were incompatible with its domestic political concerns. The AWACS sale had the potential to improve America's own military capability in the Middle East and to build the foundation for a regional security system. Yet, because of the implications of the sale for Israeli security, there was much opposition to it in Congress and the pro-Israel community. Thus, before turning to the approach of the Reagan administration to the Persian Gulf, it is important to review how U.S.–Israel relations were initially affected by the Carter Doctrine.

Israel and the Gulf—I

Despite the success of the Carter administration in negotiating a peace treaty between Israel and Egypt, diplomatic contact between the United States and Israel during the late 1970s encountered strains from a number of sources. Prime Minister Begin's intransigent position on the West Bank alienated President Carter and others in the administration.[28] American arms sales to Arab states as well as the withholding of certain transfers to Israel likewise hardened Israeli attitudes toward the United States. In the eyes of Harold Saunders, Assistant Secretary of State for Near Eastern and South Asian Affairs under Carter, the

24. Interview with President Carter, cited in Congressional Research Service, *Saudi Arabia*, 62.
25. Carter, *Memoirs*, 578–580.
26. Ambassador Alhegelan, cited in Congressional Research Service, *Saudi Arabia*, 62.
27. *Washington Post*, 1 November 1981.
28. See *Time Magazine*, "The Man From Plains Sums It Up" (11 October 1982), 62.

dialogue and understanding that had been at the core of U.S.–Israel relations were breaking down.[29] The Americans saw Israel succumbing to a wave of right-wing nationalism, while the Israelis saw the United States becoming increasingly beholden to its economic interests in the Arab world.

This hardening of relations had several effects on U.S. policy. First, officials in Washington felt that they had lost a certain amount of leverage in their dealings with Israel. Whereas in the past, diplomatic initiatives had worked well to influence Israeli policy, more coercive methods were now required. Yet, the United States wanted to appear neither at odds with the Israeli government nor implicated in all its actions. The former would reduce Arab confidence in America's ability to influence Israeli policy; the latter would make it very difficult to build a constructive U.S.–Arab dialogue. The administration settled on a policy of "evenhandedness" that involved a calculated distancing from Israeli positions. The State Department reasoned that the Saudis could not risk overt cooperation on defense matters with a country that was too closely aligned with Israeli policy.[30]

A corollary of this outlook was that Israel's participation in a region-wide security system would only harm the political climate that the administration was attempting to cultivate in the Gulf. Many in the State and Defense Departments argued that if the United States was to secure access to facilities in the Gulf littoral states, the option of basing in Israel had to be foreclosed. However, Israel's inclusion in the RDF scheme did offer several potential strategic advantages. Although the Labor party voiced opposition to the establishment of American bases in Israel, the Begin government was willing to provide "unquestioned facility access" to the United States.[31] Planners in the Pentagon saw the unreliability of bases in Turkey, Saudi Arabia, and other Arab countries as one of the main shortcomings of the RDF framework. Jeffrey Record, a prominent defense analyst, complained that "the RDF's success or failure in wartime has been staked on the momentary political calculations of potential host regimes in the Gulf."[32] Thus, Begin's willingness to provide access as well as the history of Israel's close relationship with the United States tempted U.S. planners to include Israel in the basing scheme.

For technological and geographic reasons there was also a strong case for increased reliance on Israel. In both the size of their bases and the sophistication of their equipment, the Israelis would be able to receive and service large numbers of American forces. Their air defense systems and antiterrorist network

29. Interview with Harold Saunders.

30. Interview with Randy Beers.

31. U.S. Congress, House, Foreign Affairs Committee, U.S. Security Interests in the Persian Gulf (Washington, DC: GPO, 1981), 75. For the view of the opposition Labor Party see interview with Shimon Peres, Foreign Broadcast Information Service (FBIS), 17 September 1981, Israel, 5.

32. Record, The Rapid Deployment Force, vii.

would protect against both major assaults and attempts to sabotage prepositioned stocks. In terms of staging an operation in Iran, F-15s with conformal fuel tanks could, in fact, reach most potential areas of combat from Israeli airfields.[33] Thus, in meeting strategic requirements, Israel offered many advantages as a staging area. Saudi Arabia was the most suitable in geographic terms, yet its reluctance and unreliability were serious drawbacks. Bases in eastern Turkey were also well suited geographically, but the Turks wanted to avoid any involvement in an American operation in the Gulf. Basing in Turkey also presented greater risks of escalation, because Soviet retaliation against Turkish bases would constitute an attack on NATO territory.

Despite voices in the administration calling for closer military ties with Israel, the Carter administration decided to rely exclusively on the Gulf states, Kenya and Somalia.[34] The Defense Department published an extensive list of reasons for this decision: to appear evenhanded, to prevent U.S. involvement in an Arab–Israeli war, to avoid a colonial image, and to dissuade the Arabs from offering bases to the Soviet Union.[35] However, the decision to exclude Israel from the RDF framework also clearly revealed certain priorities inherent in the Carter Doctrine. From a military standpoint, there is no question that Israel offered certain advantages that no other states in the area could provide. That the United States was willing to forego these advantages testified to the breadth of its policy objectives. The goal of the RDF was not simply to construct a projection capability; if it had been, Israel would have played a significant role. The objectives of enhancing U.S. political and strategic cooperation with Gulf states and fostering defense cooperation within the Gulf itself were equally as important as bolstering America's rapid deployment capabilities. This was a central reason for the administration's negative views of closer cooperation with Israel.

There was also a prevalent understanding within defense circles that specific agreements on military cooperation with Israel were unnecessary. Because Israel was a long term ally with common global perspectives, it was assumed that, in the event of a contingency involving the Soviet Union, Israel would play a significant role.[36] Israeli facilities were already well developed; there was no need to upgrade them. At the least, the United States could use Israeli bases; at the most, Israeli forces would be involved. Carter hinted at this in his memoirs:

33. U.S. Congress, House, *U.S. Security Interests*, 77.

34. Interview with Robert Komer. Paul Wolfowitz, who prepared a report on Persian Gulf security for the Pentagon's Office of Program Analysis and Evaluation (see Chapter 5), was one of the principal figures in the administration calling for more Israeli involvement in basing schemes for the RDF.

35. Congressional Research Service, *United States Foreign Policy Objectives and Overseas Military Installations*, 77–78.

36. This view was expressed by officials from all agencies in Washington.

"I wanted the Middle East region stable and at peace; I did not want to see Soviet influence expanded in the area. In its ability to help accomplish these purposes, Israel was a strategic asset to the United States."[37] Israel would always be available if the United States were to become involved in a regional contingency. Yet, there was no need to publicize the potential for strategic cooperation if doing so would jeopardize U.S. relations with the Gulf states.

The Reagan Transition

When President Reagan entered office in January, 1981, the Carter Doctrine was still in its formative stages. Within one year of its promulgation, the United States had succeeded in substantially improving its projection capabilities in the Gulf. Marines and their supplies had been stationed at Diego Garcia and efforts to increase sealift and airlift were under way. Nevertheless, there were certain areas in which Carter's initiatives had either failed to achieve their goals or had insufficient time to germinate. Many still doubted the ability of the RDF to deter the Soviets. The prepositioning scheme remained both uncertain and inadequate. And most importantly, the United States had failed to elicit the political cooperation of Saudi Arabia that was so essential to both constructing a regional security system and securing America's strategic access to the Gulf area.

Despite a desire to break cleanly with the policies of the previous administration, Reagan instituted few, if any, substantive changes in security policy toward Southwest Asia. But for several reasons, he did succeed in bringing to fruition certain as yet unrealized aspects of the strategy developed by Carter. Reagan was less constrained by domestic political concerns than his predecessor and was therefore able to act with more decisiveness and independence. He had the advantage of building upon a framework that was already established. Reagan saw the reaction of the Gulf states to the RDF and at least knew where the shortcomings in the strategy lay. The new president also took a more ideologically aggressive stance toward the Soviet Union. Even after the invasion of Afghanistan, Carter was never certain of Soviet intentions, and he was therefore unsure of the appropriate response. Reagan's ideological approach, however parochial, did give him a consistent framework within which to form and implement policy. Problems in all areas of the world were directly related to Soviet subversion and expansionism; Southwest Asia was a case in point.

The Reagan administration adopted two parallel approaches to furthering the security strategy for the Gulf initiated by Carter. First, Reagan hoped to change the broader framework within which Gulf states perceived U.S. intentions. Since one of the primary sources of opposition to the Carter Doctrine came from the Saudis themselves, the United States had to make a concerted effort to

37. Carter, Memoirs, 274–275.

counter or at least sidestep such opposition. The second approach was to continue offering the same incentives put forward by the previous administration.
Reagan not only accelerated those programs set into motion by Carter, but also
consummated the AWACS deal with Saudi Arabia—an arms sale that had
unparalleled consequences in the Middle East.

In an effort to "repackage" the Carter Doctrine, Reagan introduced two new
concepts—the "global perspective" and the "strategic consensus." The former
was largely for public consumption, the latter for private meetings between
Secretary of State Haig and Gulf leaders. Two months after coming to office, the
administration elaborated upon the position of the Middle East in its global
perspective: "We view the Middle East including the Persian Gulf as part of a
larger politico-strategic theater, the region bounded by Turkey, Pakistan and the
Horn of Africa, and we view it as a strategic entity requiring comprehensive
treatment to ensure a favorable balance of power."[38]

United States relations with the Gulf states were to become "part of a global
strategic situation involving our relationships to all nations of the world."[39] This
approach was more than a reflection of Reagan's ideological stance. It was an
attempt to spread the gospel of anticommunism and illuminate the Soviet
threat, thereby molding a place for the Gulf states in this broader conception of
global security. Reagan was attempting to subordinate regional sources of instability to the task of countering the Soviet threat.

The main goal of Secretary of State Haig's trip to the Middle East early in
1981 was to confirm support for this initiative. Haig conveyed to Arab leaders
the need to forge a "strategic consensus" throughout the region. For the United
States and Gulf regimes to share a primary strategic objective would improve the
chances of increased military and political cooperation. Haig asserted that solving the problem in the Gulf was "a question of the strategic realities in the
Middle East and we must not become exclusively concerned, for example, with
oil diplomacy or with Arab–Israeli differences."[40] The administration felt that
initiatives in the peace negotiations would only disrupt U.S.–Arab relations as
well as interfere with Egypt's gradual reintegration into the Arab world.[41] If
strategic concerns could subsume regional political tension, officials reasoned,
there was even hope of fostering an Egypt, Saudi Arabia, Israel triangle.[42]

38. Richard Burt, Director of the Bureau of Political and Military Affairs, in International
Communication Agency, U.S. State Department, 24 March 1981, "U.S. Building Options for
Increased Mideast Presence."

39. Congressional Research Service, *The Persian Gulf: Are We Committed? At What Cost?*
(Washington, DC: GPO, 1981), 11.

40. Alexander Haig, cited in *Financial Times*, 25 February 1981, "Haig Reiterates Change in
U.S. Mideast Policy."

41. *International Herald Tribune*, 24 February 1981, "Soviet Threat to Mideast Said to be Haig's
Priority."

42. *Financial Times*, 25 February 1981.

Haig was only encouraged to follow this approach by those in the administration who felt that progress on the Arab–Israeli front would not, in fact, ameliorate division and instability in the Arab world. In their view, the sources of strife and anti-Westernism in the Gulf were endemic to the region and not just the result of the Arab–Israeli conflict. They favored direct U.S. military and economic aid as the most effective means of addressing regional problems. There was also the question of whether substantive progress on the peace negotiations was likely. The autonomy talks had stalled, West Bank settlement was continuing, and there was no apparent basis for accommodation on either side. The United States would be wiser to concentrate on an area where there was more flexibility and consensus of interest, that of security and defense cooperation.

When Haig toured the Middle East in March of 1981, he faced a very cool reception in both Saudi Arabia and Jordan and was told unequivocally that the United States had better reassess its priorities. A Jordanian official asserted that "it is solving rather than side stepping the Palestinian issue which will defuse the possible radicalisation of the Arab states—and it is this which is providing the Soviets with their best opening in the region."[43] Unanimous rejection of the strategic consensus approach led Haig to discard the concept quite rapidly. Only two weeks after his trip to the Gulf, Haig stated, "We are not adopting any particular priority . . . to place the Soviet regional threats ahead of the urgency of progress in the peace process."[44] Thus, the Reagan administration's attempt to further its policies toward the Gulf through rhetorical means was quickly rebuffed.

By 1982, there were also other reasons for placing increasing focus on intraregional rather than Soviet threats to Gulf stability. There was a gradual reconsideration within Washington of the motives behind the invasion of Afghanistan and a diminishing concern about the likelihood of a direct Soviet move toward the Gulf oil fields.[45] The atmosphere of panic had subsided. The Soviets were mired in Afghanistan and would hardly be interested in undertaking a difficult and more dangerous engagement in Iran. Despite the fact that the Soviets were continuing to modernize their forces along their borders with Iran and Turkey, a more circumspect and cautious assessment of Soviet intentions prevailed in 1982 than in 1980.

Events within Southwest Asia also gradually diverted American attention from the Soviet threat. The Iranians in 1982 exhibited unprecedented military power with a series of isolated victories over Iraqi forces. Though the fall of Iraq was by no means imminent, the prospect of an Iranian victory heightened

43. *London Times*, 6 April 1981, "Haig Visit to Middle East Clarifies U.S. Priorities."

44. International Communication Agency, U.S. State Department, 8 April 1981, "A Statement by U.S. Secretary of State Alexander Haig."

45. *Guardian*, 17 February 1982, "Threat to Gulf Diminishes." This view was also expressed repeatedly by officials interviewed in Washington.

concern over the Gulf War both in Arab capitals and in Washington. Furthermore, as the war progressed, both combatants threatened to spread the conflict to neighboring states. In 1981, Iranian planes attacked targets in Kuwait, including, in October, a major oil facility. The Iraqi air strikes on neutral tankers in the Gulf that began in 1984 temporarily raised concern about the flow of oil and led the Kuwaitis and the Saudis to seek new air defense equipment from the United States.

Israel's invasion of Lebanon in 1982 also complicated America's approach to Gulf security. With the exception of Syria, no Arab state played an active role in the war; each essentially stood by as the Israelis drove the PLO from Lebanon. This situation led to a resurgence of more radical currents in the Arab world and forced the Saudis to distance themselves from the United States. Furthermore, Syria's dominant role in the war strengthened Assad's political position in the Middle East. His pro-Soviet stance made it increasingly difficult for the Saudis to cooperate openly with the United States. Washington's inability to influence Israeli policy in the early months of the war further damaged U.S. leverage in the Arab Gulf. Thus, the war in Lebanon not only diverted American attention from Gulf security to the Arab–Israeli conflict, it also created a climate in the Arab world that widened the gap between U.S. military strategy and the political acceptability of that strategy within the region itself.

The war in Lebanon also had a more immediate impact upon American perspectives toward military operations in the Middle East. Though U.S. Marines were sent to Lebanon in a peacekeeping capacity, they engaged in combat and suffered significant losses from sniping attacks and from the suicide bombing of their compound in October, 1983. Their involvement in Lebanon proved to take the form of just that type of unconventional combat that the military has traditionally attempted to avoid in the periphery. American troops in Lebanon were given unclear political and strategic objectives, and they faced an enemy well trained in guerilla tactics and terrorism. The episode in Beirut both made the Pentagon wary of further military engagements in the Middle East and emphasized the need for special forces and counterterrorist units.[46]

This increasing concern about intraregional conflict that emerged from the

---

46. In 1984, Secretary Weinberger gave a speech carefully delineating the circumstances in which U.S. forces should be used. The speech was made in the context of limiting further engagements in local conflicts similar to the one in Lebanon. Weinberger asserted that U.S. troops should be used "with the clear intention of winning. If we are unwilling to commit the forces or resources necessary to achieve our objectives, we should not commit them at all." He also stated that, "If we do decide to commit forces to combat overseas, we should have clearly defined political and military objectives. . . . If we determine that a combat mission has become necessary for our vital national interests, then we must send forces capable to do the job—and not assign a combat mission to a force configured for peacekeeping." See Caspar Weinberger, "The Uses of Military Power," Department of Defense News Release, no. 609–84, 28 November 1984.

Gulf War and the fighting in Lebanon was not, however, reflected in the Pentagon's contingency planning for the RDF.[47] A Soviet invasion of Iran continued to be the scenario around which planning for the RDF proceeded. The Pentagon had been instructed to prepare for this mission and was continuing to do so. As argued earlier, and especially in light of the events in Lebanon, an order to prepare for lesser non-Soviet contingencies could well have interrupted, if not stalled, the bureaucratic momentum that had gathered behind the RDF.

The continuing focus of planning for Southwest Asia on the Soviet threat was reflected in several initiatives taken by the Reagan administration. The administration recommended that the RDF be expanded from 220,000 to 440,000 men. The Pentagon wanted to earmark for the force two additional army divisions, one marine division, and five tactical air wings.[48] The Army undertook to equip a new light division that would be tailored for rapid deployment to distant regions. The ready reserve sealift fleet was also expanded, several vessels equipped with "roll on, roll off" capability, and an additional eleven depot ships sent to Diego Garcia to preposition materials.[49] The administration, revealing its concern for potential U.S. involvement in unconventional contingencies, also requested funding for additional special operation forces, including new Seals teams and Special Forces groups. By 1985, more than five divisions had been assigned to the RDF—roughly 300,000 troops (see Table 5). Congress, in discussing appropriations for these changes, pressed the administration on its strategic rationale for supplementing the size of the RDF. Secretary of Defense Weinberger unequivocally responded that "we have to have the capability to deploy enormous forces to hold and interdict and blunt the Soviet attack. That is, of course, the basis for the proposal to improve the Rapid Deployment Force that we make in this budget."[50]

A second undertaking which revealed the perspectives of the Reagan administration toward Southwest Asia was the transformation of the Rapid Deployment Joint Task Force (RDJTF) into the Central Command (CENTCOM). After almost three years of interservice squabbling over the structure of the RDF, the Reagan administration established a unified command for Southwest Asia as of January 1, 1983. The primary goal of this change was to alleviate the bureaucratic impediments that were continuing to plague the RDF's development. The creation of CENTCOM was to place the mission in Southwest Asia, at least in organizational terms, on par with military missions in Europe and East

---

47. Military interviews.

48. *New York Times*, 25 October 1982, "Special U.S. Force for Persian Gulf Growing Swiftly."

49. U.S. Congress, House, *Defense Appropriations for 1985*, Pt. 1, 162–168.

50. U.S. Congress, Senate, Armed Services Committee, *Department of Defense Authorization for Appropriations for Fiscal Year 1983*, Pt. 1, Posture Statement (Washington, DC: GPO, 1982), 10.

Table 5
FORCES AVAILABLE TO CENTCOM
AS OF 1985

Army
   1 airborne division
   1 airmobile/air assault division
   1 infantry division
   1 mechanized infantry division
   1 cavalry brigade air combat
   Rangers and unconventional warfare units
Marines
   1 amphibious division, including air wing
   1 amphibious regiment, including air group
Air Force
   10 tactical fighter wings (with support air forces)
   2 squadrons of strategic bombers
Navy
   3 carrier battle groups
   1 surface action group
   5 air/antisubmarine patrol squadrons

Source: McNaugher, *Arms and Oil*, 55, 65; and U.S.
Congress, Senate, Armed Services Committee, *Department of
Defense Authorization for Appropriations for Fiscal Year 1983*,
Pt. 1, 292.

Asia. A body with bureaucratic authority equal to that of EUCOM or PACOM would provide increasing impetus behind planning and procurement for Gulf operations. Furthermore, the REDCOM staff would cease arguing that the Gulf mission should fall under its auspices and that the RDJTF was violating the established chain of command by communicating directly with the JCS.

The symbolic significance of the change was also clear. CENTCOM was the first new regional command to be created in thirty-five years. Security considerations in the Gulf area would no longer be dealt with as being of secondary importance; Europe, East Asia, and Southwest Asia were, according to the Posture Statement for Fiscal Year 1985, "the three theaters of most critical interest" to the United States.[51] As under the RDJTF, most of the units assigned to the Central Command were also earmarked for use in other theaters. Yet, the continuous channeling of military resources and funds to the Middle East did place a strain on operations in other areas. The presence in the Indian Ocean alone impinged upon readiness in other theaters, reduced stockpiles of hardware, delayed maintenance schedules, and decreased personnel availability.[52] In

51. U.S. Congress, House, *Defense Appropriations for 1985*, Pt. 1, 33.
52. U.S. Congress, House, *Defense Appropriations for 1983*, Pt. 6, 63.

short, the Reagan administration ensured that the Carter Doctrine was not a temporary response to a particular perception of Soviet behavior, but a fixture of U.S. global security policy.

If President Reagan was to see his plans for the RDF realized, these improvements in force availability and command arrangements had to be accompanied by progress in securing regional access. The Gulf states had by no means rebuffed Carter's plans to establish the RDF, nor rejected his political initiatives for increased regional cooperation. The Saudis welcomed an "over-the-horizon" presence. The Omanis readily offered access to bases and were willing to publicize their improving ties with the United States. The Emirates and even the Kuwaitis watched with careful interest the evolving security arrangements for the region. Yet, all these states acted with great caution and restraint because of both a lack of confidence in the United States and the fear of inciting domestic opposition and regional rivalries. Saudi Arabia was the key actor that had failed to meet U.S. expectations. Carter had thought that the Saudis would stand behind both Camp David and the RDF, but was disappointed on both scores. He overestimated Saudi support for U.S. policy and the extent to which the Kingdom was willing to stand alone on specific issues. As far as shaping political currents in the Gulf was concerned, the Saudis were the most influential force. Yet, they lacked the confidence and security to take a more visible and active position. As Ghassam Salameh, a prominent analyst of Arab politics, explained, "Saudi Arabia is not a leader. It is a consensus builder. When there is no Arab consensus on an issue it prefers to stand pat rather than get out ahead of the rest."[53] In terms of gaining access to the Gulf and building political cohesion among moderate Arabs, the United States was dependent upon Saudi initiative. Thus, while the Reagan administration provided impetus to the programs that were already in progress, it also had to find a means of inducing the Saudis to play a more dominant role in regional politics.

Reagan began by accelerating many of the projects implemented by Carter: "In addition to carrying through with what has already been initiated, we are reviewing options for great access in the region, increased military construction and a greater peacetime presence."[54] The "great access in the region" referred to new arrangements that were evolving with both Saudi Arabia and Egypt. The Saudis finally agreed to preposition American supplies and "overbuild" their facilities, though they continued to reject the proposal to establish a forward base on their territory.[55] At the same time, Egypt began to show interest in

---

53. Ghassam Salameh, cited in *International Herald Tribune*, 24 January 1983, "Saudis Fail to Live Up to U.S. Expectations in Peace Talks."

54. International Communication Agency, U.S. State Department, 24 March 1981.

55. Military interviews. See also the *Daily Telegraph*, 10 March 1981, "Saudis Reject U.S. Plan for Bases as Neo-Colonial."

playing a much larger role in the security scheme. Sadat, with growing confidence in his ties with the United States, attempted to establish Egypt as America's main military ally in the area. He offered the Americans full access to both Ras Banas and Cairo West, though he refused to sign a contract for the agreement.[56] These arrangements strengthened Sadat's relationship with Washington and provided the United States a rear staging area much more suitable than that available in Somalia or Kenya.[57] As far as military construction was concerned, Reagan funneled over $2 billion into improving regional facilities. This included construction at ten different sites in Egypt, Oman, Somalia, Kenya, and Diego Garcia.[58]

Yet, behind these tangible improvements in U.S. capability was the recognition that such progress was peripheral to the main issue. The Defense Department was forthright in declaring its primary objective in the Gulf: "our overarching aim . . . [is] building up regional security."[59] And the administration knew that the realization of this goal depended upon the Saudis. In September, General David Jones, Chairman of the JCS, reminded Congress that "the *sine qua non* of the entire operation [to protect Southwest Asia] is Saudi Arabia."[60] It was because of this that the AWACS deal emerged as the most crucial element of U.S. policy toward the Gulf in 1981. This sale provided a key link between the RDF's military strategy and the political and strategic components of Gulf security for which the U.S. had been searching since 1979.

The AWACS Sale

In March, 1981, the Reagan administration recommended to Congress the sale of the AWACS arms package to Saudi Arabia. After what was one of the most heated and complex debates on foreign policy on record, the Senate approved the sale in October. Never before had a single arms agreement stimulated such controversy in Washington. And it was precisely because of its far-reaching implications that Congress took such interest in the sale. Because of the sophistication of the weaponry as well as the political message that accompanied the transaction, the deal profoundly affected the Saudis' ability to defend their oil fields, the security of Israel, and America's strategic role in the Persian Gulf. In

56. *International Herald Tribune*, 22–23 August 1981, "Sadat Aims to be U.S. Partner, Strategic Power in Middle East."

57. The reliability of Egyptian bases was called into question by Sadat's assassination. Although President Mubarak confirmed the access agreements, Sadat's death was an all too clear warning of the dangers of close cooperation with the United States.

58. International Communication Agency, U.S. State Department, 13 March 1981, "U.S. Improving Middle East and Indian Ocean Military Facilities."

59. Congressional Research Service, *The Persian Gulf*, 16.

60. General Jones in U.S. Congress, Senate, *Military Implications*, 9.

this sense, it brought to a head the crucial issues for U.S. policy in the Middle East since 1973.

To understand the role that the AWACS were to play in restructuring Gulf security, it is necessary to look at the Senate debate itself, for it was during these hearings that the administration revealed to Congress the details of its strategy. The main components of the arms package included five AWACS, F-15 enhancement equipment, and a computerized ground communications system. Senate opposition to the sale was based on two points. First, the AWACS contained a large amount of classified electronic equipment. There was concern that security in Saudi Arabia was insufficient to prevent such technology from being stolen by or sold to the Soviets.[61] Second, and more importantly, the sale would greatly decrease Israel's military edge over Saudi Arabia. The AWACS would allow the Saudis to "look" into Israel while the modified F-15s could carry out strikes throughout Israeli territory.[62] As during the Carter administration, these arguments carried a great deal of weight. Less than one month before the vote, it appeared that these points had persuaded well over half the Senate to oppose the sale.[63]

On October 28, the sale was approved by a vote of fifty-two to forty-eight. The Reagan administration and the Saudis combined their efforts to influence the outcome of the vote. As usual, the White House and the Defense Department barraged Congress with information supporting the sale. What was unusual, if not remarkable, however, was the massive corporate lobbying campaign orchestrated by the Saudis themselves. The Saudis called upon the many American companies that operated in the Kingdom to exercise influence in any way they could. The pro-Israel lobby also entered the fray. In the end, lobbying by Arab states, corporations, and especially by the White House played a key role in securing enough votes to conclude the sale.[64]

The primary considerations behind the administration's support for the sale can be put into three general categories: its effect on U.S. force capabilities, its implications for regional security arrangements, and its impact on United States–Gulf and intraregional relations. How was a single sale of weaponry to be of such broad strategic importance? Did the AWACS deal challenge a clear lesson that had emerged from the 1970s—that arms sales to the Middle East could not serve as a basis for lasting political arrangements?

As far as U.S. force projection was concerned, the sale was indispensable to

61. Ibid., 32.
62. Major General George Keegan in ibid., 99.
63. Senator Dan Quayle in ibid., 47.
64. Anthony Cordesman, *The Gulf and the Search for Strategic Stability* (Boulder, CO: Westview Press, 1984), 334. For a more detailed description of the lobbying campaign, see Judith Levenfeld, *Foreign Policy Lobbying and the 1981 Saudi Arms Sale*, and Steven Emerson, "The Petrodollar Connection."

improving American capabilities in the Gulf. By selling the package to the Saudis, the United States was effectively positioning in the most likely area of combat equipment essential to the operation of the RDF. The Pentagon's official briefing book on the sale revealed that "three years of spares for F-15s and AWACS, which would be compatible with U.S. equipment, would be stockpiled in Saudi Arabia."[65] The AWACS themselves would also be of crucial strategic importance to U.S. forces. In supporting the transaction, Secretary of Defense Weinberger revealed its merits: "[The deal would] increase the effectiveness of our own military capabilities if we were ever called upon to deploy U.S. forces to that area. The extensive logistics base and support infrastructure that will be a necessary part of this equipment package will be fully compatible with the defense needs of this whole vital area."[66] The AWACS package included an advanced command, control and communications (C^3) network as well as a ground based air defense system. General Kelley asserted that the RDF was essentially inoperative without "an air defense or air superiority network" and that he would "never let a force move into an area without that kind of protection."[67] While the air defense system would offer protection for ground forces, the AWACS would survey and coordinate combat over Saudi Arabia and as far north as the Zagros Mountains.[68] The implications of this for the RDF's Zagros Strategy need no elaboration.

Thus, in no uncertain terms the AWACS sale circumvented one of the RDF's main obstacles: the need to have large quantities of American equipment and sophisticated weaponry in the region. The United States had failed through diplomatic means to convince the Saudis to allow such prepositioning. The solution, somewhat puzzling in its simplicity, was to sell the equipment to the Saudis rather than preposition it on their territory. The obvious question concerns why the Saudis were willing to play this game. The answer lay in its potential both to enhance Saudi defense capabilities and to further attempts to establish a regional security network in the lower Gulf.

The AWACS and C^3 system necessary for the operation of the RDF would also serve as the primary components of a potential security scheme for the Gulf. According to the Pentagon, the sale "would contribute to a Gulf Air Defense system in which air defense networks could be linked, data transmitted, and air defense interceptors controlled."[69] The AWACS and the F-15s would provide the Saudis the capability to deal with smaller, intraregional contingencies, thereby allowing the United States to avoid involvement in local conflicts. In more demanding scenarios, the Saudis would also be able to provide initial air

65. U.S. Congress, Senate, *Military Implications*, 84.
66. Secretary of Defense Weinberger in ibid., 4.
67. General Kelley in ibid., 40.
68. General Stamm in Ibid., 17.
69. Ibid., 85.

coverage for U.S. forces entering the region. The United States prepared other Gulf states to be able to link their defense systems with the Saudis' new equipment. In 1981, the administration sent communications packages to both Oman and the United Arab Emirates.[70] The United States also carried out comprehensive studies of the air defense systems of Saudi Arabia, Oman, Bahrain, and Qatar. Kuwait and the United Arab Emirates had similar analyses completed.[71] Through the AWACS sale, the Saudis were acquiring the ability to lay the groundwork for a Gulf-wide defense network.

In the past, cooperative systems had failed because the impetus for coordination was lacking. No state was willing to acquiesce to the political or military dominance of another, nor were the technological benefits of cooperation worth the sacrifice in prestige or independence. Yet, the AWACS package gave the Saudis a capability so superior to that of other states (excluding Iran and Iraq, who were preoccupied with their own war) that any rivalry for military power was meaningless. And by entering into a cooperative network, other Gulf states could share in the Saudis' strength. Rather than following Nixon's scheme of designating one state—Iran—to control competition among others, the Reagan administration was hoping to foster a cooperative hierarchy led by Saudi Arabia. Saudi military predominance also confirmed its political strength in the Gulf. When put in this context, the high degree of Saudi support for the sale becomes quite understandable.

The political implications of the evolving defense system, however, went far beyond increasing Saudi leverage in the Gulf. The Reagan administration assumed the sale would improve relations between the United States and the Saudis. Riyadh's reaction to Carter's initial cancellation of the deal made it clear that the Saudis were intent on purchasing the AWACS and that their relationship with the United States was contingent upon that sale.[72] Thus, the administration saw the transfer as a means of securing its "special relationship" with the House of Saud.

Reagan also saw the potential for the United States to enhance its influence in the Gulf as a whole. This was to occur by increasing America's peacetime presence and through association with the political network that was to evolve simultaneously with the regional security system. As in Iran, the transfer of technology to the Gulf had brought in hundreds of American technicians and advisors. With equipment as complicated as the AWACS, the United States was virtually assured a military presence in Saudi Arabia for decades. It would be

70. Such improvements were part of a general modernization program and were not intended exclusively to provide a link to the Saudi system.
71. *Washington Post*, 1 November 1981. Most of the studies were done by the Mitre Corporation, one of the main contractors for the U.S. Air Force.
72. See notes 26 and 27.

1990 at the earliest before the Saudis could operate the planes themselves and even after that, "there are no plans that the United States won't have some involvement with the AWACS."[73] The mere presence of U.S. personnel solidified the strength of American influence in the Kingdom and, as the technological level of the weaponry increased, so did Saudi dependence upon U.S. assistance. Under ideal conditions, a small but crucial U.S. presence in Saudi Arabia could wield a great deal of influence and be welcomed by Riyadh.

As far as the other Gulf states were concerned, the United States felt that its evolving relationship with Saudi Arabia would also improve American influence throughout the region. Military ties would only set the stage for political as well as economic cooperation. According to Secretary Weinberger, the AWACS sale would further "Saudi efforts to develop cooperation with all of her Mideast neighbors."[74] But the administration also felt that the United States itself would play a larger role in shaping the political climate in the Gulf: "The fact that this sale demonstrates the credibility of the U.S. as a reliable security partner not only to Saudi Arabia but to other states in the region as well . . . provides the political rationale and impetus for expanded cooperation, not just in the security area but in other areas as well."[75]

There is no question that many of these statements made by administration officials during the AWACS hearings were instances of wishful thinking, if not outright exaggeration. The conception of a NATO-like alliance in the Gulf, sanctioned, if not supported, by the United States, was a model that even the most idealistic supporters of the sale could not credibly uphold. Though one can challenge the extent of the administration's vision, however, one cannot question the basic framework that it envisaged. This is because that framework was actually taking shape; the Gulf Cooperation Council (GCC) emerged simultaneously with the evolution of the AWACS strategy.

Before 1980, there had been numerous examples of defense cooperation among Gulf states. In 1962, Saudi Arabia and Jordan signed the Taif Pact as a response to attacks from Yemen. After the British withdrawal, Gulf states settled many territorial disputes without bloodshed and assisted each other in limited military operations. In 1974, Kuwait was granted access to airfields in Saudi Arabia, Bahrain, Qatar, and Abu Dhabi to assist in defending against raids from Iraq. Iran and Saudi Arabia both contributed forces to the Omani effort to quell the Dhofar rebellion.

In contrast to these examples of cooperation, however, were numerous unsuccessful attempts to further joint regional security arrangements. In 1970, Iraq proposed the formation of an Arab defense organization, but received little

---

73. General Jones in U.S. Congress, Senate, *Military Implications*, 10.
74. Secretary of Defense Weinberger in ibid., 4.
75. Ibid., 83.

support in the lower Gulf. In 1978, efforts were made to pool intelligence information; Iran, Saudi Arabia, Kuwait, Bahrain, Qatar, the United Arab Emirates, Egypt, and Sudan participated.[76] There were no concrete results. After the Shah's departure from Iran in January, 1979, further attempts were made to forge collective security arrangements in the Gulf.[77] Again, these proved to be futile. The traditional obstacles to cooperation remained: rivalry between Persians and Arabs, tension between Shiite and Sunni populations, fear of local domination, differing perspectives on the Arab–Israeli question, and divergent views of relations with external powers. By 1980, however, a combination of events and new incentives finally provided the impetus for a number of Gulf states to overcome these obstacles.

First reports of a joint council involving Saudi Arabia, Oman, Kuwait, Qatar, Bahrain, and the United Arab Emirates emerged in late 1980.[78] Ministers of these countries discussed the formation of a cooperative alliance in March of 1981 (the same month that the AWACS sale was recommended to Congress); the establishment of the GCC was formally announced in Abu Dhabi in May. The Council's first public statements addressed only economic issues, largely because of a dispute between Oman and Kuwait. Although the GCC publicly rejected any "military alliances and defense pacts between the countries of the region and foreign powers," Oman favored reliance on the United States, while Kuwait leaned toward the Soviet Union.[79] Nevertheless, it was clear that security cooperation lay behind the formation of the GCC. Nadav Safran described well these tacit assumptions: "[S]ince the GCC countries were linked by a network of bilateral security agreements, including agreements between Saudi Arabia and each of the others, the omission of specific reference to defense and security did not matter much once an integrative framework was established."[80]

During the second half of the year, however, meetings of Council members focused explicitly on security matters. This was the result of a growing consensus among members on defense issues as well as a reaction to three specific events: the intensification of the Iran–Iraq conflict, including Iranian air attacks on Kuwait; the exposure of an attempted Iranian-backed coup in Bahrain; and the formation in August of a defense pact among Libya, Ethiopia, and South Yemen.[81] Early discussion on security focused on military expenditures and the establishment of a Gulf-wide defense force. Then in late 1981 and early 1982, defense ministers of the GCC attempted to expand strategic cooperation and

76. Noyes, The Clouded Lens, 70.
77. Safran, Saudi Arabia, 355.
78. The Middle East, "Editorial," January 1981, 16.
79. Ibid., 17.
80. Safran, Saudi Arabia, 374.
81. International Herald Tribune, 3 September 1981, "6 Arab States Pledge Joint Security Steps."
See also Safran, Saudi Arabia, 378.

discussed the possibility of establishing a joint air defense network that would be coordinated by Saudi Arabia's AWACS and C³ system.[82] Although it remained to be seen whether these discussions would lead to tangible results, it was clear that the Saudis were seeking to establish this link between the AWACS deal and a regional air defense network.[83]

After decades of unsuccessful attempts, why did a Gulf defense organization finally emerge in 1981? It was clear that the Iranian revolution, the Yemen war, the Soviet invasion of Afghanistan, and the Iran–Iraq war had both multiplied and intensified the internal and external threats facing Gulf regimes. Never before was the need for cooperation perceived to be so vital. The Iraq–Iran war not only posed a tangible military threat to the region, however, it also offered a unique opportunity for an independent initiative in the lower Gulf. The war provided an excuse for excluding Iran and Iraq from the GCC. And since a large proportion of the Shiite population in the Gulf was concentrated in Iran and Iraq, this reduced a potential source of tension within the Council. The smaller Gulf states would also have been reluctant to join a Gulf-wide organization because of the dominating size and military strength of their northern neighbors. The population of GCC members was 14 million, while Iran had 39 million inhabitants and Iraq 13 million.[84]

It is difficult to determine what role the United States played in the establishment of the GCC. One can rule out any overt connection, simply because visible American participation would have precluded the involvement of Kuwait and, quite possibly, other sheikdoms. But the plans of the GCC to establish an integrated air defense system based on the Saudi AWACS were a clear indication of the indirect impact of U.S. policy on the nature of cooperation among Council members. That the defense systems of each state were, in fact, being developed to coordinate with the Saudi system was, in the words of a confidential source, "more than coincidental."[85] It is clear, however, that the GCC was deeply divided over the status of its relations with the United States. The Omanis, as the following incident illustrates, were the most pro-American. In late 1981, a prominent U.S. military officer was invited to Muscat; this was nothing unusual. Yet, for the first time, he was asked to wear a military uniform throughout his stay. The GCC happened to be meeting in Muscat at the same time, and the officer was essentially paraded before the Gulf ministers for several days.[86]

82. Safran, *Saudi Arabia*, 376–381. On the interoperability of air forces in the Gulf, see Cordesman, *The Gulf*, 621–622.

83. Safran, *Saudi Arabia*, 437.

84. United Nations Department of International Economic and Social Affairs, *Demographic Yearbook 1984* (New York, 1986).

85. In 1982, the United States took steps to further its defense cooperation with the Saudis. In February, a U.S.–Saudi Arabia joint military panel was proposed. Washington also announced plans to begin coproduction of jet aircraft with Egypt.

86. Military interview.

At the same time, the Kuwaitis had put pressure on the Omanis to distance themselves from the United States and had resisted basing strategic cooperation among GCC members on U.S. equipment.[87]

Such political divisions within the GCC prevented the Saudis from achieving the degree of regional defense cooperation that they had been seeking. As of 1987, the envisioned integrated air defense network had yet to take shape. As early as November of 1982, the GCC announced that it was reevaluating the notion of constructing a regional defense system around the Saudi AWACS.[88] These developments constituted a setback not only for the Saudis, but also for U.S. policy. Washington was understandably hopeful that an air defense network—based on U.S. equipment—would eventually be established. Furthermore, there were direct signals from the Saudis that challenged the premises of America's overall strategy for the Gulf. In February 1982, the Saudis declined a U.S. offer for an increase in joint military planning.[89] The basing arrangements that were so crucial to the operation of the RDF also became increasingly uncertain. The Saudis were less forthcoming about the use of Dhahran and the agreement with Egypt over Ras Banas lapsed. The arrangements with Egypt were never put into writing because of technical obstacles and Egyptian fears of formal ties. The U.S. Congress refused to appropriate funds under such uncertain circumstances. These developments presented a serious obstacle for an American strategy so dependent upon the reliability and cooperation of regional states. Secretary of Defense Weinberger admitted in 1982 that the United States was unable to "get the things we most need which are facilities within the Mideast countries. . . ."[90]

Nevertheless, the emergence of the GCC remained an important regional development complementing U.S. initiatives. The GCC has assumed responsibility for dealing with low-intensity local threats, precisely the type of conflict from which the United States would prefer to keep its distance. In 1983, the GCC announced the establishment of a Gulf rapid deployment force consisting of troops from Saudi Arabia, the United Arab Emirates, Kuwait, and Oman. A joint military exercise was also held.[91]

The central problem for the United States, however, superseded these purely military considerations. Simply put, Washington's political dialogue with Saudi Arabia eroded considerably during and after 1982. This is not to suggest that U.S.–Saudi relations had been particularly warm before this point. But both the Carter and Reagan administrations had overestimated both the willingness and

87. Safran, *Saudi Arabia*, 431.

88. *Contemporary Mideast Backgrounder*, "Sources of Inter-State Conflict in the Persian Gulf " (Jerusalem: Media Analysis Center, 28 November 1982), 2.

89. Safran, *Saudi Arabia*, 380–381.

90. Secretary of Defense Weinberger, cited in U.S. Congress, Senate, *Defense Authorization for Appropriations for Fiscal Year 1983*, Pt. 1, 31.

91. Cordesman, *The Gulf*, 631.

the ability of Saudi Arabia to take a leading position in Gulf politics. Behind each arms deal, the United States mistakenly perceived a more long term correspondence of political and strategic objectives. This long term correspondence, however, did not exist. By 1982, the deeper political differences between the two countries were becoming apparent. Not only did the Saudis fail to play the bold role in regional politics that U.S. officials had expected, but they also adopted policies overtly contrary to U.S. interests. Riyadh cancelled Prince Fahd's visit to Washington in 1982, reestablished diplomatic relations with Libya, actively opposed President Reagan's Middle East peace plan, and made almost no diplomatic contribution to resolving the crisis in Lebanon.[92] The clear message accompanying these moves forced American officials to view in a more sober light the limitations on U.S. relations with Saudi Arabia.

The United States had failed to recognize the extent to which the erosion of the moderate camp made it difficult for the Saudis to risk close military cooperation with the United States. With the signing of the Camp David Treaty, Egypt was cast from the Arab League. The fall of the Shah converted Iran from a status quo power to one threatening to bring radical change to the Gulf. Without Egypt and Iran, the Saudis were simply unwilling to act as the leaders of a moderate coalition.[93] After 1978, Iraq and Syria led the opposition to Camp David and set the political tone for the Arab world, a tone that was hardly conducive to close ties with the United States. When Iraq became preoccupied with the Gulf War, the Saudis were constrained by Syria's increasingly powerful position in the Middle East. These constraints upon Saudi Arabia's political role in the Gulf posed considerable problems for the implementation of U.S. policy.

Another factor placing strains on the dialogue between Saudi Arabia and the United States was the Israeli invasion of Lebanon in 1982. This chapter therefore concludes by discussing the impact of U.S.–Israel relations on the Reagan administration's approach to Gulf security.

Israel and the Gulf—II

Of the three major candidates in the 1980 presidential election, Ronald Reagan was the most outspoken in his support for Israel. Late in 1979, Reagan unequivocally stated his position:

> The fall of Iran has increased Israel's value as perhaps the only remaining strategic asset in the region on which the United States can truly rely; other pro-Western

92. See U.S. Congress, House, Foreign Affairs Committee, *U.S. Policy Toward the Persian Gulf* (Washington, DC: GPO, 1983), 21–22.
93. The best analysis of these shifting political alignments can be found in Safran, *Saudi Arabia*, esp. 352–386.

states in the region, especially Saudi Arabia and the smaller Gulf Kingdoms, are weak and vulnerable. . . . Israel has the democratic will, national cohesion, technological capacity, and military fiber to stand forth as America's trusted ally. . . ."[94]

Yet, after taking office, Reagan faced the same problem with the U.S.–Israel "special relationship" that the previous administration had. Strains in the dialogue resulted both from America's continuing search for good relations with the Gulf states and from Israeli actions that the United States could not condone. The attack on the nuclear reactor in Iraq, the annexation of the Golan Heights, and the invasion of Lebanon elicited sanctions and verbal condemnation from the United States. Likewise, the sale of AWACS to the Saudis and the absence of an American reaction to the placement of Syrian missiles in Lebanon did little to reassure the Begin government of America's commitment to Israeli security.

Nevertheless, Reagan's preoccupation with countering the Soviet threat translated into a desire to take advantage of Israel's strategic position in the region. Secretary of State Alexander Haig was one of the main proponents of capitalizing on Israel's military strength and location, especially because of Begin's strong support for the concept of strategic consensus. The Israelis understandably were quick to offer verbal support for any policy that subordinated negotiations on the Palestinian question to larger security issues.[95] As a result, the question of U.S.–Israel military cooperation did go beyond the stage of rhetoric. And the events surrounding the Memorandum of Understanding (MOU) signed between the two countries in November, 1981 revealed a good deal about the tensions within U.S. policy at the time.

The MOU on strategic cooperation emerged from a series of meetings between Haig and Israeli Defense Minister Ariel Sharon. Beginning shortly after the fall of the Shah, Sharon attempted to impress upon American officials the new strategic importance of Israel to the United States. As mentioned, many in the State and Defense Departments were opposed to the inclusion of Israel in the RDF's basing scheme. When Haig proposed to sign the MOU in late 1981, he met stiff opposition from Secretary of Defense Weinberger. It was not until President Reagan himself ordered Weinberger to acquiesce that approval from the Defense Department was forthcoming.[96] Because of such opposition to the MOU in the United States, the contents of the agreement were deliberately vague. Specific reference was made to joint naval maneuvers in the Mediterra-

94. Ronald Reagan, cited in Steven Spiegel, "The Middle East: A Consensus of Error," *Commentary* (March 1982), 24.

95. See, for example, *International Herald Tribune*, 17 January 1980, "U.S., Israel at Odds over Autonomy Issue."

96. Confidential sources.

nean, but, despite Israeli hopes that the document would focus more on RDF strategy, Israel's role in the Gulf security system was left open. There was only a reference to the potential for the "establishment of joint readiness activities including access to maintenance facilities and other infrastructures."[97] Nevertheless, in more private surroundings, Haig did admit that prepositioning supplies for the RDF did fall within the confines of the MOU.[98]

Why did the Reagan administration decide to take this step after Israel had been deliberately excluded from the RDF scheme for two years? Was this a sign that a new political framework had emerged in the Middle East that would allow the United States to engage in strategic cooperation with Israel without risking political alienation in the Gulf? It is clear that the AWACS sale was a factor in the decision to sign the MOU. The United States had made known its commitment to the security of the Gulf states; it could thus afford to cooperate with the Israelis without losing its evenhanded image. Of even more importance, however, was the need to assuage Israeli fears that had been heightened by the AWACS sale. There was concern that unless a concession was made to the Israelis, the Begin government would become more intransigent on all issues. The MOU was in part intended to soften Israeli attitudes toward U.S. policy and make possible continuation of the autonomy talks. Similar agreements were signed in 1975 and 1978 in attempts to move the Israelis to more flexible negotiating positions.[99]

The cooperative arrangements stipulated in the MOU were never tested, however, for it was suspended by the United States only weeks after its initiation as a sanction against Israel for its annexation of the Golan Heights. That the agreement was suspended so quickly was partly a reflection of the ambivalence toward it in Washington. Yet, the MOU was in force sufficiently long to elicit an Arab reaction. The Gulf states were surprisingly muted in their condemnation. They naturally disapproved of the document, but saw it as nothing new in the existing U.S.–Israel relationship and made no threats to retaliate diplomatically.[100] This raises the question of whether the Gulf states, and the Saudis in particular, would countenance military cooperation with Israel if faced with a grave threat to their security. Was the United States justified in assuming that it had to choose between the Gulf states and Israel in designing a basing strategy for the RDF? The Jordan crisis in 1970 certainly confirmed the willingness of a confrontation state to accept Israeli military assistance in the face of an extreme threat to the regime.

97. Text of agreement in *New York Times*, 1 December 1981.
98. FBIS, 16 November 1981, Israel, I–11.
99. These previous examples were in 1975 over withdrawal from the Sinai and in 1978 over the Camp David Accords.
100. See for example, FBIS, 15 October 1981, Arabian Peninsula, C-9 (statement of North Yemen President Ali Abdallah Salih).

The clearest message that emerged from the MOU, however, was that U.S. policy was in a state of flux. Having completed a crucial arms deal with the Saudis and seen an ambitious plan to restructure Gulf security take shape, the United States was reaching a vacuum in its relations with the Israelis. The administration, Congress, and the public remained firmly committed to Israel as a strategic and political ally. This attitude was reflected in the size of the aid packages to the Begin government approved by Congress. However, just how Israel was to fit into the broader perspective in the Middle East was a stumbling block in Reagan's policy. The extent to which U.S.–Israel relations deteriorated during this period was to become evident in 1982 when the war in Lebanon brought such strains to a head.

While it appears that the United States knew about and tacitly approved of the initial invasion into southern Lebanon, the Reagan administration made clear that it did not support Israeli policy throughout the war.[101] The administration's attempts to curtail the sale of certain weapons and to reduce aid to Israel indicated President Reagan's discontent with Israel's military operations in Lebanon as well as the eroding state of U.S.–Israel relations. The war also caused serious damage to America's position in the Gulf. While the Israelis bombed Beirut and beseiged the PLO, it became increasingly difficult for Arab states to maintain close ties with the United States. This factor contributed to the unanimous rejection within the Arab world of President Reagan's 1982 proposal for a Palestinian homeland to be established on the West Bank in federation with Jordan.

By 1983, the United States seemed to have burned its wick at both ends, as it were. Washington was at odds with its traditional ally in the Middle East: Israel. Similarly, U.S. relations with the Saudis, and the Arab world more generally, were at a low ebb. It became increasingly clear that the United States would not succeed in securing the durable political and strategic cooperation in the Gulf that it had been seeking since 1980. Whatever hopes remained of cultivating a fruitful political dialogue with the Saudis were dashed by the Israeli invasion of Lebanon. The resultant political climate in the Arab world led to mutual frustration within both the United States and the Gulf over Washington's continuing quest for regional access and security cooperation. The United States maintained its commitment to defend its vital interests in the Gulf with force if necessary. America's military strategy for the Gulf remained intact. Yet, the political framework in which that commitment was undertaken had changed. United States optimism about restructuring security arrangements in Southwest Asia had been tempered considerably. The initial political assumptions of the Carter Doctrine, though not abandoned, faced a period of reevaluation.

101. Ze'ev Schiff and Ehud Ya'ari, *Israel's Lebanon War* (New York: Simon and Schuster, 1984), 72–77.

Conclusions

The Carter Doctrine established a clear American commitment to use force in the Middle East to defend U.S. interests. The credibility of this commitment rested upon the development and implementation of a new military strategy for Southwest Asia. There were two prerequisites for the realization of this strategy: sufficient force projection capability and regional access. Building capability depended upon procuring additional resources, particularly lift assets, and allocating more existing resources to the Southwest Asia mission. Obtaining access was more elusive; it rested upon winning the cooperation of states allured by the prospects of U.S. security assistance, but fearful of the political repercussions of forming close ties to the United States.

Although there has been an ongoing debate since 1980 about the size and structure of the RDF, there was a consensus within both administrations about the central strategic assumptions upon which America's policy toward the Gulf was based. For both the Carter and Reagan administrations, the principal mission of the RDF was to deter a Soviet attack. In terms of procurement, this objective was reflected in efforts to increase strategic lift and intratheater mobility. The tactical aims were to harass and delay the Soviets in the northern mountains and to erect a formidable line of defense in southern Iran which the Soviets would have to confront if they were to reach the oil fields. The inconsistencies in official statements about the relative merits of adopting a deterrent/tripwire strategy as opposed to a defensive strategy were reflective of confusion about the requirements of deterrence and of ambiguity about how to measure both the strategic balance in the Gulf and the objective limits of the RDF's capability. The United States also had to address the problem of potential escalation in the Gulf; the feasibility of conventional defense by no means precluded the possibility that either adversary could use nuclear weapons. Whether any U.S. president would actually resort to nuclear or horizontal escalation as a result of conflict in Southwest Asia, however, was a question that would be answered only if the United States were to be confronted with a Soviet move toward the Gulf.

The key shortcoming in American security policy toward Southwest Asia since 1980 has been less a function of the details of military strategy per se than of the relationship between military strategy and regional politics. The feasibility of staging a major U.S. operation in Southwest Asia depended upon the cooperation of Gulf states on a wide range of issues. Before the United States could operate effectively within the region, airfields had to be enlarged, communication infrastructures built, and military supplies prepositioned. Were a deployment to take place, American troops would need access to these supplies and to facilities and bases in the theater. And most importantly, regional states would play a key role in defining the nature of the conflict. If the Soviets did invade Iran, how would the Iranians and their Arab neighbors react? Would U.S. troops be fighting in coordination with regional allies against a common enemy? Or would the United States be fighting against local troops in an effort to establish points of access? These unknowns could well determine the success or failure of America's military strategy.

This gap between strategy and political feasibility stemmed from the fact that U.S. security policy for the Gulf was based on several key political assumptions. Washington perceived that the rise of Khomeni, the Yemeni war, the Soviet invasion of Afghanistan, and the Iran–Iraq war combined to heighten the sense of insecurity within the lower Gulf. It followed that Gulf regimes would be receptive to American offers of security assistance. The United States believed that the emergence of a regional security framework would enhance political integration in the Gulf and allow local actors to assume responsibility for responding to low-intensity conflicts among or within Gulf states. The Carter and Reagan administrations also assumed that a deliberate and visible distancing from Israel would improve U.S. political leverage in the Gulf.

These assumptions proved, to varying degrees, to be accurate, but only for the short term. Though GCC members were unwilling to tolerate the establishment of U.S. bases in the Gulf, they did realize that preparations for the RDF would strengthen their own defense capabilities and make possible regional cooperation on security issues. But the United States failed to recognize that the erosion of the moderate camp after 1979 was to make it difficult for the Saudis to risk close alignment with Washington. Iraq's preoccupation with the Gulf War and Syria's important role in the conflict in Lebanon enhanced President Assad's political position in the Middle East, thereby contributing to a more radical and pro-Soviet Arab consensus. Israel's invasion of Lebanon further hindered Arab cooperation with the United States and called into question the value of Carter's and Reagan's attempts to distance themselves from the Israelis. Washington was implicated in the war by virtue of its historical relations with Israel. America's ability to influence Israeli policy—long a source of U.S. leverage in the Arab world—was also called into question by the unwillingness of the Begin government to respond to successive U.S. requests to moderate the conduct of the war in Lebanon.

American expectations of Arab cooperation were also exaggerated by Washington's preoccupation with the Soviet threat to the region after 1979. The sensitivity to regional issues that had been cultivated during the 1970s was reversed by the Soviet invasion and the ideological rigidity of the Reagan administration. The concepts of strategic consensus and global perspective were clear indications of a reorientation of America's regional political strategy. The rekindling of caustic Cold War rhetoric heightened the proclivity of the United States to view events within the Middle East—as it did in the 1950s and 1960s—primarily in an East–West context. This renewed emphasis on strategic considerations and superpower rivalry narrowed the scope and flexibility of America's dialogue with the Arab Gulf.

The United States was caught in the unenviable position of being a static external actor in the midst of a volatile and complex regional situation. The level of cooperation that emerged between Gulf states and the United States fell far short of U.S. expectations because the political strategy that accompanied the RDF was poorly designed, but also because of shifting and unpredictable political currents in the Arab world. America's military initiatives were often rebuffed because the political assumptions upon which they were based were either erroneous or obsolete. America's position in the Gulf fluctuated according to variables which the United States was unable either to control or, apparently, to understand. This does not bode well for a military strategy that is wedded to a certain set of political assumptions and dependent upon the cooperation of regional states.

The task of linking military strategy to political reality—in effect, the implementation of the Carter Doctrine—was less affected by bureaucratic dynamics and electoral concerns than was the process of policy formulation itself. This is somewhat unexpected, given that the bureaucracy essentially has sole responsibility for the execution of policy while the responsibility for formulation is shared with the White House. The key factor in the case at hand was that resistance to the RDF within the State and Defense Departments declined steadily after the decision to establish the force had been formally made. While the Carter Doctrine was still in its formative stages, these agencies brought their influence to bear: The content and presentation of policy was molded to circumvent bureaucratic resistance. Once the planning and procurement process had been set in motion, however, the State and Defense Department served largely as executors of policy. The vestiges of organizational rivalry for command responsibility in Southwest Asia continued to affect planning. There was also interagency squabbling over the details of the regional basing scheme and the role of Israel in contingency planning and preparations. In short, bureaucratic considerations affected the orientation of policy, the central issues of which had already been predetermined. A similar phenomenon applied in the electoral arena. Public opinion played an important role in determining the timing and presentation of the Carter Doctrine. Once public and congressional support had been secured, however, electoral considerations placed surprisingly few constraints upon the implementation of a new policy for the Gulf.

One of the implications of growing public and bureaucratic support for the RDF after 1981 was that the Carter Doctrine was established as a permanent feature of U.S. global security policy. In 1980, it was not yet clear if the Carter Doctrine was a temporary response to a particular set of events in the Gulf or a more substantive and long term shift in policy. With the establishment of

CENTCOM in 1983, it was evident that a permanent shift in strategic priorities had taken place. Secretary Weinberger was quite clear on this issue: "in a relative sense (although certainly not absolutely), the Free World is better off with respect to likely threats in Europe and Northeast Asia . . . than we are with respect to Southwest Asia."[102] The Carter Doctrine laid the foundation for the inclusion of the Middle East within the range of America's global military commitments.

The extension of this military commitment to the Persian Gulf reflected in conceptual terms significant continuity with U.S. global strategy during the first two postwar decades. The Carter Doctrine was based upon a reassertion of containment as it was applied in the 1950s and 1960s. The Persian Gulf, because of its oil reserves, was identified as a strongpoint of vital interest. The United States clearly spelled out a commitment to challenge with symmetrical force a Soviet attempt to control the region. Unlike the 1950s and 1960s, however, the United States in 1980 prepared itself to contain Soviet forces, not just Soviet ideology or Soviet proxies. The projection of significant U.S. force to the Gulf became essential to constructing a credible strategy of containment. The key challenge facing the United States was to implement this strategy within the existing constraints of capability, strategic geography, and regional politics.

A central feature of the security dilemma that America faced in the Persian Gulf after 1979 emanated from the fact that the United States significantly extended the scope of its global strategic commitment without a concomitant expansion in its military capability. Lift assets improved marginally, but fell far short of what was needed for a major Gulf contingency, let alone for simultaneous engagements in Europe and Southwest Asia. Such resource constraints were reflected in the operational strategy devised for the RDF; emphasis was placed on making the best use of whatever existing forces could be projected to the area. Even with sufficient capabilities, however, U.S. security policy would have been plagued by the inherent tensions between a military strategy based on static political assumptions and the volatility and unpredictability of political realities in the Arab Gulf. America's influential position in Southwest Asia— and its strategic and political perspectives toward the region—were a product of its status as a superpower. Yet, the globalism that accompanied this status led to a problematic disjuncture between military strategy and regional politics. By 1984, the United States had by no means abandoned the new policy for Southwest Asia that had emerged since 1980. But it had adopted a more realistic and sober approach to the ability of U.S. military power and military assistance to solve the dilemmas of Persian Gulf security.

102. Weinberger, cited in U.S. Congress, House, Appropriations Committee, *Department of Defense Appropriations for 1982*, Pt. 9 (Washington, DC: GPO, 1981), 8–9.

Chapter Seven

THE WESTERN ALLIANCE AND MIDDLE EAST POLICY: ATTEMPTS AT COOPERATION

Thus far, this study has been concerned primarily with U.S. policy. It has examined in some detail both the debate about Gulf security in the United States and the content of U.S. policy toward the region. In the following two chapters, the scope of the analysis is expanded to include the broader political and strategic problems that security considerations in the Middle East have posed to the Western alliance.

Since the end of World War II, European influence in the Middle East has steadily declined as a consequence of the weakening of British and French military and economic ties to the region. As a result, the Europeans have adopted a two-pronged approach to the region. On the one hand, they have attempted to influence U.S. policy as a means of having some impact upon security arrangements in the Gulf. On the other hand, European states have been careful to maintain independent policies toward the region. Similarly, the United States has made efforts to coordinate its policies with the Europeans, yet has been unwilling to sacrifice the autonomy associated with unilateral action. This tension between unilateral and collective approaches adds a new dimension to the security problem in the Gulf and raises interesting questions about the nature and process of strategic cooperation within the alliance framework.

The debate about Middle East policy within the alliance furthers the examination of the two main themes discussed above: strategy versus capability and globalism versus regionalism. America's dominant military capability makes the United States a key strategic actor in both Europe and the Persian Gulf. Yet, resource constraints dictate a trade-off between America's military commitment to Europe and its commitment to the Persian Gulf. While the Europeans have been supportive of U.S. willingness to protect Western interests in the Middle East, they do not want the United States to assume this responsibility at a cost to its continental role. The intra-alliance debate over the Middle East has also focused on the tension between global and regional perspectives. The Europeans, because they view global power through the context of colonial rule and because they are now regional powers themselves, have criticized both America's preoccupation with the Soviet threat and what they see as policies that are insensitive to regional political dynamics. The alliance debate about the Middle East thus broadens and deepens our investigation of Persian Gulf security and offers insight into the content and process of decision-making at the national and supranational level.

This chapter examines the historical record of attempts by alliance members to cooperate on Middle East policy. Similarly to Chapter 2, it seeks to identify the key issues and considerations upon which the more recent debate has focused. Chapter 8 addresses the strategic issues in more depth and analyzes NATO's attempts after 1980 to address threats to Western interests in the Persian Gulf.

Defining NATO Territory

The debate over the geographic boundaries of NATO did not end with the signing of the North Atlantic Treaty in 1949. Not only was it difficult to reach an initial agreement on the area to be covered by the Treaty, but the frequent involvement of member nations in military operations outside the specified area has repeatedly raised the question of allied support for, if not participation in, such actions. Throughout American and European interventions in the Middle East, Africa, Latin America, and East Asia, NATO has meticulously avoided adopting a formal out-of-area strategy. This restraint has persisted despite a clear recognition of the threats posed to Western security from outside Europe. As early as 1956, a NATO report asserted that "NATO should not forget that the influence and interest of its members are not confined to the area covered by the Treaty, and that common interests of the Atlantic Community can be seriously affected by developments outside the treaty area."[1] Despite such warnings, through the 1970s, the alliance did not go beyond recognizing these wider interests and offering support for individual members willing to defend them.

By 1980, the situation had changed dramatically. The primary concern of a communique issued by NATO's Defense Planning Committee (DPC) in May was the Soviet invasion of Afghanistan and concomitant security considerations in Southwest Asia. The alliance not only recognized the depth of the potential

---

1. Report of the "Three Wise Men," December 1956, in North Atlantic Assembly, Political Committee, "Interim Report of the Subcommittee on Out-of-Area Security Challenges to the Alliance" (Brussels, 1983), par. 32.

crisis in the region, but also took steps to prepare for a diversion of military assets to the Persian Gulf area.[2] There was talk of enlarging the boundaries of the alliance to include the Gulf. American, British, French, and Australian ships undertook coordinated surveillance operations in the Arabian Sea, while the Germans and Dutch both sent vessels to the Indian Ocean.[3] Why did the alliance make such a sudden shift in policy? There are two prerequisites to answering this question. The first is to identify the vital interests and fundamental strategic assumptions that formed the foundation of a Western conception—if one existed—of Gulf security. An analysis of American conceptions and policies has been presented above. It is now necessary to ask if European states shared these perceptions. The second prerequisite is to examine how the differing perceptions and interests affected alliance dynamics and shaped NATO's approach to the Persian Gulf.

During the drafting of the Treaty, the principal dispute over geographic boundaries focused on the status of colonial territories. While most of the European states wanted to include their overseas possessions under the jurisdiction of NATO, the United States adamantly opposed such inclusion and convinced other potential members to accept the Tropic of Cancer as a southern boundary. France did succeed, however, in including its Algerian Departments within the Treaty area. Article 6 reads: "an armed attack on one or more of the Parties is deemed to include an armed attack on the territory of any of the parties in Europe or North America, or the Algerian Departments of France, or the territory of Turkey or on the islands under the jurisdiction of any of the Parties in the North Atlantic area north of the Tropic of Cancer . . .." The purpose of this article was not to preclude the possibility of allied actions to the south of the Tropic of Cancer, but to ensure that an attack on colonial territories not be construed as an attack on the alliance as such.[4] Article 4 went further in delineating the potentially global scope of the alliance: "The parties will consult together whenever in the opinion of any of them, the territorial integrity, political independence or security of any of the parties is threatened." The drafters of the Treaty were also careful to omit any clause which might provide one or more states the power to prevent other members from taking military action outside the European theater.[5] Thus, although the Treaty did define a

---

2. NATO Defense Committee, Final Communique (Brussels, May 1980). Paragraph 8 asserts that "Ministers of other Countries agreed to do their utmost to meet additional burdens for NATO security which could result from the increased United States responsibilities in South West Asia."

3. Expansion of the geographic scope of NATO, though discussed in official bodies, was never considered to be a realistic option.

4. See Theodore Achilles, "U.S. Role in Negotiations that Led to Atlantic Alliance," NATO Review (October 1983), 17. The text of the NATO Treaty can be found in NATO Handbook 1983 (Brussels: NATO Information Service, 1983), 13–16.

5. Ibid., 18.

specific area that was to be NATO's primary concern, it left ample flexibility for consultation on the military operations of member states in other regions.

In 1949, the future of many of Europe's colonial possessions was uncertain. The pressure on Britain, France, Belgium, Holland, and Portugal to divest their territories was already mounting; the United States was loath to enter a security pact which explicitly sanctioned the perpetuation of the colonial system. In an effort to improve its image and economic ties to the developing world, the United States wanted to dissociate itself from European "imperialism." During the 1950s and 1960s, American criticism of European interventions to protect their territories bred resentment within the alliance. A question posed to President Kennedy in 1961 from Paul-Henri Spaak, the Secretary General of NATO, revealed a certain cynicism about America's approach to the Third World: "[I]s the United States willing, in a crunch, to sacrifice the interests of its NATO partners in order to assure itself of the support or the friendship of nonaligned countries or will it ruffle their feelings?"[6] The French were the most vocal in their attempts to muster alliance-wide support for the defense of their African territories. De Gaulle even proposed the establishment of a directoire, with French, British, and American participation, to monitor political developments in the Third World and oversee out-of-area military operations.[7] Needless to say, the Kennedy administration promptly declined the offer.

By the late 1960s, however, the respective positions of the allies vis-à-vis out-of-area contingencies began to shift. The British and French were gradually withdrawing from their outposts abroad. The United States, on the other hand, intervened in Santo Domingo in 1965 and was rapidly increasing its military presence in Vietnam. Partly as a form of retaliation, but also to improve their own image in the Third World, the Europeans were guarded, yet clear in their criticism of U.S. policy.[8] The French began to defend a strict adherence to NATO's boundaries: "[W]hy should NATO become involved [in Asia] since the area covered by the treaty is limited to Europe and the North Atlantic? Did NATO become involved in the Korean War? And when we engaged ourselves in Indochina, NATO was certainly not dragged into the conflict."[9]

The French shifted their views on the out-of-area question not because of any reinterpretation of the Treaty, but because of pragmatic considerations surrounding their positions in the developing world. They were reducing the scope of their commitments in the periphery and did not want to be drawn into undesired engagements. The United States did not seek the collective participa-

6. Paul-Henri Spaak, cited in Alfred Grosser, *The Western Alliance: European–American Relations Since 1945* (London: Macmillan, 1980), 152.

7. George H. Wittman, "Political and Military Background for France's Intervention Capability," *A.E.I. Foreign Policy and Defense Review*, vol. 4, no. 1, 12.

8. Grosser, *The Western Alliance*, 239.

9. René Pleven, cited in ibid., 215.

tion of NATO in the Vietnam War, but did expect political support and limited military aid from individual allies. America's involvement in Southeast Asia and in other regional contingencies outside Europe was also discussed in NATO councils. Thus, it was clear that the NATO Treaty—as hoped by its drafters— left the out-of-area question to be dealt with on an ad hoc basis. Such flexibility enabled the alliance to concern itself with crucial issues that lay outside Europe or the North Atlantic. Yet, it also created the potential for each regional contingency to pose a serious challenge to the cohesion of the alliance. How NATO reacted to crises in any given area was highly dependent upon the historical ties of its members to the region in question. Thus, an analysis of NATO's approach to the Middle East must begin with an examination of the interests of individual members in the region.

The Historical Background

Economic competition among the Western powers in the Middle East began well before the creation of NATO. The discovery of oil only enhanced the interest of Western states in a region that was already valued for its importance as a trade route to the East. The historical commitment of both the British and the French to the Middle East is of paramount importance.[10] Since even after the withdrawal of their forces from the area, Britain and France have remained specially sensitive to developments in the region. As will become evident, prestige and national honor have shaped their reaction to events in the Middle East as much as have strategic or economic considerations.

After the formation of NATO, the first overt clash in the alliance over Middle East policy emerged in response to the Baghdad Pact. The United States and Britain assumed responsibility for forging a defense agreement among the northern tier states after the end of World War II. The French were not included in the pact and interpreted this as an attempt to undermine their influence in the region.[11] The French were not alone in their resentment over exclusion from the Baghdad Pact. Nasser's willingness to seize the Suez Canal in 1956 was in part a response to the lack of respect accorded him by the United States and Britain. And the rift within the Western alliance that resulted from the Suez crisis rapidly superseded whatever tensions had emerged over the Baghdad Pact.

The three states that coordinated the attack on Egypt in 1956 had very different reasons for participation in the operation. The Israelis moved into the Sinai to neutralize the Fedayeen that had been carrying out raids against Israel

10. Although French priorities have shifted to Francophone Africa and the Indian Ocean, France has retained close economic ties to Arab states in the Middle East, particularly to Iraq and Lebanon.

11. Shwadran, *The Middle East*, 454.

and to open the Straits of Aqaba which had been closed by the Egyptians. The French wanted to dispose of Nasser because they believed the Algerian resistance movement would fade without his support.[12] And the British were unwilling to accept passively the affront to their national honor implicit in Nasser's seizure of the canal. British troops had withdrawn from Egypt only five weeks before Nasser's move; the psychological wounds were still fresh. What is more, the British and French relied on Persian Gulf oil for a significant portion of their energy imports and feared potential energy shortages should Nasser close the canal or blockade certain shipments.

The United States, on the other hand, felt neither a political nor a strategic need to react with force. Initially, Nasser did not block passage through the canal and Washington perceived no immediate threat to its shipping interests in the region.[13] Again, America was reluctant to implicate itself in what was a blatant perpetuation of imperialist thinking: Dulles commented, "[t]he United States cannot be expected to identify itself 100% . . . with . . . the colonial powers."[14] American oil production was also rising steadily and the United States was able to divert supplies to Europe while the canal was closed in 1956–1957.[15] For these reasons, Eisenhower remained opposed to foreign intervention. After the attack, he was enraged because of British and French willingness to act both in spite of firm American opposition and without informing him of their contemplated action. Britain and France were embarrassed by the episode and were resentful of Eisenhower's and Dulles' aloof approach as well as their seemingly contrived support for nationalistic forces in the Third World.[16]

Equal in importance to the immediate strains that resulted from the crisis were the clear differences that emerged in how the United States, Britain, and France perceived their interests in the Middle East. First, it was clear that each of the actors was motivated primarily by national interest; the notion of a collective "Western" interest had little, if any, impact. Second, French behavior was largely dictated by considerations of how the political situation in the Arab Middle East would affect French possessions in Africa. This trend was to extend into the 1980s; France's presence in the Indian Ocean and Africa continues to influence its policy toward the Middle East. Finally, it was evident that Eisenhower expected the British and French to conform to U.S. policy and was shocked by the willingness of the allies to undertake independent action. Yet, his expectations were in part a source of the problem; both the British and French were irritated by Washington's attempt to present the United States as

12. Richard Neustadt, *Alliance Politics* (New York: Columbia University Press, 1970), 14–15.
13. The Eisenhower administration proposed that an international authority be established to control shipping in the canal.
14. John Foster Dulles, cited in Grosser, *The Western Alliance*, 142.
15. Deese and Miller, "Western Europe," 182.
16. Neudstadt, *Alliance Politics*, 20–21, 57.

an ally of national liberation movements in the Third World. The lack of communication before the attack and the inflamed tempers afterward were exacerbated by these broader political issues.

The structure of the alliance itself proved to be a significant obstacle to a more coordinated and effective response to the Suez crisis. The existence of an alliance framework created clear expectations, all of which went unfulfilled. For the British and French, Nasser's move represented a direct challenge to Western interests in the Middle East. In this sense, they expected American assistance in demonstrating that the Western powers would not tolerate such challenges to their global role. The United States perceived no need for a military response and, as the de facto leader of the alliance, expected the Europeans to acquiesce. Each country interpreted the event in terms of its own interests and assumed that the alliance would serve to protect those interests. The disparity of military power among Britain, France, and the United States exacerbated this problem. Because of its military dominance, the United States expected that its position would prevail. Britain and France were indeed well aware that American participation would enhance the effectiveness of an operation in the Middle East. But European dependence upon American power, in combination with Washington's perceived exploitation of this dependence, compelled Britain and France to act without informing the United States, if only to demonstrate that they still had an independent role in the Middle East.

The final incident prior to 1973 significantly molding the relationship among the Western powers vis-à-vis the Middle East was the 1967 War. As a result of this conflict, the United States replaced the French as Israel's principal arms supplier. The consequent decline in French leverage was followed, only months later, by the British announcement of their decision to withdraw from the Gulf. British and French influence in the Middle East was being rapidly supplanted by that of the United States. From the perspective of Britain and France, the United States was not only dominating NATO strategy in Europe, but was also gradually undermining European influence in areas that lay outside NATO's jurisdiction. If European and American interests and threat perceptions had coincided, this development might not have been greeted with the chagrin that was felt in London and Paris. Yet, during the course of and aftermath of the 1973 War, it became clear that America's approach to the Middle East in general, and the Persian Gulf in particular, by no means received unanimous support within the alliance.

The Oil Crisis: A Cooperative Response?

The first section of this study dealt extensively with the impact of the October War and the consequent oil embargo on U.S. perceptions of its strategic and economic interests in the Middle East. For the most part, the Europeans shared America's assessment of the West's vulnerability to the oil weapon and, because of their high dependence on imports from the Persian Gulf, found that rising oil prices caused a serious strain on their economies. A shared perception of the problems did not, however, translate into a common approach to their solution. American and European perspectives on policy toward the Middle East diverged in three crucial areas: the Arab–Israeli conflict, the acquisition and allocation of adequate oil supplies, and the strategic posture of the West within the region.

Before turning to these policy issues, it is important to take note of an important change in the framework in which policy formulation took place. Up to this point, the consideration of a Western approach to Middle East security has led to an examination of primarily American, French, and British policy. Yet, the 1973 War and its broad impact upon the international economy, the North–South dialogue, and, potentially, the strength of Western Europe's industrial base meant that every country within NATO now paid careful attention to developments in the Middle East. The concept of an alliance approach—not just the approach of the allies—became of concrete relevance. The Middle East after 1973, because of the stakes involved, forced NATO members at least to attempt to coordinate their policies toward the region. The alliance began to address, although not through a formal process, the nature of its collective interests outside the Treaty area.

Significant divergences between American and European policy toward the Arab–Israeli conflict began to emerge between 1967 and 1973. There is no question that the 1973–1974 oil crisis was the single most important factor in convincing the Europeans to take a more pro-Arab stance on the Palestinian question—one that would distinguish their position from that of the United States. Even by 1971, however, it was clear to the West Europeans that unquestioned support for the Israelis could harm their economic relationship with the Arab states. Both because economic issues were at stake and because no other suitable forum existed, the EEC emerged as the principal organ through which an independent European position began to emerge. Throughout the 1960s, the Arabs had warned the EEC to curb its trade relations with Israel. In 1962, Arab League states threatened to "reconsider the structure of their foreign trade with the member states of the EEC as well as [their] petroleum policy. . . ."[17] After the 1967 War, it became apparent that these were not idle threats. The Arab producers attempted to halt shipments of crude to the West in order to place indirect pressure on the Israelis to withdraw from Jerusalem, the West Bank, and the Gaza Strip. During the following four years, Arab states also made numerous

---

17. Rouholla Ramazani, *The Middle East and the European Common Market* (Charlottesville, VA: University Press of Virginia, 1964), 90.

attempts to increase their control over oil industries operating on their territories, with the Algerians and Libyans finally succeeding in 1971.

The initial response of the Western Europeans to this increasing Arab pressure was poorly coordinated. Individual countries, France in particular, voiced
public criticism of America's seemingly unchallengeable support for Israeli policy. Then, in 1971, the EEC Six drafted an unreleased statement that was clearly
at odds with American policy. It called for an internationalized Jerusalem as well
as a demilitarized zone between Israel and its neighboring states.[18] After the
1973 War, the position of the EEC grew more vocal and more distant from that
of the United States. At a Community summit in Brussels in November, the
EEC (now with nine members) recognized the "legitimate rights of the Palestinians" and called for Israel to withdraw from territories occupied in 1967. In June
1977, the EEC went further and affirmed that the "effective expression of [Pal-
estinian] national identity . . . would take into account the need for a homeland
for the Palestinian people." Finally, in Venice in 1980, the Europeans called for
the participation of the PLO in the peace negotiations. Not only did this
position constitute a repudiation of American success in negotiating the Camp
David Treaty, but it also challenged a key element of Washington's diplomatic
approach: nonrecognition of the PLO.

It would be myopic to claim that the progressive drift of the EEC toward a
more pro-Palestinian stance was the sole product of an attempt to curry favor
among Arab states. As during the Suez affair, intra-alliance tensions played a
significant role. The 1967 War and Britain's withdrawal from the Gulf confirmed the decline of British and French leverage in the Middle East. The
United States became the principal arms supplier to Israel, Iran, and Saudi
Arabia, as well as the chief external diplomatic agent in the Arab–Israeli conflict. Thus, the emergence of an independent EEC position must be understood
as an attempt to challenge American dominance in the region and to reassert
Europe's role in the Middle East.[19] Even if they agreed with the substance of
American policy, the Europeans were seeking to define a *European* position. To
remain silent was to accept tacitly European subordination to American policy.
There was also pressure within individual countries for a more pro-Arab stance.
French ties with Arab states in Africa made Paris more sensitive to political
currents in the Middle East. Shifting public opinion and the power of the foreign
office establishment in both Britain and Germany contributed to shifting policies in those countries.[20] Furthermore, European states lacked the mobilized

18. Maull, "The Strategy of Avoidance," 118. The following statements on EEC policy toward
the Arab–Israeli conflict can be found in *Keesing's Contemporary Archives:* 1973–p. 26227; 1977–p.
28656; 1980–p. 30635.

19. Joan Garrat, "Euro–American Energy Diplomacy in the Middle East, 1970–80: The Pervasive Crisis," in Spiegel, ed., *The Middle East*, 90–91.

20. Maull, "The Strategy of Avoidance," 122–123.

Jewish electorate that has greatly influenced policy in the United States. Thus, it was the strong support of the United States for Israel as much as the pro-Arab inclination within Europe that led to a divergence within the alliance on policy toward the Arab–Israeli conflict.

While the consistency of American support for Israel has irritated European governments, successive U.S. administrations have, in turn, accused EEC members of submitting to the economic pressure of Arab states. The consequent mutual resentment as well as the substantive differences over policy have served as an obstacle to coordinating a Western approach—be it in the strategic or political realm—toward the region as a whole. Yet, it is clear that an independent European position was not entirely disadvantageous to EEC members. The 1973 embargo applied only to the United States and Holland; the Arabs had taken notice of the stance of other European nations. Further, a unified Western position could well have exacerbated the Arab reaction to the war. If America's close ties with Israel hindered U.S. relations with the Gulf states, then an independent European approach offered, if nothing else, an alternative channel of communication between the West and the Arab Gulf. Finally, the Europeans did succeed in strengthening their participation in the debate over Middle East policy by making their opinions known. By challenging the U.S. approach, EEC members might have invoked American ire, but they simultaneously engaged the United States in a dialogue and established a means, albeit limited, of tempering Washington's policy.[21]

Integrally related to the Palestinian question, yet of more immediate concern to all members of the alliance, was access to and the price of Persian Gulf oil. The oil crisis of 1973–1974 tested the ability of the allies to coordinate policy over a wide range of security, energy, and trade issues. The economic impact of the rise in oil prices was staggering. In 1973, the OECD nations accumulated a net trade surplus of $11 billion. By 1974, because of the high costs of oil imports, there was a trade deficit of $22 billion.[22] This imbalance, especially in Western Europe, led to steadily rising rates of inflation and unemployment.[23] Under these circumstances, the West was forced to make economic adjustments and to take steps to prevent further shortages and price increases.

The initial reaction of the NATO countries to the oil crisis was to scramble for dwindling supplies. Not only was there a lack of coordination between the United States and the EEC, but the Europeans competed among themselves for special contracts with producing states and for the reserves available on the spot market. This behavior placed extraordinary strain on demand, thereby facilitating OPEC's repeated attempts to raise prices. The Arabs made clear that the

21. U.K. House of Commons, *Afghanistan*, xxvii–xxviii, 117–118.
22. A.W. DePorte, *Europe between the Superpowers—The Enduring Balance* (New Haven, CT: Yale University Press, 1979), 208.
23. See Deese and Miller, "Western Europe," 184–185, and Chap. 3, note 4.

purpose of the embargo was to effect changes in America's negotiating position; the sanctions against the EEC were meant as inducements for the Europeans as well to apply pressure on Washington.[24] As already discussed, the EEC responded immediately by supporting Palestinian rights and calling for Israeli withdrawal from occupied territories. Yet, in the months following the embargo, the Europeans also attempted to negotiate directly with the oil-producing states to secure preferential treatment. This initiative—dubbed the Euro–Arab dialogue—was designed to create a new economic relationship between Europe and the Arab Gulf.

As early as January of 1974, several European ministers had visited the Middle East in hope of improving bilateral ties with the Gulf states. By July a formal Euro–Arab consultative council existed, with the EEC Nine and twenty-one Arab League members participating. The Nine initially offered the Arab states selective contracts guaranteeing a certain level of commodity export to the producing countries in return for preferential treatment in the allocation of oil supplies.[25] The oil-rich states in the Gulf, with their rapidly growing financial reserves, were hardly enticed by this offer. The Europeans then redirected the dialogue toward general improvements in EEC–Arab trade, with hopes of attracting the investment of OPEC members. Here too the EEC failed, as the producing states turned to the United States, Japan, and Germany as the most suitable countries for investing their revenues.[26] With few exceptions then, the Euro–Arab dialogue did not succeed in securing advantages for the EEC.[27] What it did do, however, was place even further strain on already tenuous American–European economic relations.

The Euro–Arab dialogue was reflective of broader economic problems in the industrialized West. Following President Nixon's abandonment of the gold standard in 1971, the alliance entered a prolonged period of dispute over trade and monetary policies. By attempting to establish independent economic relations with Arab states, the EEC was searching for a means of buffering the impact of the oil shortage and price rises. In 1975, the Nine also signed the Lomé Convention—a series of agreements designed to liberalize trade with the Third World. The United States perceived this as a competitive move that would damage the volume of its own trade with developing states. The Lomé Convention thus caused further tension within the alliance over trade and financial matters.

Yet, some of the most caustic exchanges between America and Europe over economic policy focused on the handling of the oil crisis itself. The EEC accused

24. In lifting the embargo, Arab leaders pointed to a favorable shift in U.S. policy toward the Arab–Israeli conflict. See Chap. 3, note 37.

25. Maull, "The Strategy of Avoidance," 129.

26. J.C. Hurewitz, "The Pervasive Crisis," in Hurewitz, ed., *Oil,* 289.

27. See *Keesing's Contemporary Archives,* 1975, 27131. The French did establish a special tie with the Iraqis by aiding them in the construction of a nuclear energy plant.

the United States of actually supporting the rise in oil prices during 1973–1974.[28] Although they did not produce irrefutable evidence, the Europeans had a strong case. Before 1973, the U.S. government had placed a protective tax on oil imports to sustain high prices for domestic production. The United States also stood to benefit from an influx of revenues into the Gulf. The growing wealth of producing states increased their interest in investing abroad, enhanced their ability to purchase arms, and created a new degree of economic interdependence between the United States and the Arab Gulf. The West Europeans were also irritated by what they perceived as America's exorbitant consumption of energy. Between 1973 and 1978, West European consumption of oil declined 2.3%. During the same period, consumption in the United States rose some 11.8%.[29] Finally, during the 1978–1979 oil shock the United States subsidized the cost of home heating fuels by $5 per barrel. The Europeans complained that this move prevented U.S. consumption from adjusting to world oil prices and therefore exacerbated the problem of high demand. These considerations fueled sentiments in Europe that Washington was doing very little to avert oil shortages and suppress prices, but was simply concerned with the short term strength of the American economy.

Washington reacted to these criticisms and to the independent European initiative toward the Arabs by proposing the establishment of the International Energy Agency (IEA). The Ford administration proposed the IEA as a means of fostering alliance cooperation in responding to potential energy shortages.[30] Established in 1975, the Agency imposed three guidelines upon its twenty-one members: to prepare a national emergency oil reserve capable of supplying domestic needs for ninety days, to be capable of reducing consumption by 10% should a shortage arise, and to devise a system for sharing available oil during a reduction in supplies.

The IEA had limited success in achieving these goals. As far as controlling allocation and consumption during a crisis, the Western response in 1978–1979 was almost as uncoordinated as in 1973. While disagreement as to whether emergency measures should be instituted paralyzed the IEA, its members again scrambled for available supplies. The reaction to the 1980 shortage was more effective, though this was in part a result of the high stocks that existed following the 1978 crisis.[31] American hopes of cultivating a unified Western stance were also dashed. The French refused to participate in the organization. The other EEC members joined in February, yet the following month made indepen-

---

28. Garratt, "Euro–American Energy Diplomacy," 94–97.

29. Robert Lieber, "Economics, Energy, and Security in Alliance Perspective," *International Security* (Spring 1980), 154–155.

30. See Wilfrid Kohl, "The International Energy Agency: The Political Context," in Hurewitz, *Oil*, 246–252.

31. Badger, "Oil Supply and Price," 132.

dent initiatives toward the Arabs without informing the United States.[32] Between June and November of 1975, while the IEA was taking shape, the Nine held three separate meetings with Arab leaders in Cairo, Rome, and Abu Dhabi.

The IEA was inadequate because it failed to provide the means through which a comprehensive energy policy could be formed. There were distinct incentives for cooperation, but also clear disincentives. On the one hand, the Europeans recognized that the United States played an integral role in the international oil market and would be crucial to offsetting the growing economic power of OPEC. Clearly, much was to be gained by sharing oil stocks and coordinating purchases. Cooperation could have reduced short term demand and therefore slowed, if not halted, the price spiral. On the other hand, the IEA was an international structure proposed and dominated by the United States and it therefore left the West Europeans in the same paradoxical position they had confronted before its establishment. The EEC wanted to dissociate itself from another institution that could well alienate both Arab states and the Third World in general. The Europeans were also suspicious of America's oil purchasing and pricing policies. Thus, there were both potential benefits and potential disadvantages to forging a collective response to the oil crisis. In order to reconcile these two conflicting impulses, most West European states joined the IEA, but were unwilling to sacrifice the option of pursuing independent initiatives in both the energy and economic fields. The result was continued strain and lack of coordination within the alliance.

An institutional problem also contributed to the inadequate response of the alliance to the energy crisis. Potential measures to counter shortages in oil and rising prices touched upon many aspects of security policy as well as energy policy. The steps under consideration ranged from taking military action in the Gulf to seeking alternative energy supplies. Yet, discussions in NATO rarely strayed into the economic realm and the EEC discussed strategic issues only under duress. The Europeans did not want to bring economic issues to NATO; Japan was not present and the Europeans feared that U.S. domination in security matters would spread to include economic concerns. A comprehensive Western approach covering both strategic and energy problems was therefore unattainable. That the EEC was expanding from six to nine members at the time further hindered its flexibility and its willingness to deal with issues that some members felt were outside its jurisdiction.

The final section of this chapter addresses the differing conceptions within NATO about the efficacy of using military force in the Middle East. Views within the alliance diverged over the broader issues of threat perception as well as the more specific aspects of strategy in the Gulf. Within hours of the outbreak

---

32. Wolfgang Hager, "Western Europe: The Politics of Muddling Through," in Hurewitz, *Oil*, 41–43.

of war in 1973, America's massive airlift to Israel, because it required refueling and overflight rights in Europe, raised the question of indirect European participation. With the exception of Portugal, the West Europeans denied the United States refueling rights on their territories. Again, the Europeans were fearful that any involvement in U.S. actions would only intensify Arab reprisals against them. Washington was understandably disgruntled by this approach. Tensions over this issue exploded, however, when the Germans discovered that the Americans were supplying the Israelis from German facilities without Bonn's consent.[33] Not only did this implicate West Germany in the war, but it was a clear indication of American willingness to undertake military operations involving the Europeans without prior consultation.

This series of events established two primary components of the out-of-area debate as it was to emerge in 1980. First, the Americans became very sensitive about whether U.S. troops in transit to Southwest Asia would be able to use European bases. This sensitivity resulted from the pragmatic considerations of overflight rights and en route access as well as the more subjective issue of European political support for U.S. operations supposedly carried out on behalf of the alliance. Second, the Europeans became extremely aware of the issue of consultation, both to avoid unwanted association with U.S. actions and to exercise their rights of partnership in the alliance.

After the cessation of hostilities between Israel and Egypt in 1973, further sources of discontent arose within NATO over long term security issues in the Middle East. While the United States reacted with great concern to the prospect of Soviet intervention in the war, the Europeans were less averse to the possibility of the joint deployment of U.S. and Soviet peacekeeping forces.[34] As far as the United States was concerned, this position revealed European naiveté about Soviet motives in the Middle East. During the mid-1970s when there was a consensus within NATO that direct Soviet advances into the region were unlikely, the divisiveness of differing perceptions of Soviet behavior was minimized. After the invasion of Afghanistan, however, this issue was to become of primary importance.

The 1973 War also broached within NATO the question of the deployment of U.S. troops to the Middle East. Although there was no formal agreement, Arthur Hartman, Assistant Secretary of State for European Affairs, asserted that U.S. forces in Europe were dual purpose and that these troops could be diverted from Europe to the Middle East without NATO approval.[35] The issue was never directly confronted because Washington decided against direct military action

33. Grosser, *The Western Alliance*, 274.
34. U.S. Congress, House, Foreign Affairs Committee, *U.S.–Europe Relations and the 1973 Middle East War* (Washington, DC: GPO, 1974), 37.
35. Ibid., 58–59.

in either the Persian Gulf or the Sinai. As mentioned earlier, the U.S. government did consider the possibility of an operation to seize the oil fields should the Arabs again attempt to deny the West access to its reserves. Discussion of this option was in itself sufficient to elicit reactions from both the Europeans and Japan urging the United States to rely on political and economic, not military, initiatives.[36]

A final source of tension within the alliance emerged from competition over arms sales to the Middle East. Despite America's growing share of sales to the region, the French continued to offer armaments to Arab states. The viability of the French arms industry depended upon exports because domestic sales were insufficient to support production of sophisticated weaponry. The United States, taking what was to become a hypocritical stance, complained that the French were selling arms to regional states in order to secure access to oil supplies.[37] More to the truth, Washington felt that its own leverage as an arms merchant was diminished because the recipient states knew they could go elsewhere if the United States refused to supply what was requested. Thus, while the French accused the United States of undercutting its arms industry, the Americans retorted that the French were selling weaponry without due consideration of strategic factors.

Conclusions

Between 1974 and 1978, the Middle East entered a rare period of relative stability. American diplomacy had succeeded in both ending hostilities between Egypt and Israel and, a few years later, effecting a peace treaty between the two countries. As far as NATO members were concerned, the flow of oil was the paramount issue. In this respect, alliance members had little about which to complain; crude continued to flow from the Gulf and oil prices actually declined in relative terms during the mid-1970s. Despite these factors, tensions over the Middle East were simmering within the alliance. The EEC Nine continued to criticize America's stance on the Palestinian question to protect their economic ties with Arab states and to reassert their political influence in the Middle East. The chaos in Iran sent oil prices soaring in 1978–1979 and the West again exhibited complete lack of coordination in coping with shortages. Mutual resentment remained over the *suave qui peut* attitude that prevailed in both 1973 and 1978. And finally, differences in perceptions of the West's appropriate strategic posture in the Middle East were held at bay because of both the relative quiet in the region and the atmosphere of détente with the Soviets.

36. For the Japanese position, see Sasagawa, "Japan and the Middle East."
37. U.S. Congress, House, *U.S.–Europe Relations—1973*, 41.

From one perspective, the record of European–American cooperation on Middle East policy during the 1970s constituted, if anything, a denial that a collective Western approach was possible. The allies appeared unable either to respond in a coordinated fashion to the oil crisis or to reach a consensual position on the Arab–Israeli conflict. The forces preventing a more unified stance were numerous. Shared interests were subsumed by economic competition; the Europeans were themselves divided over how to respond to the oil crisis; EEC members feared domination by the United States and implication in U.S. actions; the Americans resented what they perceived as Europe's political submission to the economic power of the Arab oil producers.

Yet, from another perspective, these strains that emerged were reflective of ongoing tension within the alliance between unilateral and collectivist impulses. Most West European states joined the IEA because they realized that American participation was essential to constructing an effective oil regime. The Europeans also recognized America's dominant political and military position in the Middle East and knew that to influence U.S. policy through a collective stance was to enhance their own influence in the region. At the same time, however, the Europeans so carefully formulated the Euro–Arab dialogue and an independent position on the Palestinian question precisely to avoid a unified Western stance; they actively resisted more coordination on policy. Though the Europeans took issue with the substance of U.S. policy, their primary concern in distinguishing their approach from that of the United States was to prevent the Arab world from perceiving the West as a unified political bloc. Furthermore, because an alliance approach would have been dominated by the United States, the Europeans feared that a coordinated position would diminish the independence of their foreign policy toward regions lying outside the Treaty area.

The United States as well exhibited ambivalence toward forging a collective NATO policy. On the one hand, Washington was the motive force behind the establishment of the IEA. The Ford and Carter administrations also put pressure on the Europeans to follow America's lead on the Arab–Israeli question. On the other hand, the United States used German bases in 1973 without prior consultation and reacted to independent European initiatives on energy issues and the Arab–Israeli conflict with effrontery, not with a willingness to accommodate. Washington sought the benefits of collectivism without the requisite restriction of autonomy.

The Western alliance after 1973 confronted a novel challenge. The oil crisis constituted a threat to the collective security of NATO members. And the alliance began the process of assessing shared interests and shaping an appropriate response—the IEA was a tangible result. Yet, three factors hindered the completion of that process. First, because the Middle East lay outside the boundaries of NATO, there were immediate political obstacles preventing a coordinated reaction. The Europeans feared Arab reprisals and the implications of a unified stance for the independence of their role in the Middle East. Second, because a comprehensive response involved a mix of political, economic, and strategic initiatives, it was difficult to identify an institutional structure in which to shape a coherent Western policy. Third, the relative stability of the Middle East in the mid-1970s allowed the allies to avoid confronting what were indeed divisive and politically sensitive issues.

The real problems that hindered the ability of the alliance to address security issues in the Middle East between 1950 and 1980 were political ones. During the Suez crisis, there were indeed divergent perceptions among the allies about questions of strategy; the French and British advocated the use of force, while the United States insisted upon restraint. Behind these opposing views on the efficacy of introducing military forces lay quite different views of the relationship between individual national interests and Nasser's nationalization of the canal. The Suez crisis revealed that if the alliance were to address security problems in the Middle East, it would have to start by forging a consensus on what common interests were at stake in the Middle East. The 1973 War forced allies to begin searching for this consensus, but the process was interrupted by complacency as well as by political divisions inherent in the alliance structure.

By 1980, the revolution in Iran and the invasion of Afghanistan were to destroy this complacency, heighten the sense of economic vulnerability in the West, and illuminate the need for a new security policy toward the Middle East. These factors were to bring the question of an alliance approach to the Persian Gulf to the forefront of NATO politics.

Chapter Eight

THE OUT-OF-AREA PROBLEM FOR NATO

The reaction of the Western alliance to the Soviet invasion of Afghanistan was, at the suggestion of the United States, divided into two stages. "Phase 1" concerned immediate steps—diplomatic and economic sanctions, motions of censure in the U.N., a boycott of the Olympic Games—that could be taken to express Western concern and exert pressure upon the Soviet government to withdraw its troops. "Phase 2" focused on military measures that could be pursued to adjust to the strategic implications of the presence of Soviet troops in Afghanistan and their consequent proximity to the Gulf. The primary focus of this chapter is the latter concern; namely, what steps NATO took to meet what it perceived as a new threat to its vital energy interests in the Persian Gulf. It is necessary to begin with the response in the diplomatic realm, for the behavior of NATO members during the first phase provides valuable insight into the political dynamics behind the reaction within the alliance to a crisis occurring outside the European theater.

There were several obvious reasons why developments in the Persian Gulf area were responsible for finally eliciting from NATO a more formal stance on the out-of-area question. Oil was indeed the crucial factor; in 1980 West European countries depended upon imports from the Gulf for as much as 70% of their petroleum needs.[1] Regardless of whether the Kremlin had designs on the oil fields, the instability that resulted from the Iranian revolution and the Soviet invasion increased concern among Western states about the security of oil supplies from the Gulf region. Air bases in Afghanistan also placed Soviet

---

1. U.S. Congress, Congressional Research Service, *Western Vulnerability to a Disruption of Persian Gulf Oil and Supplies: U.S. Interests and Options*, prepared for the House Foreign Affairs Committee (Washington, DC: GPO, 1983), 24.

fighter and attack aircraft closer to the Straits of Hormuz and the northern Indian Ocean. By moving into Afghanistan, the Kremlin exhibited its willingness both to occupy territory outside the Soviet bloc and to face what was sure to be a harsh Western reaction. It was the aggressive attitude and the boldness revealed by Soviet leaders, as much as the strategic implications of the invasion, that worried Western officials. In combination with the steady growth of Soviet power projection capabilities, these concerns spread alarm throughout the West about Soviet intentions. NATO's principal counter to Soviet power in the periphery had been the predominant strength of the American Navy. Yet, because of the limited size of the Persian Gulf and the threat posed by land-based air power, U.S. aircraft carriers would be particularly vulnerable within the Gulf itself. Given the proximity of Soviet troops, supplies, and air bases, the Gulf area emerged as one of the West's most strategically exposed areas outside the European theater. These factors compelled the alliance to devote unprecedented attention to Southwest Asia after 1979.

There are two central tasks to be addressed in this chapter. The first is to chart the evolution of NATO's approach to protecting its interests in Southwest Asia—and to the out-of-area problem in general—after January, 1980. The second is to identify and examine the key issues that formed the core of the debate over out-of-area strategy. The linking theme concerns how the interaction between strategic objectives and the political structure of the alliance has shaped NATO policy toward the Persian Gulf.[2]

Phase One

While Soviet troops were still pouring into Afghanistan on the first day of 1980, U.S. Deputy Secretary of State Warren Christopher met in London with the NATO ambassadors of five European states. Their goal was to forge a consensus on the immediate steps that could be taken to respond to the Soviet move. By the following week, these discussions had been moved to the more formal setting of NATO's North Atlantic Council (NAC) in Brussels. The measures under consideration were the institution of economic sanctions, the withdrawal of diplomatic personnel from Moscow and Kabul, and the boycott of the forthcoming Olympic Games in Moscow. A statement issued after the NAC meeting was reflective of attitudes within the alliance: "*Each* member state will take appropriate *individual* measures and steps" to respond to the Soviet invasion.[3] By the

---

2. For a review of the background to the out-of-area debate, see Charles Kupchan, "Regional Security and the Out-of-Area Problem," in Stephen Flanagan, and Fen Hampson, eds., *Securing Europe's Future* (London: Croom Helm, 1986), 280–286.

3. NATO North Atlantic Council, Press Release (Brussels, 15 January 1980), emphasis added.

third week in January, it was clear that there was no consensus on which measures, if any, should be adopted. American attempts to elicit a more stringent reaction were rebuffed by the Europeans and a coordinated response within NATO appeared unattainable. By the end of the month, it was not the invasion as such that preoccupied the media, but rather NATO's "disarray" and its "failure" to address the crisis.[4]

Why did it prove so difficult for the alliance to agree upon a unified response to Afghanistan? The most revealing approach to answering this question is to identify the different positions of the individual members of NATO. The United States was insistent upon a collective reaction for two reasons. First, economic and trade sanctions would be of little use if instituted by only a few countries. The Soviets could easily circumvent such measures by relying more heavily on those Western states not participating in the sanctions. Second, an American response not supported by the allies would have far less political impact upon the Kremlin than one emanating from the alliance as a whole. As far as Washington was concerned, the Soviet invasion should be seen as a threat to the security of the "free world," not as a confrontation between superpowers.

Reactions in Western Europe varied widely. Initially, there was reluctant support for American initiatives, yet little sign that individual states would participate in the sanctions. The British were the most outspoken in their support for the United States and in their willingness to take concrete steps in coordination with Washington. Prime Minister Thatcher was prepared to reduce trade links with the Soviet Union and urged that the Olympic Games be moved from Moscow.[5] The enthusiasm of the British government was tempered, however, by the reaction emerging from other European capitals. The West Germans were far less receptive than the British to American proposals. The Federal Republic was receiving large imports of natural gas from the East and was annually conducting over $5 billion worth of trade with the Soviet bloc.[6] The collapse of détente would damage relations between East and West Germany and present a serious challenge to the Christian Democratic government. Chancellor Schmidt's first reaction was to urge that the United States take the issue to the U.N.; NATO was not a proper forum in which to discuss sanctions related to Afghanistan.[7] He was prepared to condemn the Soviet invasion, yet did not want to see the incident lead to a general worsening of

---

4. See, for example, *Financial Times*, 16 January 1980, "West Fails to Agree Action Against USSR."

5. *International Herald Tribune*, 7 January 1980, "London Supports Carter; Other Capitals Lukewarm." See also House of Commons, *Afghanistan*, 2–3.

6. *New York Times*, 7 March 1980, "U.S. Worried by Allies' Afghanistan Stance."

7. *New York Times*, 5 January 1980, "Bonn and U.S. Plan Arms Talks in Wake of Soviet Afghan Moves."

East–West relations. Defense Minister Apel was more outspoken in assailing American insistence upon conformity: "what matters in the alliance is not to submit in a servile way to the will of the alliance. On the contrary, it is reasonable and imperative to bring the national interest into debate so as to arrive at results in solidarity."[8] President Carter and Chancellor Schmidt, in order to settle some of these disputes, agreed to meet on a bilateral basis to discuss Afghanistan.[9]

The French left no uncertainty about their view of collective action. By January 7, Paris had already announced that it was opposed to taking any retaliatory steps against the Soviet Union.[10] The French refused to support the imposition of sanctions against the Soviets and did not intend even to participate in efforts to reach a collective NATO position.[11] The speed and resolve with which the French rejected a coordinated response to the Soviet invasion suggested that Paris was more interested in distancing itself from NATO than in forging an allied response. That the French sent a delegation to Moscow to discuss events in Afghanistan provides further evidence that Paris was capitalizing on the split within NATO to strengthen its voice within Europe. Because of the stalemate in the alliance, France was able to take an independent and more vocal stance. With regard to Afghanistan, President Giscard d'Estaing, in an interview with *Le Monde* in February, stressed the importance of a distinctly European approach:

> Until now two major voices have been heard in the world, the United States and the Soviet Union, and other countries were only expected to voice their opinion in relation to those two. It is important to show that European powers have special relationships . . . because they exist as powers, because they have a major and growing economic and political capacity . . . and because they have special concern about the preservation of peace.[12]

The disarray of the Western response was complicated by the involvement of other political bodies in Europe. The EEC, in an unprecedented move, took up the question of sanctions at a routine meeting in mid-January. There was a consensus that member states should not undermine the effect of U.S. sanctions by selling embargoed items, but also that the fabric of détente should not be

8. Defense Minister Apel, Berlin Radio, 2 March 1980, cited in Congressional Research Service, *NATO After Afghanistan* (Washington, DC: GPO, 1980), 10.

9. *New York Times*, 5 January 1980.

10. *Le Monde*, 8 January 1980, "La France n'evisage pas de Represailles."

11. *International Herald Tribune*, 8 January 1980, "French Policy on Afghanistan Provokes Questions, Criticism."

12. President d'Estaing, interview on 7 February 1980, cited in Congressional Research Service, *NATO After Afghanistan*, 10.

irreparably damaged.[13] In February, the EEC proposed that Afghanistan be declared a neutral and nonaligned country. The plan was dropped after several weeks and would, in any case, have been of little consequence. The European Parliament also broached the issue of sanctions, yet was as unsuccessful in reaching agreement as both the EEC and NATO.

From the above discussion emerge four reasons for the failure of the Western alliance—through any of its bilateral channels or multilateral institutions—to forge a more unified approach to the invasion of Afghanistan. First, it was evident from the outset that the United States and the West Europeans had very different views about the extent to which events in Southwest Asia should affect East–West relations. In Washington, détente was "indivisible"; Kissinger's concept of linkage was still very much alive and cordial relations with Moscow could not be pursued while Soviet troops were in Kabul. The West Europeans had lived with détente for almost a decade; they were unwilling to accept the economic and political strains with the Soviet bloc that sanctions would entail.

Second, divergent views of the Soviet threat were accentuated by the move into Afghanistan. As discussed earlier, the initial American reaction was one of panic. Europeans shared a heightened perception of the Soviet military threat; that the Kremlin had acted aggressively was unchallengeable. Nor was the steady growth of Soviet power projection capabilities disputable. Nevertheless, European analyses of Soviet motives tended to focus more on the internal turmoil in Afghanistan than on Soviet designs on the Persian Gulf.[14] It was only after the hysteria subsided in the United States that more considered opinions— along the lines of those expressed in Europe—rose to the surface in Washington. Given the initial divergence between American and European perceptions of the invasion, it is easy to understand the emergence of different responses. As will soon be discussed, the issue of threat perception was to play an even more important role in the strategic response to Afghanistan.

The third factor impeding the effectiveness of an alliance response lay in the institutional diversity of the Western international community. NATO, the EEC, the European Parliament, and the U.N. all served as forums for deliberating over what steps should be taken. Each of these institutions had different delegates (although there was some overlap) and a different mandate. Agreement within any one organ was difficult enough; agreement among them all would have indeed been remarkable. To complicate matters, the individual countries, out of frustration with institutionalized channels, undertook bilateral negotiations. The United States was as active in this respect as any NATO

---

13. *The Sunday Times* (London), 13 January 1980, "NATO's Split Ranks."
14. House of Commons, *Afghanistan*, vi–xi. See also *Le Monde*, 1 April 1980, "Discordances Atlantiques."

member. The net effect, while possibly closing the gap between the two individual countries participating, was to diffuse and make more unwieldy the process of
taking collective action.

Finally, the debate within NATO over Afghanistan was deeply colored by
intra-alliance tensions that were unrelated to questions of Soviet intentions or
the efficacy of sanctions. The parallels with the situation in the mid-1970s are
striking. Once again, Europeans were resentful of American attempts to dominate alliance policy, especially in areas outside NATO's jurisdiction. In the case
at hand, tensions were exacerbated by the fact that the disputed measures were
primarily of economic, not strategic, content. The French, characteristically,
were most outspoken in their challenge to U.S. authority. In 1980, this challenge particularly piqued Washington because America's global image as well as
its leadership in the alliance had been damaged by the series of setbacks in Iran
and Afghanistan. Nor did splits within the alliance occur only on a transatlantic
basis. Though Europeans shared opposition to collective action, there was a
wide range of opinion on specific measures to be taken by individual countries.
The breadth of opinion within Europe was to widen during Phase 2. Even during
Phase 1, many on the continent questioned whether Britain had gone too far in
supporting the United States and in imposing its own sanctions. The shrill
independence of the French position was also a target of criticism. Thus, in
addition to the transatlantic confrontation, certain traditional political rivalries
unique to Western Europe contributed to disarray within the alliance.

Phase Two

There was no clear temporal division between the Phase 1 and Phase 2 responses
to the Soviet invasion. While finance ministers were discussing sanctions,
defense ministers were assessing the strategic impact of the Soviet move. It was
not until April, however, that NATO undertook extensive collective consultations on the out-of-area question in relation to the invasion of Afghanistan. By
that time, individual countries had already implemented whatever short term
measures had been decided upon. Though the disarray of Phase 1 had receded,
NATO members entered Phase 2 quite aware that a second troublesome and
potentially explosive issue had to be confronted: the protection of Western
security interests in Southwest Asia.

There was virtually no reaction in West European capitals to President Carter's State of the Union address in January, 1980. That the West Europeans
were attempting to avoid any involvement whatsoever with the RDF became
clear during the following months; they continued neither to express approval
nor to condemn America's new military commitment in the Persian Gulf. At
the outset, it was unclear how the United States was going to approach this lack

of response. Was the implementation of the Carter Doctrine, in keeping with previous American commitments outside NATO, going to be largely an American affair? President Carter answered this question himself at the end of January by admitting that the United Staates could not defend the Persian Gulf alone: It will be necessary to "coordinate . . . our efforts with nations who are not located in the region but are heavily dependent, even more than we, on oil from that region."[15] Pressure for some level of European involvement in the RDF scheme mounted through informal channels during February and March. In mid-April, Under Secretary of Defense for Policy, Robert Komer, formally presented America's case before NATO.

Komer's main goal in visiting NATO was to request that the Europeans assume at least some of the military and financial burden of deploying forces in Southwest Asia. To this end, he suggested three steps: that the West Europeans supplement their troop reserves to replace American troops diverted to the Middle East; that they be prepared to facilitate the transport of U.S. personnel across the Atlantic by making available civilian and military aircraft; and that the Europeans employ their naval and air forces to increase surveillance in the Atlantic and Mediterranean and share the burden of reconnaissance in the Indian Ocean.[16] The immediate reaction of the allies paralleled their response to the announcement of the Carter Doctrine: silence. The Europeans were attempting to avoid involvement in the RDF and were resentful of Washington's lack of diplomatic tact.[17] The RDF had been presented as a fait accompli; there was no prior consultation at NATO. Suddenly the United States expected not only European support for the Carter Doctrine, but also European willingness to contribute to the financial and material burden of defending the Persian Gulf.

By the next meeting of the Defense Planning Committee (DPC) in May, tempers had cooled and alliance members had made progress in reaching a consensus of sorts on the out-of-area question. The relevant paragraphs from the DPC final communique are quite revealing and worth citing at length:

> 5. Ministers agreed that the stability of regions outside NATO boundaries, particularly in the South West Asia area and the secure supply of essential commodities from this area are of crucial importance. Therefore, the current situation has serious implications for the security of member countries. . . .
> 6. It is in the interests of members of the Alliance that countries which are in a position to do so should use their best efforts to help achieve peace and stability in South West Asia. . . . The burden . . . falls largely upon the United States, which

15. *New York Times*, 30 January 1980, "Carter Concedes U.S. Alone Can't Defend Persian Gulf."

16. *New York Times*, 14 April 1980, "U.S. Asking Allies to Assume More of Military Burden."

17. There was unanimous agreement among European delegations in Brussels that the U.S. approach to the out-of-area issue, and especially Komer's visit, contributed considerably to tension within the alliance.

has already taken steps to enhance its effectiveness. Ministers noted that this commitment, which in certain circumstances might substantially increase, could place additional responsibilities on all Allies for maintaining levels and standards of forces necessary for defence and deterrence in the NATO area. Ministers agreed on the need for ensuring that at the same time as the United States carries out the efforts to strengthen defence capabilities in South West Asia described above, Allied capabilities to deter aggression on and to defend NATO Europe are also maintained and strengthened.[18]

The wording of these two passages was indeed hesitant. The only substantive issue addressed was the need for the Europeans to assume "additional responsibilities" in the NATO area if U.S. forces were diverted to the Middle East. Yet, the inclusion of even these vague paragraphs was in itself a significant development. The Europeans had agreed to consider the out-of-area problem through formal channels. Security in Southwest Asia was on the planning agenda. If the United States was to secure European cooperation in planning for and conducting operations in the Middle East, this was an important first step.

In assessing the implications of the DPC communique, however, several other factors must be taken into consideration. Komer did not reveal the full range of American expectations; there were several issues not contained in the DPC statement for which Washington continued to apply pressure. The question of enlarging the boundaries of NATO, though discussed by alliance members, was never considered to be a feasible option.[19] Not only was there insurmountable opposition to the concept within NATO, but there was a glaring logical inconsistency in extending the Treaty area to cover countries that were not members of the alliance and had no desire to become members.

The Carter administration did try, however, a different route to securing joint military action outside Europe. Throughout 1980, the United States repeatedly raised within the alliance the issue of a NATO rapid action force. Such a unit would operate primarily in the Indian Ocean area, be comprised of vessels and personnel from numerous member countries, and be coordinated either through NATO or on a multilateral basis at governmental levels. Though the British did take the proposal under consideration, other European members remained adamantly opposed to any joint force operating outside the Treaty area under the auspices of NATO.[20] By October, the Carter administration had acquiesced and Defense Secretary Harold Brown announced that the United States was abandoning attempts to create a joint force.[21]

18. NATO DPC, Final Communique (Brussels, May 1980).

19. Interviews at NATO. See Robert Hunter, "Safeguarding Western Interests Outside the Treaty Area." Ditchley Conference Report No. 11 (Ditchley Park, December 1982), 5.

20. U.K. Ministry of Defence, *Defence in the 1980s—Statement on the Defence Estimates 1980* (London, HMSO, 1980), vol. 1, 63.

21. U.S. International Communication Agency, 8 October 1980, "An Interview with U.S. Secretary of Defense Harold Brown."

It is worth noting that during this debate over joint deployment, a sixty-vessel fleet consisting of French, British, American, and Australian ships gathered in the Indian Ocean. Assembled largely as a response to the Iran–Iraq war, this flotilla was coordinated only on an operational level. While there was contact among military staff on the vessels, the French meticulously avoided any cooperative planning on a centralized basis.[22] Nevertheless, the mere presence of allied ships in the Indian Ocean assuaged U.S. concerns about sharing the military burden of defending the oil lanes. As will be discussed shortly, it was the political implications of coordinated action more than the added capability that officials in Washington were seeking.

One final insight into NATO's position on out-of-area strategy emerges by comparing the DPC communique with the North Atlantic Council communique issued in June. While the DPC focuses on military aspects of NATO strategy, the NAC's mandate is to address political issues. Obviously, there is a great deal of overlap among the topics discussed in the two bodies. Given the attention devoted to Southwest Asia in the DPC communique, the lack of any explicit statement about out-of-area issues in the June NAC communique represents a glaring and curious omission. The NAC limited itself to the following vague formulation: "While recognising that the security of the region [Southwest Asia] is primarily the concern of the countries there, Ministers welcomed the fact that members of the Alliance are, by reason of their relations with those countries, in a position to make a contribution to peace and stability in the region."[23]

The NAC communique revealed clearly the political sensitivity surrounding the out-of-area question; the issues were so divisive that no explicit statement could be agreed upon.[24] The DPC statement presented what the military representatives agreed should be done. Yet, there is a great deal of distance between the DPC recommendation and a concrete step on behalf of NATO members. The DPC drafts the "Ministerial Guidance" every two years. Approximately one year later, "Force Goals" are set for the following six years. These two documents serve as the basis for the annual updating of NATO's "Force Plans." It is then the responsibility of the individual member states to incorporate these directives into their national defense policies and procurement programs. DPC recommendations matter only if the political will exists to bring them to fruition. Thus, although the United States by mid-1980 might have convinced military planners

22. *Le Monde*, 22 October 1980, "Des Consultations Techniques ont eu lieu Marine Alliées pour la Securité du Trafic Petrolier."

23. NATO NAC, Final Communique (Brussels, June 1980), par. 3.

24. Interviews at NATO confirmed this point. Communique language is in itself a crucial component of the political process at NATO. As the only public declaration of NATO policy, a great deal of emphasis is placed upon wording. It is not uncommon that hours are spent negotiating over punctuation. It should also be noted that the French, who were vehemently opposed to an alliance out-of-area stance, are members of the NAC, but not the DPC.

in Europe of the need to prepare for a potential deployment of troops to Southwest Asia, it remained to be seen whether any tangible changes in strategy or reserve levels would take place.

During the next two years, tensions over the out-of-area question continued to simmer, but gradual progress was made in bringing American and European perspectives into closer alignment. The United States lowered its expectations as to what the Europeans should contribute militarily to Southwest Asia and focused its attention upon convincing its allies to assume more responsibility for defense in the European theater. These shifts reflected diplomatic concessions on the part of the United States as well as a diminishing perception of the Soviet threat to the Gulf. A delegation from the House Armed Services Committee, after a visit to Western Europe, concluded that the Europeans should be asked to support the deployment of U.S. forces to the Middle East only by compensating within Europe for the diversion of U.S. assets.[25] During the same year, a Pentagon official testified before Congress that "As far as asking our allies to leap into Southwest Asia with us, in a military sense, many of them are ill-equipped to do so, and, in fact, the total western defense against a global threat is better served by them increasing their military capabilities within their own territorial boundaries. . . ."[26]

The Europeans likewise moved toward a more accommodating position. By 1982, European countries had agreed to provide up to 600 ships and 50 aircraft to facilitate the movement of U.S. troops across the Atlantic. Several governments had also made commitments to offer transportation and logistical support to U.S. forces in Europe.[27] While there was general agreement to increase reserve levels throughout Western Europe, certain countries promised special measures. The Germans pledged to make available 90,000 reservists and to assume extra responsibility in the North Atlantic to release U.S. ships for deployment in the Indian Ocean.[28] The French and the British also undertook steps to bolster their own rapid deployment capabilities.

The shifting positions of both the Americans and the Europeans were reflected in NATO communiques. While references in the DPC statements to out-of-area strategy became more detailed, the NAC finally began to take a public stance, albeit limited. In December of 1981, the NAC recognized that the alliance must prepare for contingencies outside Europe: "In their consultations [on global security] allies will seek to identify common objectives. . . . Those

25. U.S. Congress, House, Armed Services Committee, *North Atlantic Treaty Organization—An Alliance of Shared Values* (Washington, DC: GPO, 1982), 70.

26. U.S. Congress, House, Appropriations Committee, *Military Construction Appropriations for 1983*, Pt. 5 (Washington, DC: GPO, 1982), 257.

27. U.S. Congress, Senate, *Defense Authorization for Appropriations for Fiscal Year 1983*, Pt. 1, 282–286.

28. House of Commons, *Afghanistan*, xxx and U.S. Congress, House, *NATO—An Alliance of Shared Values*, 71.

allies in a position to do so will be ready to take steps outside the Treaty area to deter aggression and to respond to requests by sovereign nations for help in resisting threats to their security or independence."[29]

By the Bonn Summit the following June, further progress had been made in transforming the will to cooperate on the out-of-area question into concrete policy steps. The fourteen members participating in the integrated defense structure identified three crucial measures: All members must consult with allies fully on any issue that affects NATO security; efforts must be made by all members to compensate for the diversion of U.S. troops and lift capabilities to Southwest Asia so as not to expose the central front; the Europeans should be prepared to facilitate the movement of U.S. troops to regions outside the NATO area.[30] As will be discussed shortly, a wide gap remained among the allies as to what consultation, compensation, and facilitation entailed. Nevertheless, the Bonn Document revealed that substantial progress had been made since 1980, and it came to serve as a watershed in thinking about out-of-area operations. NAC communiques since June of 1982 have reflected the decisions taken at Bonn, and these guidelines have served as the core of NATO's approach to the out-of-area question into 1987.

Political agreement on these measures, however, has not been followed by concrete efforts to implement them. The record of adherence to the Bonn Summit agreement since 1982 has been, at best, erratic. As far as consultation on out-of-area operations is concerned, the record is mixed. The British did inform NATO before undertaking their operation in the Falklands and the United States consulted at least some European allies before staging an air raid on Libya in April, 1986. Furthermore, U.S. and European peacekeeping forces coordinated operations in Beirut following the 1982 Israeli invasion of Lebanon. The United States did not, however, consult its allies before intervening in Grenada and the French have undertaken several operations in Chad without prior discussions in the alliance.

Turning to facilitation, Washington agreed to offer logistical support to the British during the Falklands War and London allowed U.S. bombers to operate from bases in England during the U.S. attack on Libya. On the other hand, the French denied Washington overflight rights during the Libyan raid and the British faced widespread European condemnation of their involvement in the operation. Italy and the United States also clashed over the use of Italian bases and the handling of terrorist prisoners during the *Achille Lauro* affair. In short, it appears that consultation and facilitation will occur only on an ad hoc basis. The requirements for secrecy and short term planning in staging overseas operations also reduce the likelihood that individual allies will discuss intended operations in NATO councils.

29. NATO NAC, Final Communique (Brussels, December 1981), par. 9.
30. Document on Integrated NATO Defense—Bonn (Brussels, 10 June 1982), 2.

Finally, and most importantly, there is no sign that the Europeans have taken or intend to take the steps necessary to compensate for the potential diversion of U.S. assets. The greatest shortfalls would occur in logistics capability, munitions stockpiles, and troop reserves. Although several European states have marginally expanded their programs in these areas, these efforts have done little to address the problems that a U.S. operation in Southwest Asia would present for conventional deterrence and defense in Europe.[31] During 1983 and 1984, NATO's International Secretariat conducted a study on the impact of an American deployment to the Gulf area on European security. The report appeared in late 1984 and was entitled "Study on the Implications for NATO of the U.S. Strategic Concept for Southwest Asia." The report was delayed by a dispute between Turkey and Greece over a passage concerning operations in the Aegean Sea.[32] As a result, its recommendations for compensation were not included in the 1984 Force Goals. A second impact study has been requested, but it will not be until the late 1980s that concrete proposals to raise European reserve levels to compensate for the potential diversion of U.S. forces will be incorporated into NATO's long term force planning.

The allies have failed to respond more substantively to the Bonn Summit agreement in part because, since 1982, the out-of-area issue has gradually receded from the limelight of alliance politics. American fears of a Soviet move into Iran grew less intense, as did concern about a potential cutoff of oil resulting from the Iran–Iraq war or other intraregional conflicts. The Bonn Summit also served to defuse some of the political tension that had mounted between 1980 and 1982. Alliance efforts to address the out-of-area issue grew less frenetic and adopted a more long term perspective.

The continuation and intensification of the Gulf War has also shifted the focus of the out-of-area debate. The emphasis of the dialogue has switched from a Soviet contingency in Iran to the potential consequences of the Iran–Iraq conflict. There have been four principal concerns among the allies: that the fighting will spread to neighboring states; that the conflict will lead to a cutoff or reduction of oil supplies, especially if attacks on oil installations and tankers

31. Under the current configuration of the RDF, a full deployment to Southwest Asia would involve up to 400,000 troops. Given that it could well utilize virtually all of the U.S. strategic lift capability, another six U.S. divisions might have no way to get to Europe. Among major European countries, only the British, Italians, and Germans have substantially raised force levels (reserve and active) between 1980 and 1985 (about 20,000, 17,000, and 15,000 respectively). Moreover, these increases reflect long term programs and are not indicative of specific efforts to respond to the depletion problem. Dutch force levels have actually declined by about 5,000 troops. As far as lift capability is concerned, the British and French have both purchased a small number of new lift aircraft and are stretching existing planes. The overall impact, however, is minimal: The French and British each have one squadron of strategic lift aircraft, while the United States has seventeen. International Institute for Strategic Studies, *The Military Balance* (London, 1980–1986).

32. North Atlantic Assembly, "Interim Report-1984," 7.

continue; that a victory for either side will throw the regional political situation into disarray; and that the continuing hostilities will provide the Soviets opportunities for direct or indirect involvement in regional affairs. [33]

Though no firm consensus has been reached, the allies have sought to maintain neutral positions. Since 1983, support has shifted marginally toward the Iraqis, largely in response to successive Iranian victories. The United States also renewed efforts during the tanker war to bolster the air defense capabilities of local states. The Saudis succeeded in shooting down an Iranian plane in June of 1984.

The American Position

Given the above chronology of NATO policy toward the out-of-area question, it is now possible to examine in more detail the positions of the various countries within the alliance. To begin, it is necessary to understand the reasons for America's insistence on European involvement, especially in light of the history within the alliance of avoiding joint action in operations outside the Treaty area. We will then explore why the Europeans, in a collective sense, first ignored America's overtures and then gradually moved to a more accommodating position. And finally, the attitudes and capabilities of specific European countries will be examined. Their individual interests in the Persian Gulf area have had considerable influence on the evolution of NATO's strategy toward Southwest Asia.

When placed in the historical context of the Middle East, it is not difficult to understand American attempts after 1980 to involve the Europeans more deeply in Persian Gulf security measures. Until 1968, Britain was the primary external power maintaining a military presence in the Gulf, while the French and the Americans made significant contributions. After the British withdrawal, the United States assumed responsibility for protecting Western oil interests in the area, yet did so largely through the assistance of Iran and Saudi Arabia. After the United States made the decision in 1980 to increase its own military strength in the region, the pressure placed upon the Europeans to devote military resources to the Gulf was in many ways an attempt to revert to the situation existing before the British withdrawal. Not only would a sharing of defense responsibility ease the burden on America, but some officials in Washington also felt that the Europeans, because of their historical ties to the region, would be more suitable agents for external intervention. [34] This argument was support-

33. See ibid., 12–13.
34. See Peter Foot, "Beyond the North Atlantic: The European Contribution," Aberdeen Studies in Defence Economics, no. 21 (Aberdeen, 1982), 4–6.

Table 6
POTENTIAL WEST EUROPEAN CONTRIBUTIONS TO A NATO DEPLOYMENT
TO SOUTHWEST ASIA[a]

Country	Amphibious forces		Air transportable forces		
	Commando	Marine	Airborne	Air portable	Specialist
Belgium			1 regt		
Denmark					
France		1 bn	1 div	1 div	1 lt bde
West Germany			3 bdes		
Greece	1 bde	1 regt	1 bde		
	1 bn	1 bn			
Italy		3 bns	1 bde		
Netherlands		2 gps			
Norway					
Portugal	1 regt				
Spain	4 coys		1 bde	1 bde	
Turkey	1 bde	1 bde	1 bde		
United Kingdom	3 gps		2 bns	1 bn	1 regt

[a]Key: regt, regiment; bn, battalion; div, division; bde, brigade; gps, groups; coy, convoy.
Source: Peter Foot, "Beyond the North Atlantic," p. 33 and *The Military Balance 1981–1982* (London:
International Institute for Strategic Studies, 1981).

able as long as the contingency at hand remained quite limited. The British,
because of the presence of their military personnel in Oman and their continued
commercial ties to other Gulf states, could indeed play an important role in
controlling a small regional conflict. But as far as any large-scale intervention
was concerned, the Europeans were far less well equipped than the Americans.

When President Carter first announced that the United States could not
defend the Persian Gulf alone, he was not suggesting that European involvement was essential to projecting a credible deterrent force to Southwest Asia. As
we will soon see, he was concerned primarily about the political implications of
joint deployment and about the problem of troop depletion in Europe. The
military capability that the Europeans could contribute to a large operation in
the Gulf was actually quite limited (see Table 6).[35] And in those areas where
the United States was in most need of added assets—primarily sealift and airlift—the Europeans were least able to respond.[36] The question of airlift, in terms

35. With the exception of the British and French, other European members of NATO maintain
minimal capability for long-distance projection. The French maintain the strongest intervention
capability. For a detailed analysis of European capabilities, see ibid., and Peter Foot, "Improving the
Capabilities for Extra-European Contingencies: The British Contribution," Aberdeen Studies in
Defence Economics, no. 18 (Aberdeen, 1981).

36. Both the French and the British relied upon U.S. airlift for their respective operations in

of both the RDF's mission in Southwest Asia and the reinforcement of the central front, presented the most serious logistical problem. Using all available military airlift, the United States, as of 1982, would have faced considerable problems in transporting a 220,000–man unit to the Gulf. Not only would such a deployment have taken much longer than the Pentagon thought acceptable, but it could have deprived the United States of the lift necessary to reinforce the central front.[37] Furthermore, there would have been a 20% drop in the number of troops available to fight in Europe should U.S. forces have been sent to Southwest Asia. Under President Reagan's larger configuration for the RDF, the corresponding figure would be as high as 33%.[38] The drain on combat service forces would be particularly severe. One study estimated that a deployment of the RDF to the Gulf would divert some 49,000 service personnel from potential use in Europe. This would deprive three U.S. divisions in Europe of their necessary communications and logistics support.[39] These potential depletions in both lift and reinforcement capabilities could have had a hazardous impact on European security, and the United States had no choice but to raise the issue in Brussels.

Financial considerations also colored American behavior. Since the 1950s there has been a continuous debate within the alliance about the appropriate division of fiscal responsibility among member states. Through successive administrations, Congress has repeatedly complained that Americans absorb too much of the financial burden of defending Europe. After 1980, Congress argued that the Europeans, especially in light of their heavy dependence on Middle East oil, should share the expense of preparing for military intervention in the Gulf area. Several European members, however, claimed that they were already unable to maintain NATO's guideline of a 3% annual increase in defense spending. Further, implicit in the recognition that Europe should share fiscal responsibility for defending the Gulf was the assumption that operations in Southwest Asia should fall under NATO auspices. This was a link the West Europeans were loath to make. Congress increased pressure on the administration to seek European assistance by indicating that funding for the RDF might be contingent upon allied willingness to share the burden. Thus, the viability of America's own plans for the Gulf became dependent upon European cooperation on the out-of-area issue. Senator Gary Hart spoke for many members of

---

Zaire and Zimbabwe. Even after the procurement of a new strategic lifter, French airlift capabilities remain limited. See Pierre Delachenal, "Aéromobilité et Dissuasion—Quel Avenir pour un Transport Aérien Militaire?" *Défense Nationale* (November 1982).

37. U.S. Congressional Budget Office, *Rapid Deployment Forces: Policy and Budgetary Implications* (Washington, DC: GPO, 1983), 29–32.

38. Ibid., xvi-xxx.

39. Ibid. 50.

Congress when he questioned whether the United States should be prepared to "intervene on behalf of European nations for their supplies of oil even if we don't need them."[40] To be assured of funds for the RDF, the administration had to pursue the out-of-area question in NATO councils. And administration officials needed more than private assurances of European cooperation. They needed to present to Congress a clear declaration from both the DPC and the NAC that NATO as a collective unit was taking steps to address security concerns in Southwest Asia. This was a primary motivation for American insistence that the out-of-area issue be addressed in the final communiques.[41]

In addition to congressional pressure and the potential for a diversion of U.S. troops from Europe, one additional factor influenced the strength of American conviction that the Europeans should assume some responsibility for out-of-area preparations. In the late 1970s NATO strategy for defending the central front was shifting toward an increased emphasis on conventional deterrence. This shift entailed not only a significant rise in military expenditure, but also a change in weapons procurement policy. Given the limitations on European defense budgets and the inertia present in all weapons production programs, the move toward bolstering conventional capabilities was progressing very slowly. The out-of-area issue offered an opportunity for the United States to provide momentum for this change in strategy.[42] The call for the Europeans to compensate for a diversion of U.S. troops by raising conventional force reserve levels served as a means through which the United States could pursue these broader planning goals.

America's position on the out-of-area debate was also shaped by intraalliance political dynamics. NATO emerged somewhat shaken from the confusion that ensued during the Phase 1 reaction to Afghanistan. Following numerous splits within NATO over Middle East policy and the embarrassing failure of U.S. policy toward Iran, the rejection of the sanctions program presented a particularly serious challenge to Washington's leadership role in the alliance.[43] The out-of-area issue, as a central aspect of alliance strategy over which the Europeans and Americans were divided, emerged as a primary channel through which the United States could reaffirm its control within NATO.[44] The Reagan administration therefore adopted an especially uncompromising position on Southwest Asia.

40. U.S. Congress, Senate, Armed Services Committee, *Defense Authorization Appropriations for for Fiscal Year 1983*, Pt. 6, 3748.

41. European delegations mentioned that U.S. representatives were forthright about their need to secure concessions in the communiques to placate Congress.

42. Congressional Research Service, *NATO After Afghanistan*, 12.

43. Congressional Research Service, *Crisis in the Atlantic Alliance: Origins and Implications* (Washington, DC: GPO, 1982), 16–19.

44. For the European perception of this attitude, see Helmut Schmidt, "Saving the Western Alliance," *The New York Review of Books* (31 May 1984).

A second consideration emerges from America's own perception of its weakened global position. After 1979, the American public and the U.S. government were less certain of the direction of American foreign policy than at any time since World War II, with the possible exception of the years during the Vietnam War. Critics repeatedly claimed that U.S. behavior in the international arena lacked direction, that America had no foreign policy as such. Spurred on by the debate over the deployment of intermediate-range nuclear missiles (INF), much of this criticism emanated from Western Europe. The question of American sensitivity to European criticism is complex. On the one hand, Washington has been known to act unilaterally and without consulting its allies. On the other, especially during times of low domestic confidence in foreign policy, American administrations have been quite sensitive to reactions from European capitals.[45] The uncertain political atmosphere in 1980 meant that the Carter administration was concerned with the reception of its policies both in Europe and on a global scale. The United States was not content with verbal support for its approach to the Persian Gulf; it also sought to present its policy as part of a joint undertaking. As in Korea in 1950, American policy was not to be perceived as global expansionism, but as the American contribution to defending the interests of the Western world. This contributed to the desire in Washington to secure a joint force for the Indian Ocean and, failing that, a force coordinated at the military level. The mere presence of vessels from allied countries tempered American uncertainty about its foreign policy and made clear to regional states as well as to the Soviet Union that it was "the West," not just the United States, that was committed to maintaining a military presence in the Indian Ocean.

The European Position

The motives behind the European approach to the out-of-area issue are much more difficult to characterize. This is a result of the many voices that comprise a European position as well as the erratic response of the Europeans to U.S. overtures. Before turning to the perspectives of individual countries, an attempt will be made to summarize those considerations both for and against adopting a formal alliance approach to Southwest Asia. The following question provides a suitable starting point: Did the Europeans gradually agree to contribute to the out-of-area effort because of an appreciation of the strategic need to do so or because of the pressure applied by the United States? In other words, in approaching the out-of-area question, were the Europeans responding to security

45. See Congressional Research Service, *Crisis in the Alliance*, 25–29, and Hunter, "Safeguarding Western Interests," p. 5.

considerations in Southwest Asia or reacting to U.S. policy and attempting to influence it through alliance mechanisms?

Initial European resistance to involvement in America's plans for the Persian Gulf was largely the product of the factors discussed in the previous chapter: resentment of U.S. domination of the alliance, fear of implication in U.S. actions in the Middle East, and concern over U.S. perceptions of the Soviet Union and the indivisibility of détente. The Europeans were aware that the U.S. government and particularly the Reagan administration were attempting to revitalize America's role in the alliance. They were particularly sensitive to both the absence of consultation over the Carter Doctrine and the manner in which the United States unilaterally informed the alliance that U.S. troops might be diverted from Europe. It was this type of behavior that led European ministers to urge their colleagues not to submit to the "servile will" of the United States.

Even after both sides had reached an agreement at the Bonn Summit (the consultation–compensation–facilitation formula), the Europeans were skeptical of American intentions. History had shown that the United States, as well as other members of NATO, acts first and consults afterward. On this issue, the Foreign Affairs Committee of the House of Commons remarked that the alliance must begin by "improving as a matter of urgency, machinery for consultation between the United States of America and its allies on threats to Western interests outside the NATO area. . . ."[46] There was equal concern over abuse of the facilitation proviso. While the United States wanted ironclad guarantees that it would have access to European bases in the event of a major operation in Southwest Asia, the Europeans insisted that each eventuality had to be addressed on an ad hoc basis. The Europeans had not forgotten the 1973 war during which the United States had used German bases without prior consultation in Bonn.

As the oil flow from the Gulf was potentially at stake, the Europeans were again hesitant to associate themselves too closely with U.S. policy. While the Arab–Israeli question provided a ready source of contention, the key issue in 1980 was whether a strong Western military posture in the Gulf would secure oil supplies or simply lead to further instability in the region. There was a consensus on both sides of the Atlantic that the most serious threat to the stability of the Gulf region came from intraregional sources. Yet, there was a wide divergence, especially after the Soviet move into Afghanistan, about the likelihood of a Soviet invasion.[47] The United States believed it was necessary to take visible steps in order to deter Soviet aggression; the RDF was to fulfill this function. The Europeans focused primarily on internal threats and were more inclined

46. House of Commons, *Afghanistan*, xxxii.
47. Congressional Research Service, *The Persian Gulf: Are We Committed? At What Cost?* 25.

toward political and economic initiatives in the region.[48] Not only could a visible American presence alienate Arab Gulf states in peacetime, but it would be of little use except in the worst case scenario—a Soviet invasion of Iran. Furthermore, a U.S. military buildup in Southwest Asia could well provoke an aggressive Soviet response and strain East–West relations. Thus, the Europeans felt that the United States was both overreacting and doing so in a fashion that could harm Western interests. A House of Commons report on events in Southwest Asia captured accurately European frustration: "There is a misunderstanding both within the Western alliance and between the Western alliance and Soviet Union over the meaning of détente."[49]

What appeared to the Europeans as muddled thinking within the Pentagon did little to restore their confidence in U.S. policy. As discussed earlier, there were organizational problems in the command structure of the RDF, as well as a number of competing approaches to its operational strategy. If the Pentagon was itself unclear about what the RDF was to do, how could the allies be expected to support it? The Europeans were particularly concerned by the Reagan administration's plan to increase the size of the RDF. If the main function of the force was to deter the Soviets, why was the United States preparing for sustained combat in the region?[50] Did the Pentagon believe that the United States could defeat the Soviets in Iran? This issue was especially problematic in light of the impact that the larger RDF would have on reinforcements available for Europe.

Finally, European opposition to involvement in out-of-area operations was based upon realistic assessments of limited material and financial resources. The Europeans recognized that, under ideal circumstances, concrete steps should be taken to address security threats existing outside the Treaty boundaries. Yet, they did not want to assume responsibilities that they were incapable of meeting. In the words of former British Prime Minister Edward Heath, "[w]e have to ensure that when we make a strategic decision which is announced, like the fact that the Gulf is a vital interest of the Alliance, we have also got the resources to carry through the necessary defence of the area if it is to be required."[51]

A brief look at economic and demographic trends in Europe points to the severity of the domestic factors constraining European behavior. The sluggishness of the European economy, as reflected in its low growth rates and high unemployment, has virtually precluded the possibility of a rise in defense expenditure. During the 1980s, the Europeans have fallen behind the NATO guideline of a 3% growth rate in defense spending per year. In 1986, real increases in

48. North Atlantic Assembly, "Interim Report-1983", 5.

49. House of Commons, *Afghanistan*, xxx.

50. See Henri Labrousse, "Une Stratégie de Dissuasion pour le Golfe?" *Défense Nationale* (April 1982), 79–80.

51. Edward Heath, cited in House of Commons, *Afghanistan*, 181.

British, French, and West German defense spending will fall between zero and 2%.[52]

Demographic trends are also beginning to place severe constraints on manpower. West Germany, which contributes some 50% of the ground troops stationed on the central front, will face the greatest shortfall. In the next decade, available manpower in the Federal Republic will be reduced by almost one-half because of a sharp decline in the birthrate that began in the 1960s.[53] Even with an upturn in the European economy and the expansion of the reserve program, a serious depletion will be unavoidable. Efforts to address the compensation issue would mean increasing the number of non-German European troops dedicated to the central front, a move which would entail high political and economic costs for the countries involved.

Given such multifaceted opposition to the demands put forth by the United States, how can Europe's eventual involvement in the out-of-area problem be understood? Why did NATO eventually incorporate planning for a contingency in the Persian Gulf into its policymaking cycle? To begin, the Europeans did not deny that events in Southwest Asia could potentially pose a grave security threat to NATO. European governments disagreed with the United States about the seriousness of that threat and how best to address it, given the economic and political limitations within the alliance framework. Yet, when it became evident that the United States could well send its troops to Southwest Asia regardless of objections within the alliance, the Europeans were forced either to take compensatory steps or to face a potential shortfall in reinforcements and supplies. This consideration precluded the possibility that the Europeans could, as they did initially, simply ignore American pressure.

As the debate on out-of-area security evolved, it became increasingly clear that if the Europeans hoped to influence U.S. policy, they had to engage the Americans in a constructive dialogue. To stonewall the issues was to give Washington complete freedom in formulating policy toward Southwest Asia; to discuss the issues in NATO councils was to provide some means of tempering U.S. behavior. As expressed by a British Parliamentary Committee, "if European countries are to remain full partners with the USA in the Alliance and be in a position to exert their influence, every effort must be made to share burdens in the defence and diplomatic fields."[54] Some extended this argument by calling for the strengthening of independent European power projection capabilities. If European nations maintained substantial strike forces, they could wield leverage over the United States by contributing their units to or withholding them from

52. Francois Heisbourg, "Conventional Defense: Europe's Constraints and Opportunities," in Andrew Pierre, ed., *The Conventional Defense of Europe: New Technologies and New Strategies* (New York: Council on Foreign Relations, 1986), 72.

53. Ibid., 74.

54. House of Commons, *Afghanistan*, xxx.

the RDF.[55] Again, it was not the added capability that was at stake, but the political implication of European participation in joint deployments.

The Europeans were concerned about influencing not only the content of U.S. policy, but also its general orientation. One of the principal reasons behind NATO's decision to deploy American intermediate-range missiles had been to prevent the "decoupling" of the United States from Europe in the event of a Soviet attack through the central front. In a similar sense, the Europeans feared that America's interests outside NATO's boundaries—specifically in the Middle East and East Asia—might decouple the United States from its close ties with Europe. If the Europeans did not show at least some support for America's efforts outside the area, then the strength of America's military commitment to Europe could well be diminished. They did not fear that the United States would abandon the defense of the NATO area, but that America's economic and strategic priorities might shift to other regions. A second concern, voiced in more conservative circles, was that Washington's willingness to accept global responsibility could well be undermined by persistent European reluctance to contribute to the effort. Though many in Europe criticized the escalating nature of superpower competition in the Third World, they did not want to see the United States move toward an isolationist posture. In the words of one British parliamentarian, "is there not the danger . . . of the Americans drifting if not into some form of isolationism then into a western hemisphere continentalism, and leaving the Europeans to fend for themselves?"[56]

Implicit in European concern about the "drift" in U.S. policy was the assumption that the cohesion of the alliance should, at times, take precedence over divergent perspectives on strategy. The gradual shift toward compromise on the out-of-area issue by both the Americans and the Europeans was reflective of a mutual recognition of this factor.[57] At the Bonn Summit, the Americans did not achieve their initial goals, while the Europeans were far more involved in the out-of-area scheme than they had originally intended. Both sides had made compromises in their positions to preserve the political integrity of the alliance.

On balance, then, European acquiescence on the out-of-area debate was more the product of U.S. pressure than of growing European appreciation of the need for a new approach toward the Gulf. The Europeans perceived the strategic need to address the troop depletion problem, but reserve levels could have been raised without entering into a formal agreement on out-of-area strategy. Furthermore, because of demographic and economic constraints, the Europeans failed to raise reserve levels as stipulated in the Bonn Summit declaration, suggesting that the agreement was the result of symbolic politics, not the product of strate-

---

55. Michael Howard, cited in ibid., 212–213.
56. Eldon Griffiths, cited in ibid., 189–190.
57. Brzezinski relates this notion to general alliance decisions. See *Power and Principle*, 308, and Heath in ibid., 181.

gic necessity. While the Europeans by no means feared that the United States would abandon them, they perceived clear costs associated with their continuing noncompliance on the out-of-area problem. As negotiations proceeded, it became clear that European intransigence could lead to at least some degree of decoupling or strategic drift. Acquiescence on the out-of-area question proved preferable to risking U.S. alienation and the consequent strain on alliance relations.

The Individual Voices

How the policies of the individual countries within Europe affected NATO's approach to Southwest Asia is the focus of the final section of this chapter. Since 1979, the West Europeans have enjoyed surprising success in coordinating their policies toward Southwest Asia. There was initially a wide divergence of opinion on the application of sanctions in response to both the Iranian revolution and the Soviet invasion of Afghanistan. Britain was most supportive of America's lead, the French, most opposed, and the other European states often vacillating between these two extremes. Yet, in both cases the numerous positions grew closer largely to strengthen Europe's voice within the alliance. This trend repeated itself during the out-of-area debate. The following discussion will focus first on the British and French approaches to the out-of-area question. Then the German approach will be examined, followed by that of the Dutch— as representative of the smaller member states. Finally, this section will address the attitudes of the southern flank countries, because of their unique strategic position vis-à-vis operations in Southwest Asia.

The 1979 British Defence White Paper contained no explicit reference to joint out-of-area activities and cited a NATO study to convey its assessment of Soviet behavior: "in general the foreign and other policies of the Soviet Union, including its concept of détente . . . [are] not likely to undergo any fundamental change."[58] In the 1980 White Paper, the Thatcher government made clear its commitment "to play a full part in firm collective Western responses to Soviet encroachments." Such responses could well include military action, and NATO members should "where appropriate, act together."[59] It was clear that events in Afghanistan had had a profound impact upon British defense policy. The above statements supporting collective military action were not made with reference to Britain's remaining territorial possessions, but were directed toward Southwest Asia.

This shift in declaratory policy was backed by concrete changes in force

58. U.K. Ministry of Defence, *Statement on the Defence Estimates 1979* (London: HMSO, 1979), 10.

59. U.K. Ministry of Defence, *Statement on the Defence Estimates 1980* (London: HMSO, 1980), 39, 42.

planning. In 1974, Britain had dismantled its Joint Airborne Task Force against the will of numerous Conservative members of Parliament and the judgment of the Foreign and Commonwealth Office (FCO). There was also a steady decline during the 1970s in Britain's sea power and force projection capabilities.[60] By 1980, attitudes had shifted dramatically; numerous steps were taken to rebuild the country's intervention capabilities. Thirty Hercules aircraft were lengthened, special equipment for airborne intervention stockpiled, a parachute assault team trained, and a command and control headquarters for emergency operations established.[61] Efforts in this area were intensified after the Falklands War, as the logistical requirements of the conflict in the South Atlantic had illuminated weaknesses in Britain's sea power and force projection capabilities.[62]

Yet, it was British support for collective out-of-area responsibilities that mattered most in the alliance, not these specific changes in force planning. Even with this buildup, Britain's ability to contribute to an alliance operation in the Gulf area remained very limited. Into early 1981, however, the Thatcher government publicly defended the RDF and even expressed reluctant support for a global NATO force. In March, the Prime Minister herself referred to "an urgent need for a new defence policy beyond the North Atlantic."[63] That statements such as these influenced the treatment of the out-of-area issue in NATO was evident. The French, Germans, Italians, Dutch, and Danes chastised the British government for its outspoken position. *Défense Nationale*, the unofficial mouthpiece of the French military establishment, wrote that Mrs. Thatcher had alienated the Arab world and "evoked the well-known spectres of colonialism and imperialism."[64]

This strong criticism of the British stance must be viewed in light of the fact that in 1981, there was gathering momentum behind the concept of forging a more distinct European defense identity: Increasing attention focused on reviving the Western European Union (WEU) as a potential forum for defense cooperation. The British position on out-of-area strategy, because it ran contrary to that of most other European states, undermined such attempts to forge a more cohesive voice. Within this context, Britain was particularly sensitive to European criticism of its stance on Gulf security. Under pressure from European governments and from a Ministry of Defence that preferred not to weaken

60. Interview with John Weston. The FCO has traditionally complained that the decline in projection capabilities has damaged Britain's diplomatic strength in the Third World.

61. U.K. Ministry of Defence, *Statement on the Defence Estimates 1981* (London: HMSO, 1981), 32.

62. U.K. Ministry of Defence, *The Falklands Campaign: The Lessons* (London: HMSO, 1982), 30–32.

63. *Guardian*, 3 March 1981, "Thatcher Pledge on Gulf Force Irks Colleagues." For a comprehensive summary of the evolution of the British position, see John Reed, "Out-of-Theatre Operations—A New Imperative for Europe," *Defence* (March 1983).

64. *Défense Nationale*, "Menaces sur les Puits du Golfe" (July 1981), 42.

Britain's continental commitment, the Thatcher government's support for a formal out-of-area strategy in NATO gradually declined in the second half of 1981. Successive White Papers placed increasing emphasis on "diplomacy, development aid and trade policies" as the most appropriate means of addressing instability in the Third World. Nevertheless, Britain had already ensured that the Europeans were deeply involved in the out-of-area debate.

The principal voice limiting the extent of that involvement was emanating from Paris. Two decades earlier, the French would have welcomed joint efforts to deal with Middle East security. In 1960, President de Gaulle remarked that "if there is not an agreement among the principal participants of the Atlantic Alliance toward other countries outside of Europe, how will it be possible indefinitely, to maintain the Alliance in Europe?"[65] This French commitment to its regional military role outside the boundaries of NATO has remained strong into the 1980s. Although numerous French colonies have gained independence since de Gaulle's presidency, as of 1982 there were still some 26,000 French soldiers stationed in Africa and the Indian Ocean region.[66] The area in which de Gaulle's statement has become radically obsolete, however, concerns the French perspective on collective action within NATO.

Since the topic was first broached in NATO in 1980, the French have been adamantly opposed to an alliance-wide approach to security measures in Southwest Asia. They argued that NATO's primary and, indeed, only concern should be the defense of Europe and North America. Out-of-area issues should be addressed, by definition, through structures outside the alliance. For NATO to assume defense responsibilities beyond its boundaries would be to undermine the very foundation of the alliance. The considerations behind this position were integrally linked to France's original reason for withdrawing from NATO's military structure: to maintain an independent foreign policy. Not only would acquiescence on the out-of-area issue constitute submission to American dominance within the alliance, but it would lead to a de facto increase in European reliance on U.S. strategy and military power. The United States, because of its military capability, would be a likely participant, and probably the dominant one, in most out-of-area operations. A formal NATO approach to Southwest Asia would mean that all European members, either through participation or implication, would be involved in a primarily American undertaking. This situation would, in the words of one French military official, reduce the European states to "demi-etats."[67]

65. Charles de Gaulle, cited in Wittman, "France's Intervention Capability," 12.

66. Francois Charollais and Jean de Ribes, Le Défi de l'Outre-Mer l'Action Extérieure dans la Défense de la France, Cahier no. 26 (Paris: Foundation pour les Etudes de Défense Nationale, 1983), 313.

67. Interview with General Prestat.

While it might appear that this objection should have clearly defined the impact of the French position on the out-of-area debate, it did not do so. This was largely because France maintained that as long as planning and operations took place outside the auspices of NATO, the members of the alliance should maintain a strong capability for military action beyond the European theater. The French offered support for America's commitment to deter the Soviets in the Persian Gulf.[68] They contributed a portion of their Indian Ocean fleet to the joint flotilla in the Gulf of Oman and stated that they would be prepared "in the last resort, to participate in military operations in conjunction with our allies. . . ."[69] The French did make it clear, however, that their presence in the Indian Ocean was to protect national, not Western, interests.[70] France was concerned about the independence of the decision to participate, not the independence of its military operations as such. The French realized that the United States would likely be the dominant military power in joint missions in the periphery. Yet, this was acceptable as long as French or, for that matter, European participation was the result of bilateral consultation outside the formal alliance framework. Thus, although the French opposed an out-of-area capability for NATO as such, they exhibited their willingness to undertake joint military action.

The French also took steps to improve significantly their own intervention forces. In 1978–1979 the Force d'Intervention was expanded through the addition of a new alpine unit. The Mitterrand government pursued further steps to strengthen France's regional military capabilities. Before his election, Mitterrand asserted that "it would be necessary to strengthen the power of our intervention forces."[71] After taking office, he supervised the reorganization of the French Army into the Force Assistance Rapid (FAR), an integrated unit for operations both within and outside the European theater. Within the FAR, the 31st Brigade, the 9th Marine Infantry, and the 11th Parachute Division—47,000 soldiers in all—were earmarked as units for rapid intervention outside Europe.[72]

Thus, the French projected two contradictory impulses into the out-of-area debate—one through rhetoric and one through example. In essence, Paris was demonstrating its own vital concern with developments outside Europe, yet was suggesting that NATO as an institution should not share that concern. This was a tenable position for the French because of their independent intervention capability. However, other European countries without such capability could hardly turn to the Western European Union or any other European defense

68. Labrousse, "Une Stratégie de Dissuasion pour le Golfe?" 76–77.
69. Amiral Schweitzer, "Une Stratégie pour la France," *Défense Nationale*, (July 1981), 32.
70. Foot, "Beyond the North Atlantic," 24.
71. Francois Mitterand, cited in *Le Monde*, 8 October 1981, "Une Vocation Prioritaire."
72. French Ministry of Defense, *Information Note a l'Attention des Chefs de Corps 1983* (Paris: Service d'Information de Relations Publiques des Armées, 1983), 8.

organization to protect their economic or political interests abroad; NATO was the only one that could provide effective military options. This factor left some of the smaller and less powerful European states in a difficult predicament.

The Germans felt the full impact of this dilemma. They recognized the vulnerability of their interests in the Persian Gulf, but their constitution restricted the scope of their military operations to the protection of the homeland. Through what means could Germany contribute to the defense of the Gulf?

Initially, Bonn was opposed to discussing Southwest Asian security measures in NATO. The Minister of Defense argued that the topic lay outside the auspices of the alliance and should, in any case, be addressed through diplomatic and economic, not military initiatives.[73] Bonn suggested that an alliance-wide approach was unnecessary, but that individual countries should contribute in any way possible to the stability of the region.[74]

By the end of 1980, in response to the Iran–Iraq war, American pressure, and the political inducements discussed above, Germany's position began to shift. The Germans sent a number of vessels to the Indian Ocean—an act which, although ostensibly for training purposes, had a symbolic impact on the alliance. In addition, Bonn agreed to assume increased responsibility in the Atlantic if U.S. ships were diverted to Southwest Asia. By March, 1981, the Germans had gone even further: "The Federal Republic would not contribute directly to such a force [for intervention in Southwest Asia] though it might, in certain circumstances, make some transport facilities available."[75] The German position had progressed significantly, yet was still guarded. The Germans made it clear that the offer of facilitation was contingent upon both the nature of the conflict and prior consultation. By the NATO conference in Bonn in June of 1982, the Germans were willing to support the consultation–compensation–facilitation formula as long as the Americans were willing to uphold their commitment to consult before acting. In light of the events in 1973 and the crucial issues at stake, the Germans wanted both to be informed about and to approve of any action involving their forces or their territory. Thus, an out-of-area strategy could not be more formal than the consultation process itself. And since the content of any consultation was wholly dependent upon the contingency at hand, an appropriate alliance response could be forged only on an ad hoc basis. The Germans had agreed to enter the debate, yet had drawn a line past which they were unwilling to venture.[76]

73. U.S. Congress, Senate Armed Service Committee, *Europe and the Middle East: Strains on Key Elements of America's Vital Interests* (Washington, DC: GPO, 1982), 5.
74. Peter Foot, "Problems of Equity in Alliance Arrangements," Aberdeen Studies in Defence Economics, no. 23 (Aberdeen, 1982), 36.
75. *Guardian*, 4 March 1981, "Allies Worried by Mobile Forces Plan."
76. Interviews with the German Delegation, NATO.

The Dutch and other northern European countries were far less compromising. Though the Dutch had traditionally attempted to bridge the political gap between NATO's primary and lesser powers, their limited projection capabilities restricted the strength of their voice within the alliance on the out-of-area issue. This predicament enhanced the Dutch perception of the importance of the consultation process in their overall participation in NATO. This is not to suggest that their military contribution was insignificant, but that it was of less de facto importance than that of the British or the Germans. The Dutch recognized that consultation on out-of-area contingencies had not only been limited in the past, but would continue to be limited in the future. In situations warranting rapid intervention, military considerations often preclude discussions within the alliance. Thus, the Dutch were opposed to an out-of-area strategy for NATO on the grounds that it would diminish the autonomy of their foreign policy; it would widen the scope of activities falling under the auspices of the alliance while potentially reducing the input of the smaller countries into the nature of those activities.[77]

Greece and Turkey, though by no means major powers within the alliance, did not share the Dutch perspective. This was largely because of their proximity to the Persian Gulf area. In the event of a deployment to Southwest Asia, both countries could well play a vital role. Access to Greek ports and airfields would facilitate the transport of forces and supplies to the Gulf. More importantly, airfields in eastern Turkey would place American tactical fighters within range of key targets in Iran. In light of the likelihood that Turkey and Greece would be directly involved in an operation in the Gulf area, the governments of both countries favored that such an undertaking be framed within the context of the alliance. Otherwise they might be singled out for Soviet retaliation while other NATO members remained uninvolved. Granted, it is difficult to envisage a scenario in which Soviet attacks against the southern flank would not lead to a wider conflict. Yet, if the Greeks and Turks were to participate in an operation in Southwest Asia, they would want to be able to rely on NATO's deterrent umbrella.

It is evident that there was by no means a consensus within Europe about the out-of-area problem. The British favored the adoption of an alliance strategy, yet their position was tempered by pressure from the continent. The French opposed any NATO approach as such, yet simultaneously made clear their commitment to maintain the capability and will to undertake military operations in the periphery. A wide range of perspectives separated the other European members, with each reacting to its particular political and geographic position within NATO. This diversity weakened Europe's collective voice within the alliance and hindered a primary European goal—resisting American dom-

77. Interviews with the Dutch Delegation, NATO.

ination of the issue. Nevertheless, by the middle of 1982, NATO was able to reach an interim agreement on the out-of-area issue necessitating compromises by all parties concerned. But the provisions agreed upon were tenuous ones, as exemplified by the erratic record of adherence to the principles put forth in the Bonn Summit declaration.

Conclusions

If political acceptability is the measure of success within the alliance, then the Western allies did succeed in forging a solution to the out-of-area question. The allies collectively addressed difficult and sensitive issues and reached logical conclusions. The attention devoted to regional security meant that during the next crisis in the periphery, the alliance would at least be prepared to confront the proper political and strategic problems.

When taking hard strategic issues into consideration, however, the outcome was clearly suboptimal. Unilateral concerns dominated collectivist impulses. By 1987, despite significant compromise on behalf of individual member states, few substantive issues were resolved. The problem of troop depletion still existed. Although the Europeans agreed in principle to compensate, no concrete steps were taken to address the potential 20–33% shortfall that would result from a U.S. deployment to the Middle East. This issue presented particular problems for the West Germans for purely demographic reasons: They face a stark decline in the number of men eligible for national service. The United States also failed to secure the access and overflight arrangements that it had been seeking. Given the relative transparency of both threats and interests in the Persian Gulf, why was a more satisfactory response not forthcoming?

Despite the broad scope of the debate over out-of-area strategy, only one concrete strategic consideration lay behind the extensive discussions within the alliance on Persian Gulf security. This single issue was how to compensate for the potential shortfall in U.S. reinforcements for Europe that would result from an American deployment to Southwest Asia. Officials in both the United States and in Europe recognized the gap between America's global strategy and its capability. The implementation of America's military strategy for the RDF would impair the implementation of NATO's military strategy for Europe. The problem was by no means insignificant. Not only would the deployment of the RDF drain American manpower, but it would also utilize virtually all the lift assets needed to ferry men and equipment to Europe. Given that a Soviet–American confrontation in the Middle East would increase the likelihood of hostilities in Europe, neither the United States nor the Europeans were willing to overlook this potential loophole in the strength of Europe's conventional defense. The solution—urged by the United States and reluctantly accepted by the Europeans—was for the European states to increase their manpower and military stockpile reserves by whatever levels possible. Whether reserve levels in Europe in fact increase remains to be seen.

Why did the out-of-area debate never address the core strategic issues that shape Persian Gulf security, the difficult questions that concern the feasibility and conduct of military operations in Southwest Asia? Given the high dependence of the West European states on Gulf oil, their reluctance to assume more responsibility in constructing security arrangements is, at first, quite puzzling. Two explanations are readily apparent. First, the Europeans simply did not have the capability to contribute significantly to the effectiveness of an American operation in the Persian Gulf. Because of the glaring discrepancy between American and European force projection capabilities, the question of European participation in a regional strike force was never an issue of much strategic importance. Constraints on European manpower and defense expenditures also predetermined a reluctant response to Washington's request for compensation within the European theater. The second explanation concerns the timing of America's attempts to secure a formal alliance approach toward the Gulf. When a U.S. delegation went to Brussels in April of 1980 to discuss out-of-area strategy, the RDF had already been unilaterally established. Washington had made a de facto commitment to send forces to the Gulf to protect the flow of oil. The Europeans could therefore afford to be "free riders."[78] There was little impetus for them to expend resources if the United States had demonstrated a willingness to assume full responsibility for the extended military commitment.

In addition to these strategic and economic considerations, the political dynamics of decision-making in NATO offer further explanation of the apparent tension within the alliance between unilateral and collective approaches to Persian Gulf security. Four broad issues are relevant: the impact of domestic electoral considerations, the differing perceptions within the alliance of global and regional issues, the politicization of strategy, and the bureaucratization of decision-making.

Because of the shortfall in U.S. reinforcements for Europe that an American deployment to the Gulf would entail, the Carter and Reagan administrations felt compelled to broach the out-of-area issue in NATO. The manner in which the United States presented the problem, however, was shaped in large part by congressional demands that the Europeans share the burden of defending the Gulf. When legislators spoke of linking appropriations for the RDF to progress on the out-of-area issue, both administrations felt pressed to secure at least some evidence of European willingness to contribute to the emerging arrangements for

78. For more theoretical examinations of the dynamics of alliance relationships and the concept of "free rider," see Mancur Olson, *The Logic of Collective Action* (Cambridge, MA: Harvard University Press, 1965), and Russell Hardin, *Collective Action* (Baltimore, MD: Johns Hopkins University Press, 1982).

Gulf security. Implicit in the funding problem was a more subtle issue. American strategy was based upon the supposition that the continued flow of Gulf oil was crucial to the viability of the Western economy. Yet, because the Europeans were much more dependent upon Middle East oil than the Americans, it was primarily Europe that stood to benefit from U.S. efforts to protect the Gulf. Thus, if the administration was to justify its Gulf policy to Congress and the American people, it had to secure European approval, if not European participation.

The European members of NATO faced similar domestic constraints. The European public did not support further increases in defense spending, especially when several states faced difficulties in meeting existing NATO commitments. The INF debate also provided significant momentum to the peace movements throughout Western Europe. In Britain, the Ministry of Defence, not unlike the Pentagon, was opposed to devoting more resources to regional missions. In West Germany, those critical of adopting an out-of-area role pointed to the limits placed on the scope of military action by the constitution. The call for a more distinct European defense identity also made it difficult for individual governments to support America's position in the out-of-area debate. Because of these domestic and intra-European pressures, it was extremely difficult for any European government to support the inclusion of a formal out-of-area strategy in NATO policy. The decisions taken in NATO councils had to fall within the limits set by these domestic political considerations. It is for this reason that council communiques played such an important role in the debate. The American delegation needed some tangible sign of European acquiescence; the European delegations could go only so far in accommodating U.S. demands. In short, the policy positions that emanated from Brussels reflected the common recognition that decisions had to be tailored for public consumption.

This is not meant to suggest that, with the exception of the troop depletion problem, substantive strategic issues played no role in shaping the debate over out-of-area strategy. Indeed, divergent perceptions of appropriate global and regional strategies impaired the ability of the alliance to forge a more coherent response to the Soviet invasion of Afghanistan. For the Europeans, a harsh reaction to Moscow's aggression was simply not worth the decline in East–West relations that would inevitably follow. In their effort to preserve at least some of the benefits of détente, the Europeans resisted American attempts to impose a wide range of diplomatic censures and economic sanctions. Divergent perceptions of exactly what was at stake in an overall decline in East–West relations was thus a principal obstacle to orchestrating a collective *diplomatic* response to the Soviets.

Of more importance than considerations of East–West relations in shaping the *strategic* response, however, were divergent conceptions of how best to approach the quagmire of regional security. In broad terms, the Europeans feared

American reliance on military as opposed to diplomatic initiatives. If used without great caution, the RDF could well incite problems, not solve them. Furthermore, the British and French each viewed the Middle East through their own particular historical prism. The British wanted to maintain their political influence in the Gulf; the French were concerned with their economic interests and the implications of regional conflict for stability in North Africa. Although the Western allies shared a common concern for access to Gulf oil, differing peripheral interests and divergent approaches to regional security impaired the formulation of a more substantive NATO policy for the Persian Gulf.

Another key factor concerns the politicization of the debate over out-of-area strategy. From the outset, the discussion of Persian Gulf security within NATO took place within the context of an American–European confrontation over policy. American recommendations, precisely because they came from Washington as opposed to Bonn or London, met with stiff resistance in NATO councils. That the United States came to Brussels having made a unilateral decision about the RDF certainly did little to ameliorate Washington's hegemonic image. Addressing the troop depletion problem, for example, was as important to the Europeans as to the Americans. Nevertheless, the Europeans initially ignored this issue as well. Regardless of its context, the source of American policy became one of its key liabilities. The politicization of the debate over strategy not only polarized American and European perspectives, but also constrained the nature of the dialogue between the two camps. In the end, the Europeans used the alliance network to temper U.S. policy, not to propose alternative security arrangements. Their approach can best be described as one of damage limitation: What was the minimum extent to which the Europeans could acquiesce before eliciting a punitive response from the Americans or engendering drift in Washington's strategic priorities? It is by no means surprising that this negotiating strategy produced a less than optimal outcome.

Finally, it is important to consider how NATO's bureaucratic structure shaped the approach of the alliance toward regional security problems. At the outset of the debate, the initial bargaining positions of alliance members fell at opposite ends of a preference spectrum. The Americans sought joint participation in a regional strike force; some European members resisted even broaching the topic in alliance councils. Delegations came to Brussels with a minimum and maximum preference ordering. The dynamics of the bargaining process thus involved searching for the lowest common denominator: an outcome which would not violate the maximum position of the least interested European state while still meeting America's minimum requirements for a settlement. The process was one of satisficing, not optimizing. This was reflected in the outcome of the debate. The compensation–consultation–facilitation formula was very vague and was left to ad hoc interpretation. Realistically, little had been achieved in terms of constructing a concrete out-of-area strategy. This was in part a reflection of the fact that there was no easy solution to the problem. Earlier chapters revealed the magnitude of the strategic dilemmas involved in projecting significant power to Southwest Asia. Nevertheless, alliance mechanisms had produced a suboptimal outcome which, although lacking in strategic rationale, met the key test of political acceptability.

Essential to understanding the relationship between initial bargaining positions and policy outcomes was the role that communique drafting played in the decision-making process. As the principal sources of NATO policy open to the public, the DPC and NAC communiques serve as vital political tools for the individual delegations. Shifts in policy that are intended to meet domestic political demands must be reflected in these documents. In a debate as highly politicized as that over out-of-area strategy, communique language played an especially vital role. Extended discussions on the wording of the passages concerning Southwest Asia came to take the place of substantive dialogue about strategy. This phenomenon detracted from the extent to which the NATO bureaucracy or the individual delegations viewed the out-of-area issue as one of crucial importance to the formulation of NATO policy. There was widespread recognition that the outcome of the debate would have limited implications for alliance strategy.

NATO's lengthy planning cycle also contributed to the somewhat deflated context in which the debate took place. Even if the political will had existed to respond to the crisis in the Persian Gulf with certain shifts in force procurement or deployment, such changes would have occurred at a very slow pace. There is a considerable time lag both between the drafting of Ministerial Guidance and the formation of Force Plans and between the setting of those directives and their incorporation into national defense policies and programs. If the entire decision-making process ran smoothly, it would take a minimum of five years to see any significant shift in NATO strategy reflected in national planning. Given that bureaucratic inertia or resistance could well lengthen considerably this time lag, there was pervasive skepticism among NATO's permanent staff and within delegations that the out-of-area debate would ever play a significant role in shaping international or national defense planning. From the outset, there appeared to be widespread recognition that little could be done to alter NATO's rigid Eurocentrism.

These conclusions suggest that NATO as presently constituted is unprepared and unable to address adequately regional threats to Western security. It is also safe to assert that the alliance has reached its limit in terms of formulating a formal out-of-area strategy in peacetime. And in wartime, given the cumbersome structure of the alliance, the Western powers are most likely to cooperate through bilateral and multilateral channels outside the NATO framework. Were the Soviets to invade Iran, for example, it is clear that the United States would take immediate countermeasures. Individual European states could well participate, yet the urgency of the situation would make it highly unlikely that any party would attempt to involve the alliance collectively. That NATO—the central component of the Western security framework—is unable to address threats to Western interests in the Middle East is another aspect of the dilemma of security in the Persian Gulf.

Chapter Nine

THE DILEMMAS OF PERSIAN GULF SECURITY

Not until 1979 did the United States confront directly the full scope of the three strategic dilemmas of Persian Gulf security. Through the first three postwar decades, the tension between strategy and capability did not emerge because the United States perceived as very unlikely a direct Soviet move into Southwest Asia and because the British, until the 1970s, maintained a military presence in the Gulf. The tensions between globalism and regionalism and between unilateralism and collectivism, however, became readily apparent during the 1950s. America's overriding concern with Moscow's intentions in the Middle East and its tendency to interpret developments within an East–West rather than a regional context took root in the late 1940s and intensified through the late 1950s. The key policy initiatives during this period—the Truman Doctrine and the Eisenhower Doctrine—were both responses to perceived shifts in the nature of the Soviet threat to the region. Eisenhower's reaction to the rise of Nasserism, the Iraqi revolution, and the political turmoil in Lebanon in 1958 revealed a preoccupation with stopping the spread of communism, not with understanding or responding to Arab nationalism.

The question of collective Western efforts to address security problems in the Middle East also emerged during the 1950s. The uncoordinated response to the Suez crisis in 1956 was the first of many examples of attempted alliance cooperation that were to fail. In the early postwar years, it was the Europeans that were attempting to lure the United States into collective action. By the 1970s and 1980s, the roles were reversed: The United States sought to persuade reluctant European states to participate in cooperative energy and security programs. Regardless of the positions of the actors, however, it was clear by the late 1950s that the formulation and implementation of security policy toward Southwest Asia was to be a divisive issue within the Western alliance.

The tangible implications of these strategic dilemmas were moderated, however, by the absence of imminent external or internal threats to the West's position in the Middle East. During the 1950s and 1960s, the Western powers maintained political dominance in the region vis-à-vis the Soviet Union. Concern about a direct Soviet move into Southwest Asia remained low. The Soviets gradually enlisted regional allies, but did not appear able either to replace the Western powers as the principal external actor in the region or to undermine their points of strategic access. Furthermore, it was not until the late 1960s that the Arab–Israeli conflict became explicitly linked to the escalating Cold War in Southwest Asia.

The intraregional situation was somewhat more ambiguous. On the one hand, the British maintained a presence in the Gulf until the early 1970s and succeeded in securing a relatively quiescent political order on the Arabian peninsula. Most of the oil production in the region was handled by Western-owned companies, a situation which suggested few obstacles to securing adequate supplies at low prices. And apart from the Suez incident and repeated terrorist raids and counterattacks, Arab–Israeli tensions did not escalate to the level of full-scale military conflict until 1967.

On the other hand, there were clear signs that anti-Western sentiment was spreading geographically and growing in intensity. Anti-Western regimes emerged in Egypt, Syria, Iraq, South Yemen, and Libya. States in the Gulf resented the continuing foreign presence in the region. Oil-producing states objected to the loss of national revenue resulting from profit-sharing agreements with foreign oil companies. These political currents became apparent through attacks on British positions in the Gulf and through successive attempts by Arab states to nationalize the oil companies operating on their territories. The political objectives of regional powers were becoming increasingly incompatible with the political and strategic objectives of the West.

As a result of the 1967 War, the British withdrawal from the Gulf, and the 1973 October War, these growing indications of the structural challenges facing the West's position in the Middle East came to a head. The 1967 War widened the radical/moderate split within the Arab world, a development which the Soviets recognized as an opportunity for enhancing their leverage in the region. The Soviet decision to support the PLO and break diplomatic relations with Israel was a final step transforming the Arab–Israeli conflict into an explicitly East–West confrontation. The British withdrawal from the Gulf in the early 1970s threatened to throw the region into political chaos. There was also concern that the British departure would invite renewed Soviet attempts to build its regional influence. Finally, the Arab states emerged from the 1973 War with a new degree of economic and political power. Not only did the vulnerability of the Western economy become manifest, but U.S. relations with the Arab world were now on a new and more tenuous footing.

Despite Washington's traditional preoccupation with global concerns, the United States reacted to these developments with uncharacteristic and admirable sensitivity to intraregional considerations. Wary of the dangers of establishing a new foreign presence and constrained by the political impact of its involvement in Vietnam, the United States responded to the British withdrawal by appointing and enabling Iran to assume responsibility for security arrangements in the Gulf. Washington countered the new political power of oil producing states by constructing a network of interdependent relationships—based on strategic and economic cooperation—with pro-Western regimes in the region. Successive administrations also adopted a more active approach to the Arab–Israeli peace process. The goals were to restrict the opportunity for Soviet entry provided by divisions in the Arab world, to enhance U.S. leverage with Arab states, and to bring peace to the region. The stability of oil prices during the mid-1970s, the steady progress in Arab–Israeli peace negotiations, and the decline of Soviet influence in the Middle East were reflective of the success of this adroit diplomatic approach.

The success of U.S. policy, however, also depended upon the accuracy of key political assumptions and the stability of certain political conditions. In the sense that these assumptions were susceptible to obsolescence and these conditions open to radical change, the 1970s were a decade of illusion about the relative invulnerability of U.S. interests in Southwest Asia. The United States became well aware of the strategic and political problems involved in securing access to Persian Gulf oil. Yet, a specific set of rare but convenient circumstances served to obscure or, at least to temper, inherent problems in America's strategic position in the Middle East.

First, détente confirmed the belief, prevalent throughout the 1950s and 1960s, that the Soviets presented no direct military threat to Southwest Asia. The political setbacks the Soviet Union suffered in association with the 1973 War suggested that its indirect political threat to the region was waning as well. In short, containment seemed to be working well and certainly required no new outlay of military resources. Second, the Shah was willing to assume responsibility for essentially all conceivable intraregional military missions. This absolved the United States of the need to develop its own military capability in the region. The core elements of American security policy toward Southwest Asia— U.S. deployments, force structure, force readiness, and contingency planning— were predicated upon the stability of the Shah's regime and the overwhelming regional superiority of his military. Finally, the formation of a strong moderate consensus around Iran, Saudi Arabia, and Egypt nurtured a political atmosphere within the Middle East conducive to American interests. Within this conservative climate, the Saudis were willing to take a bold and overtly pro-American stance both within OPEC and within the Arab world. The political climate also contributed to progress in the Arab–Israeli peace process. From a global and a regional perspective, the view from Washington was a very favorable one.

The events of 1979 revealed that the sources of America's favorable perception of its strategic position in Southwest Asia were indeed circumstantial and ephemeral. Within a period of twelve months, the key global and regional assumptions upon which U.S. policy was based had eroded. The Soviet invasion of Afghanistan heightened fears of direct and indirect Soviet advances into Southwest Asia. Iran, the power the United States had designated and enabled to defend U.S. interests in the Gulf, was no longer willing to fulfill this role. In terms of intraregional politics, the Tehran–Riyadh–Cairo alignment behind the pro-American consensus had crumbled. Iran was brandishing a new form of radicalism, Egypt had been expelled from the Arab League, and Saudi Arabia was foundering, caught between moving closer to the United States and seeking the political security of alignment with Syria and Iraq. These events exposed and exacerbated the three strategic dilemmas that the United States faced in the Gulf, dilemmas that had been held in abeyance by a combination of diplomatic skill and pure luck.

Strategy versus Capability

Events in Iran and Afghanistan illustrated glaring limitations on the efficacy of military force as a policy instrument and illuminated the severe constraints on U.S. capability in the region. United States military power—and the threat to employ it—proved to be of little use in either crisis. The Carter administration reasoned that the use of force would only exacerbate problems in Iran. The failure of the hostage rescue mission only enhanced the sense of impotence in the United States. A military response to the Soviet invasion was also unfeasible. It made little sense to risk a confrontation with the Soviet Union over the status of Afghanistan.

The most difficult problem was not how to use military force in an immediate sense, however, but how to respond to the long term implications of the changing strategic environment in Southwest Asia. The fall of the Shah meant the absence of a dominating regional power whose political and strategic objectives coincided with those of the United States. America undertook steps to bolster its own regional military capability—to assume responsibility for responding to intraregional conflicts in the Gulf. This process was interrupted by the Soviet move into Afghanistan. And although the invasion changed the objective strategic situation only marginally, American perceptions of the Soviet threat to the Gulf changed radically. The United States assumed a new and much more demanding military mission: responding to a Soviet invasion of Iran.

By 1980, containment no longer meant arming regional surrogates to prevent the spread of Soviet influence. Whether or not the Kremlin was actually considering a move toward the Gulf was irrelevant; the United States perceived its strategic vulnerability in the region and decided that developing the capability to deter and to resist a Soviet thrust was essential to the implementation of containment in Southwest Asia. For the first time in the postwar era, the United States was contemplating the possibility of fighting a land war against the Soviets in the Gulf area. This mission required far more military capability than planners ever envisaged sending to the Middle East.

The prospect of erecting a credible deterrent in Southwest Asia was daunting. In 1979 the United States was wholly unprepared to undertake a major military operation in the Middle East. Sufficient forces, lift, and regional infrastructure were lacking. There was not even an office in Washington responsible for carrying out thorough contingency planning for operations in the Gulf area. The nearest reservoir of U.S. military power was in the Pacific, thousands of miles from the Gulf. Aircraft carriers, America's principal means of projecting power in the periphery, would have been of little use in Iran unless operating in conjunction with ground combat forces. Marine units, traditionally responsible for ground missions in distant regions, were hardly sufficiently equipped or numerous enough to confront armored Soviet columns.

Difficult choices and a certain amount of strategic finesse succeeded in minimizing, if not overcoming, these obstacles. An unwieldy and bureaucratically competitive planning process driven by persistent civilian intervention produced arrangements for the RDF that clearly reflected innovation within the military establishment. The composition of the RDF and its operational strategy made good use of whatever forces were available for a contingency in Southwest Asia. The force was designed to take advantage of the terrain and the mobility of light troops—the only units that could be transported quickly to the Gulf. The United States succeeded in erecting a force that could significantly hamper, if not halt, a Soviet move into Iran. In combination with the options of nuclear and horizontal escalation—and the uncertainty surrounding these options—the RDF's capability did provide a strong and credible U.S. deterrent in Southwest Asia.

Unresolved questions do, however, remain. A debate on the optimum size of the RDF continues, driven by differing opinions about both the requirements of conventional deterrence and how to evaluate the effectiveness of the RDF against Soviet forces were it to be deployed in Iran. Given the low credibility of an American nuclear response to Soviet aggression in Southwest Asia, what level of conventional capability is sufficient to deter the Soviets? Is it enough to hamper significantly the Soviet advance or should the United States seek to devise a strategy for denying the Soviets access to the oil fields?

Assuming that the conventional defense of Iran is feasible—as this study argues in Chapter 5—the current size of the RDF (over six divisions) provides as much deterrent power as a larger force and presents as strong and credible a deterrent as the United States needs or is capable of buying. Simple comparisons of the number of the divisions that each side could send into Iran are meaningless. Once the differences between American and Soviet divisions and the advantages that accrue to the defender are taken into account, claims of massive Soviet superiority appear unfounded.

A five- to six-division RDF offers substantive deterrence at several levels. It would be able to interdict Soviet columns in the northern mountains, raising the stakes and costs for the Soviets and buying time for heavy U.S. divisions to arrive in Khuzestan. The American line of defense in the south would be capable of severely injuring if not defeating Soviet forces entering Khuzestan from the few available roads in the Zagros Mountains. While this force would by no means ensure that the United States could stop the Soviets, it would deny the Soviets the option of blitzkrieg and erode their confidence about achieving a quick and easy victory, if victory at all. This strategy thus meets the core requirement of conventional deterrence. A Soviet invasion would clearly be a costly and risky undertaking; the Soviets could by no means be confident of being able to achieve their objectives. A third level of deterrence would rest upon U.S. nuclear and horizontal escalation, however unattractive these options appear to be. A larger RDF adds little, if any, deterrent capability at any of these three levels. In fact, given that a seven- or eight-division force would require more manpower and lift than the United States would be willing or able to commit to Southwest Asia, a larger force structure would actually undermine the credibility of America's deterrent posture. Nevertheless, confusion over the requirements of deterrence and over how to measure the objective limits of U.S. military power in the Gulf continues to fuel the debate over the RDF's strategy and force structure.

Erecting a credible deterrent in Southwest Asia has not been achieved without a reassessment of America's regional strategic priorities and a recognition of the fact that America's strength in Europe and East Asia could well suffer from a U.S. deployment to the Middle East. Within the context of this acknowledgment of strategic overextension, the United States has found a temporary balance between its military strategy and its capability in Southwest Asia. Were simultaneous conflicts to breakout on different fronts, however, this state of overextension would no doubt lead to difficult sacrifices of at least some of America's global commitments.

Globalism versus Regionalism

While the tension between strategy and capability, within the context of these qualifications, has been at least temporarily resolved, the gap between military strategy and regional politics has not. And it is this strategic dilemma that has posed the most urgent and most serious problem for American policy toward Southwest Asia since 1979. It is now possible to define more accurately the nature of this problem and to address three key questions. First, how has this tension between globalism and regionalism manifested itself? Second, what were its sources? Third, is it possible to correct or to compensate for the disjuncture between military strategy and political reality within U.S. policy?

From the outset, the Carter Doctrine was based upon illusory political assumptions. In the wake of the fall of the Shah and the Soviet invasion of Afghanistan, the United States sought an independent military capability that would reduce America's dependence on regional surrogates. Reliance on Iran had worked well for over a decade. Yet, the revolution illustrated that even the regime assumed to be the most stable in the region was susceptible to unpredictable and radical change. The United States was left in a position of glaring strategic vulnerability. The RDF was to enable the United States to take matters into American hands and to assume responsibility for defending its own vital interests.

These goals faced several obstacles at the regional level. To begin, the RDF by no means provided the United States with the independent military capability that it had been seeking. The cooperation of regional states remained essential to the deployment of U.S. troops and the conduct of American operations in Southwest Asia. To implement its strategy, the United States needed to undertake extensive preparations; it attempted to secure forward bases, to forge a "strategic consensus," to preposition materiel, and to enlarge facilities in the theater. While these activities were crucial to the operation of the RDF in a military sense, they impaired its capabilities in a political sense. The political ramifications of America's strategic entry into Southwest Asia made it increasingly difficult for regional states to risk military cooperation with the United States. Yet, such cooperation was in itself crucial to securing strategic entry. The United States developed the RDF because it was a global power. Yet, the feasibility of implementing the RDF's military strategy was jeopardized by a wide range of factors linked to America's global status: the political liabilities associated with America's strategic posture; America's role in the Arab–Israeli conflict; the reluctance of regional states to appear allied with or dependent upon Western "imperial" power; and the hesitancy of local actors to become more deeply involved in the escalating superpower rivalry in Southwest Asia.

The RDF's military strategy reflected a global orientation in a second important sense. America's new security framework for Southwest Asia centered on responding to a Soviet move toward the Gulf. Assumptions about contingency planning, force structure, and operations were based upon the scenario of a U.S.–Soviet confrontation. There was, however, a wide range of potential military contingencies in the Gulf that could have threatened either the stability of pro-Western regimes or the flow of oil itself. A spillover of the Iran–Iraq war, an Iranian attempt to close the Straits of Hormuz, or a coup in Saudi Arabia are cases in point. It was far more likely that the RDF would be deployed to respond to one of these smaller scenarios than to confront the Soviets in Iran. An RDF designed to respond to a Soviet thrust might indeed have sufficient assets to deal with these scenarios. Yet, a smaller contingency is by no means an easier one to win. Insufficient attention was devoted to how to use these assets in lower levels of conflict. There were few units in the RDF trained to deal with unconventional warfare and planning for such contingencies was inadequate. As U.S. involvement in conflicts in Vietnam, the Middle East, and Grenada and the more recent Iraqi attack on the USS *Stark* in the Gulf itself have shown, the American military has not been particularly effective in dealing with lower levels of conflict and unconventional threats. Granted, GCC forces may be able to cope with some such contingencies without U.S. assistance. But, as recent events in the Middle East have exhibited, U.S. troops deployed in the region would likely face an enemy well versed in terrorist and guerilla tactics.

Washington's global orientation also produced a disjuncture between U.S. security policy and the broader political context shaping America's position in the Gulf. The United States consistently exhibited what could be called "perceptual imperialism." It tended to project its perspectives onto local actors and assumed a close correspondence between American and regional perceptions of the strategic situation in Southwest Asia. The rising Soviet threat was to bring the security concerns of the United States and the Arab Gulf into closer alignment. According to American logic, this situation was to increase the dependence of regional powers on U.S. security assistance. Strategic cooperation was not only to enhance the military capabilites of the United States, it was also to serve as the basis for a broader political dialogue. In return for security assistance, the United States expected the Saudis to play a favorable role in the Arab–Israeli conflict and to preserve stability in OPEC production and pricing policy. Washington was by no means oblivious to the fact that close ties to the United States came not without political liabilities. Yet, the key assumption was that the immediate concern for national security would offset the more ambiguous threat posed by political alienation in the Arab world.

These calculations were unfounded for several reasons. Neither the Saudis nor other states in the Gulf shared America's preoccupation with the Soviets. Of far more immediate concern were the Gulf War, potential Iranian attacks on neighboring territory, and attempts to disrupt tanker traffic. To cope with these threats, GCC states indeed wanted to enhance their air defense capabilities and worked toward establishing a rudimentary regional defense system based on American equipment. But, while the United States saw a long term correspondence of interest behind each major arms transfer, the Saudis saw an opportunity to improve their strategic position in the Gulf. The recipients of U.S. weaponry felt neither compelled nor politically able to fulfill America's quid pro quo— broader strategic and political cooperation. The Saudis were well aware that the United States, given its declared military goals in the region, urgently needed strategic access and was willing to sell arms to achieve it. In this sense, the Saudis had a comparative advantage in their relationship with the United States, not vice versa. Riyadh could obtain the weaponry it wanted, yet still keep American forces at a safe distance. As a result, the United States was able neither to cultivate the strategic consensus nor to maintain the political leverage that it expected. While the United States played a key role in shaping the strategic situation in the Gulf, its role in shaping political currents in the Arab world was far less central. The U.S.–Saudi strategic relationship, while at the core of America's perception of the Gulf, was only one component of the view from Riyadh.

As a result of these differing perceptions, Washington was frequently baffled by the behavior of the Saudis and insensitive to the intraregional pressures that they faced. Since 1979, the United States has been pressing the Saudis for cooperation at a time when the political environment in the Gulf has hardly been conducive to closer ties with Washington. America's illusory expectations led to frustrations on both sides and, by the end of 1982, to a serious deterioration in the U.S.–Saudi "special relationship" which has not yet been repaired.

The Reagan administration's more recent efforts to sell arms to Iran consti- tutes yet another manifestation of the misguided logic that has informed—or mis- informed—U.S. regional security policy. The arms deal had little, if any, chance of achieving either of the objectives that the administration seems to have been pursuing: effecting the release of American hostages in Lebanon or improving relations with the Khomeni regime. Furthermore, even if the transfer had led both to the release of the hostages and to the moderation of Iran's anti-Ameri- can rhetoric, it is difficult to envisage the long term rationale that lay behind the policy initiative. Occasional infusions of arms to Iran will hardly prevent the taking of U.S. hostages or assuage the deep-rooted anti-Western sentiment that emerged with the Iranian revolution. Once again, U.S. decision-makers misread the political environment in Iran and placed far too much confidence in the leverage that can be derived from the sale of military hardware.

The divergence between American perspectives and regional realities was also reflected in the strong military bias of America's overall approach to the Gulf. After 1979, the United States relied heavily on initiatives in the military realm as its key source of leverage in Southwest Asia. This is not to suggest that American policy was militaristic. On the contrary, the United States, even after the declaration of the Carter Doctrine, has exhibited great caution in using military force in the Middle East. But Washington has relied almost exclusively on initiatives in the security realm as its principal lever in the Persian Gulf. American dependence on arms sales and other security arrangements has esca- lated steadily since the 1960s. This preoccupation with strategic considerations naturally led to a neglect of other political and economic sources of influence. This was no more evident than in America's relationship with Iran; after a decade of basing its close relations with the Shah on arms sales, Washington was virtually paralyzed when forced to confront the political upheaval associated with the revolution. Furthermore, the influence secured by arms sales was, in most cases, only temporary. Weapons transfers usually represented an alliance of convenience, not a long term correspondence of interests or objectives.

Perhaps American political culture favors the use of force over the use of persuasion in dealing with cultures alien to its own. Perhaps this bias was a reflection of the belief that it is more difficult to address the ideological and social causes of political change than it is to alter the policies of other states by offering hardware. Whatever the cause, America's concentration on military initiatives and considerations produced a security policy that made strategic sense, yet only within the scope of a very narrow and superficial set of political assumptions.

The Sources of Globalism

What were the sources of these misperceptions and America's globalist orientation? To begin, the Cold War has cast U.S. perceptions of the Middle East— and all peripheral regions—into a rigid mold. The extension of American power into the periphery is predicated upon and justified by an image of global U.S.– Soviet competition. In the postwar years, containment has been the central concept shaping America's regional security policies. Shifts in U.S. security policy toward the Middle East have corresponded to changes in the perceived requirements of containment. In the 1940s and 1950s, the Truman and Eisenhower Doctrines were responses to the ideological challenge posed by the Soviets. In the late 1960s and 1970s, the United States engaged in an arms sales race with the Soviet Union to preserve the military superiority of pro-Western states and to counter the Soviet search for regional surrogates. Since 1979, brought about by a shift in U.S. perceptions of the direct Soviet threat to Southwest Asia, the central focus of U.S. policy has been to deter a Soviet move into the Gulf.

The United States has cast its conception of national security—and based its doctrine, force structure, and contingency planning—around the notion of containment. The applicability of containment to the periphery, however, assumes two preconditions. First, the United States must be confronting either Soviet forces or Soviet ideology. Second, the threat to U.S. interests must take the form of a deterrable event—one that can be avoided by the threat to use or the use of military force.

The problem is that many situations in the periphery do not meet these two preconditions; containment alone has served as an inadequate doctrinal basis upon which to construct an effective and comprehensive regional strategy. There are numerous threats to U.S. interests in the Gulf which are unrelated to

220 THE PERSIAN GULF AND THE WEST

Soviet military power or ideology. Similarly, the spread of Arab nationalism, Islamic fundamentalism, or civil rebellion cannot be deterred by the threat of U.S. intervention. Given the nature of the Cold War, the United States must indeed confront the direct military threat and the indirect political threat that the Soviets pose to U.S. interests in the Persian Gulf. Yet, reliance on containment has narrowed the scope of America's vision; regional considerations have been subsumed within concern about the Kremlin's intentions. This has led to the formulation of security policy that rests on unreliable, if not unsound, political foundations.

The primacy of containment in American thinking about regional security lies at the root of the global bias within U.S. policy. This bias has been shaped by both cognitive and bureaucratic factors. First, the global orientation of U.S. policy has been driven by the cognitive biases of decision-makers. Compare, for example, the American response to the revolution in Iran with the U.S. reaction to the Soviet invasion of Afghanistan. Washington reacted sluggishly and reluctantly to events in Iran. The first high-level review of U.S. Iranian policy took place almost ten months after the beginning of civil disturbances. Even after the Shah's departure, planning to respond to developments in Iran moved with excruciating slowness. In contrast, the invasion of Afghanistan, an event of less immediate strategic significance, galvanized the top echelon of decision-makers into action. The administration sought to impose sanctions in coordination with the West Europeans; the Carter Doctrine was introduced; preparations for the RDF proceeded with quickened pace. Washington showed much greater sensitivity and eagerness to respond to the Soviet move than it did to a regional development that potentially had far greater long term implications.

Part of the reason for this sluggish reaction to the revolution was the high degree of confusion in Washington over how best to respond to events in Iran. The White House favored firm support for the Shah. The State Department urged that Iran move toward coalition government. And throughout Washington, there was a great deal of uncertainty about the nature of the political instability in Iran and how best to cope with it. As Henry Kissinger suggested in his memoirs, the United States lacked a coherent approach for dealing with political change in the Third World:

> Assuming we had understood the peril [of revolution in Iran], what should the United States have advised? Do we possess a political theory for the transformation of developing countries? Do we know where to strike the balance between authority and freedom, between liberty and anarchy in feudal societies? . . . The fact is that we lack a coherent idea of how to channel the elemental forces let loose by the process of development.[1]

Personal descriptions of the crisis reveal a pervasive sense of confusion in Washington. Brzezinski viewed the revolution as presenting an "acute moral and

1. Kissinger, *Years of Upheaval*, 672–673.

political dilemma" for the United States and, despite his confidence in the Shah, Brzezinski perceived "a strange sense of ambiguity about him."[2] Secretary of State Vance commented that "we are operating with too limited an understanding of Iranian political realities."[3] Late in 1978 he sent a telegram to his ambassador in Tehran, William Sullivan, stressing that "it is essential repeat essential to terminate the continued uncertainty."[4] Ambassador Sullivan captured the atmosphere of confusion and frustration in Washington with the title of his study of what Iran after the Shah might look like: "Thinking the Unthinkable."[5]

As a result of this uncertainty, officials simply avoided dealing with the crisis. Brzezinski admitted that "until the crisis became very grave, the attention of top decision makers, myself included, was riveted on other issues. . . ."[6] Gary Sick, Iran specialist in the NSC, while recognizing that this delay was in part a product of the administration's preoccupation with SALT II and Camp David, concisely summarized the implications of pervasive uncertainty for the decision process:

> At least equally important for the relative lack of attention paid to Iran during this critical period was the underlying realization that there were no attractive options available to Washington. Civil rebellion poses painful dilemmas . . . . [S]ince there were very few realistic policy options available, and since any substantial change in policy involved actions that were certain to be politically distasteful or worse, people were inclined to keep their thoughts to themselves. The combined effect was to stifle communication, to breed suspicion and to encourage procrastination in the hope that the situation would resolve itself somehow.[7]

As many studies of decision-making have shown, individuals facing difficult decisions and uncertainty pay selective attention to the external environment, distort incoming information, and fail to consider fully available options.[8] Rather than seeking initiatives crafted for the crisis at hand, decision-makers minimize uncertainty by altering their perceptions of the crisis until it appears to be more manageable within the context of a fixed repertoire of options and

2. Brzezinksi, *Power and Principle*, 371, 361.

3. Cyrus Vance, *Hard Choices: Critical Years in America's Foreign Policy* (New York: Simon and Schuster, 1983), p. 328.

4. Brzezinski, *Power and Principle*, 375.

5. Ibid., 367.

6. Ibid., 358.

7. Sick, *All Fall Down*, pp. 66–67.

8. For discussion of the cognitive processes that accompany stress and the psychological mechanisms that lie at the root of this aversion to uncertainty see Steinbruner, *The Cybernetic Theory of Decision*, pp. 47–139; Robert Jervis, *Perception and Misperception in International Politics* (Princeton, NJ: Princeton University Press, 1976), 117–203; and Irving Janis and Leon Mann, *Decision Making* (New York: Free Press, 1977), 45–80.

beliefs. These cognitive tendencies cause people, whether under stress or not, "to fit incoming information into pre-existing beliefs and to perceive what they expect to be there."[9]

If the gap between American perceptions and political reality was the product of these cognitive tendencies, what type of behavior would U.S. officials likely have exhibited? Given that the Carter administration faced a high degree of uncertainty and frustration, what policy repertoire and pre-existing beliefs would American decision-makers turn to under these circumstances? As discussed above, thinking about regional security has been dominated by the notion of containment. American officials therefore tend to define security in terms of containing the Soviet Union and deterring Soviet or Soviet-sponsored aggression.

This conception of security was clearly reflected in the timing and substance of the U.S. reaction to the crises in Southwest Asia. American officials initially reacted reluctantly and with little coherence to the Iranian revolution. When forced to formulate a substantive response, they focused on the Soviet threat. Their reaction to the Soviet invasion of Afghanistan stands in stark contrast. Washington responded with alacrity because it was precisely this type of contingency that the national security apparatus has been calibrated to meet. Though more difficult to respond to in purely military terms, the prospect of a U.S.–Soviet confrontation was a definable and familiar threat, one that fit neatly into the policy repertoire that has emerged to implement containment. For the individuals and organizations involved in the decision-making process, focus on the Soviet threat reduced uncertainty and relieved the frustration that had mounted over Washington's inability either to understand or to cope effectively with the Iranian revolution. Furthermore, by late 1979, the administration was under growing domestic pressure to demonstrate American resolve. President Carter realized that "[t]he public was . . . becoming more restive with each passing week because of our seeming impotence in dealing with international crises."[10] The need for a definitive policy response fueled the need to concentrate on the Soviet threat.[11]

    9. Jervis, *Perception and Misperception*, 143.
    10. Carter, *Memoirs*, 489.
    11. Decision-makers were subject to both unmotivated and motivated biases. In the former case, an individual perceives what he expects to perceive because of his belief system. In the latter, an individual perceives what he wants or needs to see because of cognitive failure associated with decisional stress. In the case at hand, the primacy of containment in American thinking about regional security led decision-makers to view events within an East–West framework. The political chaos in Southwest Asia and the frustration and fear it produced in Washington led to complementary cognitive failures that caused officials to pay selective attention to incoming information and to focus on the Soviet threat. Both biases led to the same types of misperception. For further discussion of this distinction see Richard Ned Lebow, *Between Peace and War—The Nature of International Crisis* (Baltimore, MD: Johns Hopkins University Press, 1981), 101–119.

Officials in the Carter administration, stymied and frustrated by radical political change in Iran, altered their perceptions of the crisis in Southwest Asia and viewed events in terms that were more familiar and with which they felt better able to cope. This cognitive bias helps to explain why decision-makers in 1979 initially perceived accurately the gravity of developments in Iran on their own terms, but then began to concentrate on the potential for Soviet manipulation or penetration well before the invasion of Afghanistan. A coherent policy response to the events in Southwest Asia crystallized only with increasing concern about the Soviet threat. The Soviet invasion of Afghanistan justifiably heightened U.S. concern about the Kremlin's intentions. But it also meant the further subordination of intraregional concerns to East–West considerations. Brzezinski in his memoirs hinted at the perceptual shift that precipitated the crystallization of policy: "The Soviet invasion of Afghanistan meant that henceforth any action taken by us toward Iran had to be guided, to a much larger extent than heretofore, by its likely consequences for regional containment of Soviet ambitions."[12]

This conceptualization of the problem—one that relates confusion over the nature of radical political change to a cognitive tendency to concentrate on the Soviet threat—is consistent with the exclusive focus of the RDF on a U.S.–Soviet confrontation, and with Washington's illusory assumptions about the dynamics of intraregional politics. American officials simply ignored or paid selective attention to incoming information. This bias is also consistent with the overall military orientation of U.S. policy. The need to understand the crisis within the context of containment suggests why the United States perceived the chaos in the Gulf in terms of deterrable events and insisted on making public commitments to use force in the region when the introduction of U.S. troops would hardly have prevented, and may well have exacerbated, many of the apparent threats to U.S. interests. It is also true that U.S. misperceptions of events in the Middle East and exaggeration of the Soviet threat were most pronounced during the other key period of radical change in the region: 1956–1958.[13] Furthermore, American globalism was least pronounced—and U.S.

12. Brzezinski, *Power and Principle*, 485.

13. There are remarkable parallels between the 1956–1958 and the 1979–1981 cases. As in the latter period, U.S. misperceptions and exaggeration of the Soviet threat seem to have been driven by confusion over the nature of nationalism and radical movements more generally. Despite Eisenhower's preoccupation with the Soviet threat and communism (see chapter 2), his memoirs reveal a significant degree of uncertainty about the causes of political change. General Qassim, who led the coup in Iraq that triggered the Lebanon landing was "something of a mystery figure whose basic purposes were never made plain." Eisenhower remained unconvinced about even Nasser's true colors: "If he was not a Communist, he certainly succeeded in making us very suspicious of him." In fact, though Eisenhower spoke constantly of communist penetration of the Middle East, he seemed to recognize that his assessment was based on belief, not on fact. In justifying the Lebanon invasion, he could not go beyond stating a "deep-seated conviction" that the chaos had been caused by

sensitivity to regional dynamics highest—during the period in which the Arab world experienced relative political stability: the 1970s. American inability to understand and to cope with radical political change and the associated cognitive bias favoring focus on the Soviet threat deepen understanding of the misperceptions that lie at the root of American globalism and the persistent disjuncture between military strategy and political reality.

A second key factor contributed to the global orientation of U.S. policy: organizational structures and bureaucratic dynamics. Preparations for the RDF reveal in detail a global bias within the planning process. Early in 1979, planning to address U.S. strategic vulnerability in the Gulf concentrated on intraregional contingencies. When the White House instructed the Pentagon to commence planning for the RDF, the Joint Chiefs and individual services reacted with little enthusiasm. The military had historically resisted the formation of a regional strike force largely because it would divert resources from the central mission against the Soviets. In part because of this lethargic reaction, the focus of contingency planning for the RDF was switched from intraregional missions to the task of responding to a Soviet invasion. As discussed in Chapter 4, this shift occurred well before the Soviet invasion of Afghanistan and officials confirmed that it was intended at least in part to serve as a means of overcoming bureaucratic inertia. Confronted with a more familiar mission and one that required a sizable expansion of the defense budget, the services no longer avoided involvement in planning for the Gulf but began to compete for participation in the RDF. Service rivalry and the politics of command arrangements also drove planning toward the most demanding scenario. A mission that involved all four services was more likely to receive support throughout the military bureaucracy. It was also necessary to postulate a scenario that would warrant the establishment of a new command structure. An independent authority with primary responsibility for Southwest Asia—first the RDJTF, then CENTCOM—proved essential to provide the organizational momentum needed to bring the concept of the RDF to fruition.

Not all agencies favored or directly contributed to this concentration on the Soviet threat. The State Department was concerned about the potential adverse effects of the RDF on regional politics and was initially opposed to the establishment of the force on these grounds. Paradoxically, however, this opposition to the RDF eventually served to focus bureaucratic attention on global considerations. Organizational squabbling among the State Department, the Defense

---

communists. Eisenhower, *Waging Peace*, 288, 265, 266. The timing of perceptual changes is also similar to that of 1979–1981. The administration reacted to the Suez crisis with restraint and saw little evidence of Soviet manipulation. As in 1979, focus on the Soviet threat grew only as nationalism and anti-American sentiment gained momentum and pressure for a substantive policy response mounted.

Department, and the National Security Council forced those pushing for a new Gulf strategy to seek a lowest common denominator of sorts. While there was wide disagreement both among and within agencies over whether and how to respond to regional instability, there was far more cohesion over the familiar problem of whether and how to cope with Soviet aggression. The new policy had to be packaged to minimize bureaucratic obstacles. In the context of designing a new security policy for the Middle East, a process which involved enlisting the support of the many agencies and offices responsible for the area (not to mention Congress), this meant focusing attention on the Soviet Union.

Interagency rivalry contributed to American globalism in a second important respect. The split between the NSC and the State Department over U.S policy toward the Gulf was reflective of the different interests and perspectives of the individuals making up each organization. Generalists, who are concerned primarily with broader East–West issues, dominate the NSC and the top echelon of decision-making. The State Department, on the other hand, contains many career regional experts concerned mainly with studying and interpreting local dynamics in the Middle East.

In the early stages of the Iran crisis, these differing organizational perspectives stymied the formulation of a coherent policy. As Brzezinski notes, "disagreement within the U.S. government widened as the situation in Iran deteriorated."[14] As the chaos in Iran intensified, however, so pressure for a substantive U.S. response mounted within Washington and the electorate. As a result, the locus of decision-making shifted toward the White House, favoring the opinions of the generalists in the NSC and neglecting those of the career regional specialists in the State Department. Furthermore, it is precisely during these periods of crisis that stress-induced cognitive biases favoring focus on the Soviet threat would be most pronounced among top decision-makers, widening the rift with regional experts. The White House therefore constricted the normal channels of policy formulation as a means of both circumventing State Department opposition to its policies and streamlining the decision process. It is clear that the NSC similarly orchestrated the sale of arms to Iran during the Reagan administration. In both 1979–1980 and 1986–1987, State Department officials complained that the NSC had overstepped its bounds and dominated the decision process. Given that area experts had, for the most part, been excluded from decision-making, it is not puzzling that the policies that emerged lacked sensitivity to regional realities.[15]

14. Brzezinski, *Power and Principle*, 371.
15. Parallels with the 1956–1958 period are again striking. As in 1979–81, there was a significant rift between the top echelon of decision-makers and the career bureaucrats. Eisenhower and Dulles were concerned primarily with the Soviet threat and halting the spread of communism. Regional experts in the Department of State and CIA favored accommodating the rise of Arab nationalism and attempting to develop good relationships with newly emerging regimes. As the

In essence, the global bias within U.S. security policy has been the product of complementary cognitive and bureaucratic components. American inability to respond to political change and preoccupation with containment have skewed U.S. policy toward the Gulf and shaped the Soviet-centric nature of the bureaucracy. The structure and process of decision-making have also shaped American thinking and ensured that regional concerns are often subsumed by global ones and that the system as a whole is calibrated to react to the Soviet threat, not to regional realities.

For these reasons, America's strategic perspectives and those of regional states have been on divergent paths. Especially since 1979, increasing American concern with the Soviet threat—and the political and strategic implications of that concern—has not been compatible with intraregional developments. The United States developed a military strategy for fighting the Soviet Union that relied heavily on the cooperation of Gulf states. The Gulf states, and particularly Saudi Arabia, found it increasingly difficult to risk such cooperation with the United States, though they were attracted by the prospects of enhancing their own defense capabilities. The Saudis indeed faced serious military threats which the United States assisted them in addressing. Yet, they did not share America's perception of the Soviet threat or of the need to wed themselves inextricably to America's military strategy, especially in light of the increasingly radical orientation of the Arab political consensus led first by Iraq and later by Syria.

The United States could indeed have improved upon its sensitivity to these issues and attempted to integrate more fully regional concerns into the formation of its security policy toward Southwest Asia. The RDF could have been oriented more toward intraregional contingencies. U.S. expectations about securing strategic cooperation with regional states could have been more realistic and efforts to obtain regional access more subtle. These measures would not have removed the long term sources of the strategic problem the United States faces in the area, however, simply because America's political—and hence strategic—position in the Middle East is dependent upon a complex set of variables over which Washington has very little control. The tension between globalism and regionalism may be reduced by increased sensitivity to the problem and by ensuring that area specialists are integrally involved in the formulation of policy, yet the requirements of America's broader strategic objective of

---

situation worsened and pressure for some type of response mounted, Eisenhower and Dulles took charge of policy, excluding regional experts from the decision process. One official commented that the State Department staff "felt totally out of touch with the Secretary of State [Dulles], that the communications were erratic or non-existent. Policy discussions were issued as fiats and often without proper consultation." Emmet John Hughes quoted in John Foster Dulles Oral History Project, Princeton University, Archives, 22 April 1965, 24. See also Spiegel, *The Other Arab–Israeli Conflict*, 60–61.

deterring the Soviet Union will continue to conflict with the political objectives of regional states. The United States faces the enduring prospect of having vital interests in an area that is close to the Soviet Union, politically volatile, and inherently ambivalent, if not hostile, to the United States as a global power.

Unilateralism versus Collectivism

While the United States has attempted to address these strategic problems in the Gulf on a unilateral basis, it has also sought the assistance of its NATO allies. Since 1973, the Western allies have made repeated efforts to coordinate their approaches to Middle East security issues. The United States, through its leadership position in the alliance, has attempted to bring European perspectives into closer alignment with its own. The West Europeans have likewise tried to exercise direct influence on U.S. policy through formal consultation and indirect influence through establishing a moderating independent position on key issues. This process, however, has not resulted in converging perspectives. Instead, the United States, under the broader guise of its Middle East policy, has developed a distinct agenda specifically to manage alliance relations. There were essentially two separate components to America's approach to Southwest Asia. One addressed concrete strategic and political issues pertinent to Gulf security. The other focused on steps that could be taken within the alliance to complement America's unilateral initiatives: sharing oil stockpiles, preparing for a diversion of U.S. troops from Europe, and arranging overflight rights for U.S. materiel en route to Southwest Asia. These were all issues somewhat peripheral to the central questions of Persian Gulf security.

The effective division of U.S. security policy toward the Persian Gulf into two distinct agenda was reflected in the outcome of the out-of-area debate itself. Within the narrow context of alliance management, NATO members succeeded in solving the problem at hand. There was clear international cooperation; intensive negotiation moved member states from their initial bargaining positions and produced a general agreement of intent at the Bonn Summit in 1982. But in a larger context—namely, that of addressing the broader strategic issues at stake—such cooperation looks far less impressive. NATO members indeed reached an agreement, but it was one that essentially pushed aside a politically sensitive issue without producing an adequate solution. The alliance may have temporarily succeeded in preempting further internal divisions, but it left open the more important question of how NATO would respond to a major international conflict in Southwest Asia.

The failure of the alliance to reach a more substantive solution is somewhat puzzling given the common interests at stake and the relatively transparent threats that existed. The fall of the Shah, the Soviet invasion of Afghanistan, and the outbreak of the Gulf War combined to present a threat to Western interests far more immediate than the presence of Soviet troops along the central front. Although in a territorial sense these developments were outside NATO auspices, the alliance provided an existing framework that could facilitate communication and cooperation.

No single reason explains why more fruitful cooperation did not emerge. The previous chapter identified four interrelated problems that hindered progress on the out-of-area issue. First, there were concrete differences among alliance members over how best to respond to the turmoil in Southwest Asia. The perspectives of the allies diverged because of their individual historical ties to the Middle East and because of conflicting opinions as to whether military or political initiatives would be most effective in countering the perceived threats. Second, the politicization of the debate stimulated competition between the United States and the West Europeans over issues that were actually peripheral to considerations of Gulf security. Third, the structure of the NATO bureaucracy itself presented an obstacle to attempts to include the Persian Gulf within the purview of alliance planning. Divisions between the Defense Planning Committee and the North Atlantic Council, the length of the planning cycle, and the unique nature of communique politics limited the ability of the alliance to formulate a coherent out-of-area policy. Fourth, and most importantly, economic and demographic trends in Europe severely restricted the extent to which the Europeans could devote resources either to participate in regional missions or to compensate for the diversion of U.S. troops from Europe.

The absence of a more substantive solution also raises the broader question of just how much correspondence there was between U.S. and European motivations for a collective response. The United States and the West Europeans clearly had shared interests in the Persian Gulf. Furthermore, they recognized the need for and the logic of a cooperative approach toward the region. And it was this recognition that led to repeated attempts to coordinate their policies toward the Middle East. The problem was that each had a differing conception of the benefits to be derived from a collective stance. The United States wanted the autonomy of unilateral action, but also sought the legitimacy and military convenience (compensation, strategic access) associated with alliance-wide cooperation. The Europeans desired the global influence and added capability of a collective stance, yet, within the context of an alliance dominated by the United States, were unwilling to sacrifice the political legitimacy and sovereignty associated with a unilateral (or a European) approach.

Both parties sought the benefits of collectivism. But their specific interests in cooperating intersected in only a very limited way. As a consequence, successive attempts at coordination produced little in the way of substantive results. The pursuit of common interests in the Middle East was submerged within a more narrow vision of separate national interest that emerged in the context of competitive alliance politics. It was this tension between the expectation of coopera-tion and the reality of political limitation that led to oscillation between uni-lateral and collective approaches to Gulf security within the Western alliance.

Implications for Policy

The implications of this study for U.S. policy toward Southwest Asia are indeed quite sobering. The United States faces enduring strategic problems in the Persian Gulf which, given the limitations on American military capability and the dependence of the Western economy on Gulf oil, do not lend themselves to short term solutions. The Soviets will continue to pose a military threat to the region, leaving the United States with the task of maintaining the conventional deterrent already acquired and improving its ability to transport forces to South-west Asia. At the same time, the United States must address the question of maintaining access to Gulf oil, in terms of both managing its relations with Gulf states and protecting oil fields and tankers from potential attack.

Several steps can be taken, however, to improve America's strategic position in Southwest Asia. As argued above, the most serious weaknesses in U.S. policy have resulted from the tension between globalism and regionalism, the gap between the assumptions upon which military strategy is based and the political realities of the Gulf. Decision-makers in the United States must recognize that the problem is a perceptual and cognitive one, deeply rooted in America's approach to regional security in the postwar era. Containment alone is insuffi-cient to guide policy; it must be complemented by a notion of regional security that is more sensitive to local political change and to events that cannot be deterred by the use of U.S. military power. American decision-makers and scholars must address the difficult question of how to cope with radical political change. Dealing with revolutionary states has been one of the most perplexing problems facing the United States since 1945. Beginning with the Truman administration, successive administrations have been frustrated by the political volatility of regimes in the Middle East. Accommodating revolutionary states or simply doing nothing, rather than isolating or threatening them, may well be a more productive strategy in the long term. Distant acceptance of radical regimes may be a viable means of limiting the regional and global implications of revolu-tion in the periphery. Whatever the outcome of inquiry on these issues, greater understanding of and sensitivity to radical change will ameliorate the cognitive roots of American globalism that have plagued U.S. policy in the Middle East.

Given the bureaucratic sources of American globalism, integrating area spe-cialists more fully into the decision-making process—especially during periods of crisis—will also facilitate the formulation of more appropriate regional strat-egies. As argued above, it is during periods of radical political change and the frustration and uncertainty that it causes in Washington that the cognitive and bureaucratic processes stimulating U.S. globalism are most pronounced. But it is also these periods of crisis in which the input of regional experts is most needed. As the recent scandal over the arms sale to Iran demonstrated, the NSC must not be allowed to formulate and implement initiatives outside the purview of the other organizations responsible for foreign policy.

Within the context of the Persian Gulf, the United States should adopt a more cautious and realistic assessment of the regional environment. Washington should expect less overt cooperation and less consistency from the Saudis and other conservative states. Lower expectations will reduce pressure on Riyadh and force the United States to recognize the unreliability and unpredictability of its allies in the region. This, of course, does not mean abandoning the diplomatic dialogue with regional states, but pursuing that dialogue from a more distant and cautious perspective. An overbearing approach not only makes the Saudis fearful of cooperation, it leads them to believe that America's commitment to them is inviolable. A small dose of uncertainty could induce them to consider more carefully the importance of American assistance. Distance and restraint should also guide U.S. involvement in the Iran–Iraq war. The Reagan administration has already paid dearly for its attempts to influence Iranian policy by seeking to improve relations with so-called moderate elements within the political elite. The escort of tankers into the northern Gulf is similarly ill-advised, increasing the likelihood that the United States will become more deeply mired in the Iran–Iraq conflict.

In terms of hardware considerations, the establishment of the RDF has been a very favorable development. The breadth of America's military options in Southwest Asia and in other peripheral areas has been improved considerably. By procuring additional lift assets, the United States is able to use more efficiently existing military resources. And, most importantly, planners have begun the long-neglected task of addressing how and under what circumstances the United States would want to engage its troops in a conflict in the Gulf area. It is important, however, that more attention be paid to responding to non-Soviet contingencies in Southwest Asia. The current size of the RDF (up to six ground troop divisions, ten air wings, and three carrier task forces) is sufficient to fulfill its deterrent role and to respond to intraregional conflicts. But more flexibility in operations and in planning would enhance the RDF's ability to address lesser contingencies. Much thought has been given to how many forces the United States might need in Southwest Asia; more thought needs to be given to how those forces might be used. The Iraqi missile attack on the USS Stark made clear the need for a reassessment of the role and operation of U.S. forces in the Gulf.

In the long term, the United States should seek to ameliorate or, if possible, to eliminate at least one source of the strategic dilemmas that it faces in the Gulf. The obvious step (and one that is within the realm of possibility) is for the

West to reduce its dependence on Persian Gulf oil. Limited progress has already been made in this respect. The United States and the West Europeans have begun to diversify their sources of supply; states outside the Middle East are producing a greater share of world consumption. Diminishing reliance on Gulf oil would not ease the tension between strategy and capability with respect to implementing containment; the United States would still face a Soviet military threat and would still need to obtain regional access to conduct any sizable operation. The gap between military strategy and political reality would, however, be reduced, simply because America's position in that political reality would be simplified and strengthened. The Gulf states could no longer wield the oil weapon as their key source of leverage, thereby improving America's bargaining power in the region. A close economic relationship would continue because of the mutual benefit to both producing and consuming nations. Yet, access to Persian Gulf oil would no longer be a vital interest of the West. This would reduce the number of potential scenarios in which the United States would perceive a need to intervene militarily in the region. It would also mean that if America's deterrent eventually failed to prevent a Soviet move toward the Gulf, the United States would have the option of strategic withdrawal without abandoning access to a resource vital to the strength of the Western economy.

Despite the fact that the United States, because of its military capability, will remain the dominant Western power in the periphery, efforts will continue to share among the NATO allies the burdens of regional security. During the past three years, the turmoil in Southwest Asia has quieted, an oil glut has depressed prices, and fears of a Soviet move into the region have subsided. The failure of direct air attacks on tankers in the Gulf to disrupt supplies has also reduced fears of an impending oil shortage. As a result of these developments, the out-of-area debate has receded from the limelight of alliance politics.

The problem, however, is a looming one. The next crisis stemming from developments in the Gulf—whether a spreading of the Gulf War, an Iranian attempt to close the Straits of Hormuz, or a drastic rise in oil prices—will again focus the attention of NATO members upon security issues in Southwest Asia. The allure of a collective approach will compel the allies to seek a coordinated response. Yet, the same issues that have hindered cooperation since 1973 are likely to reemerge: wide disparities in force projection capability, European fears of U.S. dominance of both NATO and Third World security policies, and differing perceptions of how best to cope with the apparent threats to Western interests.

Several steps can be taken to temper and to circumvent these deep-rooted perceptual differences between American and European approaches to regional security problems. The allies should establish a standing consultative group within NATO to address security issues in peripheral areas. By creating a forum separate from the principal councils and other committees in NATO, officials would be able to address out-of-area problems in a less politically charged atmosphere. It is important that this council be under NATO auspices simply to maintain the credibility of its recommendations.

While the scope and specificity of discussions in a NATO council on out-of-area issues would be limited by political constraints, the committee could be used for the discussion of general developments in the periphery, for individual members to give notice of intended operations, and for setting force levels and reinforcement requirements. Particularly important in this respect are European efforts to increase their reserve levels, thereby assuming more responsibility for their own defense needs and releasing American forces for peripheral missions. It is unrealistic to expect the Europeans to be able to compensate for a potential 20–33% shortfall in U.S. reinforcments. Yet, special attention should be placed on increasing the number of logistical support units, because an American deployment to Southwest Asia would draw heavily on service personnel. Arrangements should also be made for the use of European civilian aircraft to ferry U.S. forces to the continent. While the growth of European amphibious and air transportable forces should not be neglected, more emphasis should be placed on strengthening force levels and munitions stockpiles in Europe.

While general issues should be discussed in this NATO council, concrete strategic cooperation between the allies should occur on a multilateral, not a collective basis. Because it is simply too politically sensitive to coordinate regional security policies in a formal alliance framework, agreements on cooperation should be made among individual states. In more conceptual terms, multilateralism offers a middle road between unilateralism and collectivism. It provides the autonomy and sovereignty associated with a unilateral approach without sacrificing the benefits of cooperation.

The capability and will for extensive coordination indeed exist. The British and French have recently expanded their rapid deployment capabilities and, in their respective engagements in the Falklands and Chad, exhibited their willingness to use force to protect their interests in the periphery. The Germans, Italians, and Dutch have recently sent vessels on "training missions" outside European waters, revealing at least some interest in extending the scope of their military responsibilities. France, Italy, and Spain are in the process of expanding their aircraft carrier programs. In the Pacific, the Japanese have recently indicated that they might expand their security role in East Asia, and the Australians continue to maintain an important naval presence in the South Pacific/Southeast Asia region.

The key point is that among those states that have common interests in the Third World, the potential exists for more cooperation on sharing the burdens associated with regional security. On a multilateral basis, individual members of the alliance should pursue a wide range of measures that include: contingency planning for specific operations; steps to improve the interoperability of projection forces; arrangements for specific states to assume responsibility for sur-veillance and naval patrol in designated regions; agreements on the sharing of intelligence. More coordinated intelligence and surveillance operations would play an important preventive role by improving the ability of the allies to address regional security problems before the outbreak of hostilities. Should one or more parties decide to intervene, these measures would also facilitate cooperation on an operational level.

These steps will enhance the ability of the West to protect its interests in the Third World. Nevertheless, the projection of power in the periphery will remain a difficult task and offer elusive rewards. Whether to protect access to natural resources, to contain the Soviets or Soviet proxies, or to defend political inter-ests, American or European forces fighting in distant regions would face con-siderable obstacles. Transporting large numbers of troops and securing access will always present intractable difficulties. Unless invited by regional powers, it is unlikely that Western forces will receive a warm reception in any area of the periphery. This factor not only could restrict access, but also, given the pro-liferation of precision weapons to many smaller countries, could significantly hamper an attempt by external forces to intervene militarily. Furthermore, it is clear that any large deployment of forces outside the Treaty area will have serious implications for the conventional defense of Europe. This attaches added strategic and political significance to the decision to engage in protracted mili-tary conflict in the Third World.

These factors suggest that NATO's vital interests in Southwest Asia will remain extremely vulnerable until the West is able to eliminate its dependence on Persian Gulf oil. This strategic and economic vulnerability is structural, not circumstantial, in nature. Optimism derived from the current oil glut or the continuing stalemate in the Gulf War is illusory. Only by disengaging its vital interests from Southwest Asia will the West begin to find a lasting solution to the unique strategic dilemmas that it faces in the Persian Gulf.

BIBLIOGRAPHY

Government Documents

I. U.S. Government Documents [published in Washington, DC by the Government Printing Office (GPO), unless otherwise stated]

U.S. Arms Control and Disarmament Agency
    World Military Expenditures and Arms Transfers 1971–1980, ACDA Publication no. 115, Washington, DC, March 1983.
    The International Transfer of Conventional Arms, Washington, DC, September 1973.
U.S. Congress, Congressional Budget Office, *Rapid Deployment Forces: Policy and Budgetary Implications*, 1983.
U.S. Congress, Congressional Research Service
    Western Vulnerability to a Disruption of Persian Gulf Oil Supplies: U.S. Interests and Options, prepared for the House Foreign Affairs Committee, 1983.
    Congress and Foreign Policy—1981, prepared for the House Foreign Affairs Committee, 1982.
    Crisis in the Atlantic Alliance—Origins and Implications, prepared for the Senate Foreign Relations Committee, 1982.
    Executive–Legislative Consultation on U.S. Arms Sales, prepared for the House Foreign Affairs Committee, 1982.
    Changing Perspectives on U.S. Arms Transfer Policy, prepared for the House Foreign Affairs Committee, 1981.
    The Persian Gulf: Are We Committed? At What Cost?, prepared for the Joint Economic Committee, 1981.
    Saudi Arabia and the United States—The New Context in an Evolving "Special Relationship," prepared for the House Foreign Affairs Committee, 1981.
    Soviet Policy and United States Response in the Third World, prepared for the House Foreign Affairs Committee, 1981.
    Nato After Afghanistan, prepared for the Senate Foreign Relations Committee, 1979.
    United States Foreign Policy Objectives and Overseas Military Installations, prepared for the Senate Foreign Relations Committee, 1979.

235

United States Military Installations and Objectives in the Mediterranean, prepared for the House International Relations Committee, 1977.

Oilfields as Military Objectives, A Feasibility Study, prepared for the House International Relations Committee, 1975.

U.S. Congress, House of Representatives

Department of Defense Appropriations for 1985, Hearings before the Appropriations Committee, Pt. 1, 1984.

U.S. Policy Toward the Persian Gulf, Hearings before the Foreign Affairs Committee, 1983.

Department of Defense Appropriations for 1983, Hearings before the Appropriations Committee, Pts. 1 and 6, 1982.

East–West Relations—U.S. Security Assistance, Hearings before the Foreign Affairs Committee, 1982.

North Atlantic Treaty Organization—An Alliance of Shared Values, Report to the Armed Services Committee, 1982.

Department of Defense Appropriations for 1982, Hearings before the Appropriations Committee, Pt. 9, 1981.

Effect of Iraqi-Iranian Conflict on U.S. Energy Policy, Hearings before the Government Operations Committee, 1981.

U.S. Security Interests in the Persian Gulf, Report of a Staff Study Mission to the Persian Gulf, Middle East and Horn of Africa, to the Foreign Affairs Committee, 1981.

East–West Relations in the Aftermath of the Soviet Invasion of Afghanistan, Hearings before the Foreign Affairs Committee, 1980.

U.S. Interests In, and Policies Toward the Persian Gulf, 1980, Hearings before the Foreign Affairs Committee, 1980.

Conventional Arms Transfer Policy, International Relations Committee, 1978.

Proposed Aircraft Sales to Israel, Egypt, and Saudi Arabia, Hearings before the International Relations Committee, 1978.

The Persian Gulf 1975: The Continuing Debate on Arms Sales, Hearings before the International Relations Committee, 1975.

The Persian Gulf 1974: Money, Politics, Arms and Power, Hearings before the Foreign Affairs Committee, 1974.

Proposed Expansion of U.S. Military Facilities in the Indian Ocean, Hearings before the Foreign Affairs Committee, 1974.

New Perspectives on the Persian Gulf, Hearings before the Foreign Affairs Committee, 1973.

U.S.–Europe Relations and the 1973 Middle East War, Hearings before the Foreign Affairs Commitee, 1973.

U.S. Congress, Senate

Department of Defense Authorization for Appropriations for Fiscal Year 1983, Hearings before the Armed Services Committee, Pts. 1 and 6, 1982.

Europe and the Middle East: Strains on Key Elements of America's Vital Interests, Report to the Armed Services Committee, 1982.

Department of Defense Authorization for Appropriations for Fiscal Year 1982, Hearings before the Armed Services Committee, Pt. 1, Posture Statement, 1981.

Arms Sales Package to Saudi Arabia, Hearings before the Foreign Relations Committee, Pts. 1 and 2, 1981.

Military and Technical Implications of the Proposed Sale to Saudi Arabia of Airborne Warning and Control Systems (AWACS) and F-15 Enhancements, Hearings before the Armed Services Committee, 1981.

Department of Defense Authorization for Appropriations for Fiscal Year 1981, Hearings before the Armed Services Committee, Pt. 1, 1980.

U.S. *Security Interests and Policies in Southwest Asia,* Hearings before the Foreign Relations Committee, 1980.

U.S. *Military Sales to Iran,* A Staff Report to the Foreign Relations Committee, 1976.

Multinational Corporations and United States Foreign Policy, Hearings before the Foreign Relations Committee, 1974.

U.S. Defense Security Assistance Agency, *Foreign Military Sales and Military Assistance Facts,* Washington, DC: Data Systems and Reports Division, 1974.

U.S. Department of State, *United States Policy in the Middle East, September 1956–June 1957,* no. 6505, Near and Middle Eastern Series 25, 1957.

II. British Government Documents [published in London by Her Majesty's Stationery Office (HMSO)]

U.K. House of Commons

Statement on the Defence Estimates, Second Report from the Defence Committee, 1981.

Afghanistan: The Soviet Invasion and Its Consequences for British Policy, Fifth Report from the Foreign Affairs Committee, 1980.

Statement on the Defence Estimates, Second Report from the Defence Committee, 1980.

U.K. Ministry of Defence

Statement on the Defence Estimates, 1979–Cmnd. 7474, 1980–Cmnd. 7826–I, 1981–Cmnd. 8212–I, 1982–Cmnd. 8529–I, 1983–Cmnd. 8951.

The Falklands Campaign: The Lessons, Cmnd.–8758, 1982.

The United Kingdom Defence Programme: The Way Forward, Cmnd.–8288, 1981.

III. French Government Documents

French Ministry of Defense, "Information Note a l'Attention des Chefs de Corps," Paris: Service Information de Relations Publiques des Armées, 1983.

IV. Other Documents

The Gulf Committee, *Documents of the National Struggle in Oman and the Arabian Gulf,* 9th June Studies, London, 1974.

John Foster Dulles Oral History Project, Princeton University Archives.

North Atlantic Assembly, Political Committee, "Information Document of the Subcommittee on Out-of-Area Security Challenges to the Alliance," Brussels, 1983.

———, "Interim Report of the Subcommittee on Out-of-Area Challenges to the Alliance," Brussels, 1983 and 1984.

North Atlantic Treaty Organization, North Atlantic Council, *Final Communiques* and *Press Releases,* Brussels, 1950–1983.

———, Defense Planning Committee, *Final Communiques* and *Press Releases,* Brussels, 1950–1983.

Secondary Sources

V. Books and Articles

Allison, Graham, *Essence of Decision—Explaining the Cuban Missile Crisis.* Boston, MA: Little, Brown, 1971.

Allard, Kenneth, "Soviet Airborne Forces and Preemptive Power Projection," in *Parameters* (December 1980).

The American Assembly, *The United States in the Middle East.* Englewood Cliffs, NJ: Prentice Hall, 1964.

The Arab Research Centre, *Oil and Security in the Arab Gulf.* Proceedings of an International Symposium, London, 1980.

Art, Robert, and Waltz, Kenneth, eds., *The Use of Force.* Lanham: MD, University Press of America, 1983.

Ayoob, Mohammed, "The Superpowers and Regional 'Stability': Parallel Responses to the Gulf and the Horn," in *The World Today* (May 1979).

Badger, Daniel, and Belgrave, Robert, "Oil Supply and Price: What Went Right in 1980?", Energy Paper no. 2. London: Policy Studies Institute and the Royal Institute for International Affairs, 1982.

Beling, Willard (ed.), *The Middle East—Quest for an American Policy.* Albany, NY: State University of New York Press, 1973.

Bell, Raymond, "The Rapid Deployment Force, How Much? How Soon?" in *Army* (July 1980).

Ben Zvi, Abraham, "Regionalism and Globalism: The Problems of American Relations Toward the Middle East, 1950–1976," in *International Problems* (Fall 1976).

Betts, Richard, *Surprise Attack: Lessons for Defense Planning.* Washington, DC: Brookings Institution, 1982.

———, *Soldier, Statesmen, and Cold War Crises.* Cambridge, MA: Harvard University Press, 1977.

Black, Stanley, "Learning from Adversity: Policy Responses to Two Oil Shocks," Essays in International Finance, no. 160. Princeton, NJ: Princeton University Department of Economics, Dec. 1985.

Blechman, Barry and Kaplan, Stephen, *Force without War—U.S. Armed Forces as a Political Instrument.* Washington, DC: The Brookings Institution, 1978.

Brodie, Bernard, *Escalation and the Nuclear Option.* Princeton, NJ: Princeton University Press, 1966.

Brown, Harold, "U.S. Security Policy in Southwest Asia: A Case Study in Complexity," Address delivered at the Johns Hopkins Foreign Policy Institute. Washington, DC, April 1981.

Brzezinski, Zbigniew, *Power and Principle—Memoirs of the National Security Advisor, 1977–1981.* London: Weidenfeld and Nicolson, 1983.

Calleo, David, *The Atlantic Fantasy: The U.S., NATO, and Europe,* Studies in International Affairs, no. 13. Baltimore, MD: Johns Hopkins University Press, 1970.

Carter, Jimmy, *Keeping Faith—Memoirs of a President.* New York: Bantam Books, 1982.

Charollais, Francois, and de Ribes, Jean, *Le Défi de l'Outre-Mer—l'Action Extérieure dans la Défense de la France,* Cahier no. 26. Paris: Foundation pour les Etudes de Défense Nationale, 1983.

Chubin, Shahram, *Security in the Persian Gulf 4: The Role of Outside Powers.* Aldershot: Gower Publishing Co. Ltd., for the International Institue for Strategic Studies, 1982.

———, "Soviet Policy Towards Iran and the Gulf," Adelphi Paper no. 157. London: International Institute for Strategic Studies, 1982.

———, "U.S. Policy and Persian Gulf Security for the 1980s," Daedalus (Fall 1980).

Cordesman, Anthony, *The Gulf and the Search for Strategic Stability: Saudi Arabia, the Military Balance in the Gulf, and Trends in the Arab–Israeli Military Balance.* Boulder, CO: Westview Press, 1984.

Cottrell, Alvin, ed., *Sea Power and Strategy in the Indian Ocean.* Beverley Hills, CA: Sage, 1981.

Cottrell, Alvin, ed., *The Persian Gulf States—A General Survey.* Baltimore, MD: Johns Hopkins University Press, 1980.

Cottrell, Alvin, and Moorer, Thomas, *U.S. Overseas Bases: Problems of Projecting American Military Power Abroad,* Georgetown Center for Strategic and International Studies, The Washington Papers, vol. 5, no. 47. Beverly Hills, CA: Sage, 1977.

Critchlow, James, "Minarets and Marx," in *The Washington Quarterly* (Spring 1980).

Darby, Philip, *British Defence Policy East of Suez, 1947–1968*. Oxford: Oxford University Press, 1973.

———, "The West, Military Intervention and the Third World," in *Brassey's Annual—Defence and the Armed Forces*. London: William Clowes and Sons, Ltd., 1971.

David, Stephen, "Realignment in the Horn: The Soviet Advantage," in *International Security* (Fall 1979).

Dawisha, Adeed, and Dawisha, Karen, eds., *The Soviet Union in the Middle East: Policies and Perspectives*. London: Heinemann for the Royal Institute of International Affairs, 1982.

Dawisha, Adeed, "Saudi Arabia's Search for Security," Adelphi Paper no. 158. London: International Institute for Strategic Studies, 1980.

Dawisha, Karen, "The U.S.S.R. in the Middle East: Superpower in Eclipse?" *Foreign Affairs* (Winter 1982–1983).

———, "The Soviet Union and the Middle East: Strategy at the Crossroads?" in *The World Today* (March 1979).

DePorte, A.W., *Europe Between the Superpowers—The Enduring Balance*. New Haven, CT: Yale University Press, 1979.

Deese, David, and Nye, Joseph, eds., *Energy and Security*. Cambridge, MA: Ballinger, 1981.

Delachenal, Pierre, "Aéromobilité et Dissuasion: Quel Avenir pour un Transport Aérien Militaire?" in *Défense Nationale* (November 1982).

Divine, Robert, *Eisenhower and the Cold War*. New York: Oxford University Press, 1981.

Dunn, Keith, "Constraints on the U.S.S.R. in Southwest Asia: A Military Analysis," in *Orbis* (Fall 1981).

The Economist, "Defending the Gulf: A Survey," 6 June 1981.

———, "Rim of Prosperity, the Gulf: A Survey," 13 December 1980.

Eilts, Hermann, "Security Considerations in the Persian Gulf," in *International Security* (Fall 1980).

Eisenhower, Dwight, *Waging Peace*. Garden City, NY: Doubleday and Co., 1963.

Eley, John, "Towards a Theory of Intervention—The Limitations and Advantages of a Transnational Perspective," in *International Studies Quarterly* (Summer 1972).

Emerson, Steven, "The Aramco Connection," in *The New Republic*, 10 May 1982.

———, "The Petrodollar Connection," in *The New Republic*, 17 February 1982.

Epstein, Joshua, *Strategy and Force Planning: The Case of the Persian Gulf*. Washington, DC: Brookings Institution, 1987.

———, "Soviet Vulnerabilities in Iran and the RDF Deterrent," in *International Security* (Fall 1981).

Flanagan, Stephen, and Hampson, Fen, *Securing Europe's Future*. London: Croom Helm, 1986.

Foot, Peter, "Beyond the North Atlantic: The European Contribution," Aberdeen Studies in Defence Economics, no. 21. Aberdeen University, 1982.

———, "Problems of Equity in Alliance Arrangements," Aberdeen Studies in Defence Economics, no. 23. Aberdeen University, 1982.

———, "Improving Capabilities for Extra-European Contingencies: The British Contribution," Aberdeen Studies in Defence Economics, no. 18. Aberdeen University, 1981.

Freedman, Lawrence, ed., *The Troubled Alliance—Atlantic Relations in the 1980s*. London: Heinemann, 1983.

Gaddis, John Lewis, *Strategies of Containment—A Critical Appraisal of Postwar American National Security Policy*. New York: Oxford University Press, 1982.

Ganin, Zvi, *Truman, American Jewry, and Israel 1945–1948*. New York: Holmes and Meier, 1979.

Grosser, Alfred, *The Western Alliance: European-American Relations Since 1945*. London: Macmillan, 1980.

Haas, Richard "Filling the Vacuum: United States Foreign Policy Towards Southwest Asia, 1969–1976." Oxford University D. Phil. thesis, 1982.

Hardin, Russell, *Collective Action*. Baltimore, MD: Johns Hopkins University Press, 1982.

Hartley, A., "American Foreign Policy in the Nixon Era," Adelphi Paper no. 110. London: International Institute for Strategic Studies, 1974.

Hauner, Milan, "Seizing the Third Parallel: Geopolitics and the Soviet Advance into Central Asia," in *Orbis* (Spring 1985).

Heikal, Mohammed, *Sphinx and Commissar—The Rise and Fall of Soviet Influence in the Arab World*. London: Collins, 1978.

Hoagland, Jim, "Sauci Arabia and the United States," in *Survival* (March 1978).

Hoffmann, Stanley, *Contemporary Theory in International Politics*. Englewood Cliffs, NJ: Prentice-Hall, 1971.

Hudson, Michael, *Arab Politics—The Search for Legitimacy*. New Haven, CT: Yale University Press, 1977.

Hunter, Robert, "Safeguarding Western Interests Outside the NATO Area," Ditchley Conference Report no. 11, Ditchley Park, 1983.

Huntington, Samuel, *The Common Defense—Strategic Programs in National Politics*. New York: Columbia University Press, 1961.

Hurewitz, J.C., ed., *Oil, the Arab–Israel Dispute, and the Industrial World—Horizons of Crisis*. Boulder, CO: Westview Press, 1976.

———, ed., *Soviet–American Rivalry in the Middle East*. New York: Praeger, 1969.

International Institute for Strategic Studies, *The Military Balance*. London, annual.

Jabber, Paul, "U.S. Interests and Regional Security in the Middle East," in *Daedalus* (Fall 1980).

Janis, Irving, and Mann, Leon, *Decision Making*. New York: Free Press, 1977.

Jervis, Robert, *Perception and Misperception in International Politics*. Princeton, NJ: Princeton University Press, 1976.

Kaiser, Karl, et al., "Western Security: What Has Changed? What Should Be Done?" New York: Council on Foreign Relations, 1981.

Kennedy, Edward, "The Persian Gulf: Arms Race or Arms Control?" in *Foreign Affairs* (October 1975).

Kennedy School of Government, Case Program, "Shaping the National Military Command Structure: Command Responsibilities for the Persian Gulf," Case no. C95-85-628. Cambridge, MA: Harvard University, 1985.

Keohane, Robert, *After Hegemony—Cooperation and Discord in the World Political Economy*. Princeton, NJ: Princeton University Press, 1984.

Kissinger, Henry, *Years of Upheaval*. London: Weidenfeld and Nicholson and Michael Joseph, 1982.

———, *The Troubled Partnership—A Reappraisal of the Atlantic Alliance*. New York: McGraw-Hill, 1965.

Komer, Robert, "Maritime Strategy vs. Coalition Defense," in *Foreign Affairs* (Summer 1982).

Krasner, Stephen, *Defending the National Interest—Raw Materials Investments and U.S. Foreign Policy*. Princeton, NJ: Princeton University Press, 1978.

Labrousse, Henri, "Une Stratégie de Dissuasion pour le Golfe?" in *Défense Nationale* (April 1982).

———, "Enjeux et Défis dans le Golfe et l'Océan Indien," in *Défense Nationale* (July 1981).

Laffin, John, *The Arab Mind, A Need for Understanding*. London: Cassell, 1975.

Lebow, Richard, *Between Peace and War: The Nature of International Crisis*. Baltimore, MD: Johns Hopkins University Press, 1981.

Lee, David, *Flight from the Middle East—A History of the Royal Air Force in the Arabian Peninsula and Adjacent Territories, 1945–1972*. London: HMSO, 1980.

Legum, Colin, ed., *Crisis and Conflict in the Middle East—The Changing Strategy: From Iran to Afghanistan*. New York: Holmes and Meier, 1981.

Legvold, Robert, "The Superpowers: Conflict in the Third World," in *Foreign Affairs* (Spring 1979).

Lehman, John, and Weiss, Seymour, *Beyond the Salt II Failure*. New York: Praeger, 1981.

Leitenberg, Milton, and Shaffer, Gabriel, eds., *Great Power Intervention in the Middle East*. New York: Pergamon Press, 1979.

Lellouche, Pierre, and Moisi, Dominique, "French Policy in Africa: A Lonely Battle Against Destabilization," in *International Security* (Spring 1979).

Lenczowski, George, "The Arc of Crisis: Its Central Sector," in *Foreign Affairs* (Spring 1979).

Levenfeld, Judy, "Arguments, Appeals and Arm-Twisting: Foreign Policy Lobbying and the 1981 Saudi Arms Sale," unpublished Senior Honors Thesis, Government Department, Harvard University, 1983.

Levy, Walter, "Oil and the Decline of the West," in *Foreign Affairs* (Summer 1980).

Lieber, Robert, "Economics, Energy and Security in Alliance Perspective," in *International Security* (Spring 1980).

Louis, Wm. Roger, *The British Empire in the Middle East 1945–1951, Arab Nationalism, The United States, and Postwar Imperialism*. Oxford: Clarendon Press, 1984.

MccGwire, Michael, and McDonnell, John, eds., *Soviet Naval Influence—Domestic and Foreign Dimensions*. New York: Praeger, 1977.

MccGwire, Michael, ed., *Soviet Naval Policy—Objectives and Constraints*. New York: Praeger, 1975.

McNaugher, Thomas, *Arms and Oil, U.S. Military Strategy and the Persian Gulf*. Washington, DC: Brookings Institution, 1985.

Mangold, Peter, "Shaba I and Shaba II," in *Survival* (May/June 1979).

———, *Superpower Intervention in the Middle East*. London: Croom Helm, 1978.

Mansur, Abdul, "The American Threat to Saudi Arabia," in *Armed Forces Journal* (September 1980).

Marr, Phebe, *The Modern History of Iraq*. Boulder, CO: Westview Press, 1985.

Mearsheimer, John, *Conventional Deterrence*. Ithaca, NY: Cornell University Press, 1983.

Meyer, Gail, *Egypt and the United States*. Rutherford, PA: Fairleigh Dickinson University Press, 1980.

Mortimer, Edward, *Faith and Power—The Politics of Islam*. New York: Vintage Books, 1982.

Myers, Kenneth, ed., *NATO—The Next Thirty Years: The Changing Political, Economic and Military Setting*. London: Croom Helm, 1983.

Nakhleh, Emile, "The Palestine Conflict and U.S. Strategic Interests in the Persian Gulf," in *Parameters* (March 1981).

Neustadt, Richard, *Alliance Politics*. New York: Columbia University Press, 1970.

Newsom, David, "America Engulfed," in *Foreign Policy* (Summer 1981).

Novik, Nimrod, "Weapons to Riyadh, U.S. Policy and Regional Security." Tel Aviv: Tel Aviv Center for Strategic Studies, 1981.

Noyes, James, *The Clouded Lens—Persian Gulf Security and U.S. Policy*, Hoover Institution Publication no. 206. Stanford, CA: Hoover Institution Press, 1979.

Olson, Mancur, *The Logic of Collective Action*. Cambridge, MA: Harvard University Press, 1965.

Perlmutter, Amos, "American Policy in the Middle East: New Approach for a New Administration," in *Parameters* (June 1981).

Pierre, Andrew, ed., *The Conventional Defense of Europe: New Technologies and New Strategies*. New York: Council on Foreign Relations, 1986.

———, *Arms Transfers and American Foreign Policy*. New York: New York University Press, 1979.

Poirier, Lucien, "La Greffe," in *Défense Nationale* (April 1983).

Quandt, William, *Saudi Arabia's Oil Policy*. Washington, DC: Brookings Institution, 1982.

———, "Comment," in *Arab Oil and Economic Review* (February 1980).

Ramazani, Rouhollah, "Security in the Persian Gulf," in *Foreign Affairs* (Spring 1979).

———, *The Persian Gulf—Iran's Role*. Charlottesville, VA: University of Virginia Press, 1972.

———, "The Settlement of the Bahrain Dispute," in *Indian Journal of International Law,*" vol. 12, no. 1, 1972.

———, *The Middle East and the European Common Market*. Charlottesville, VA: University of Virginia Press, 1964.

Record, Jeffrey, *The Rapid Deployment Force and U.S. Military Intervention in the Persian Gulf*. Cambridge, MA: Institute for Foreign Policy Analysis, July 1981.

Reed, John, "Out of Theatre Operations—A New Imperative for Europe," in *Defence* (March 1983).

Ross, Dennis, "Considering Soviet Threats to the Persian Gulf," in *International Security* (Fall 1981).

Roumani, Maurice, ed., *Forces of Change in the Middle East.* Worcester, MA: Worcester State College Press, 1971.

Rubinstein, Alvin, ed., *The Great Game, Rivalry in the Persian Gulf and South Asia.* New York: Praeger, 1983.

———, "The Soviet Union and the Arabian Peninsula," in *The World Today* (November 1979).

Safran, Nadav, *Saudi Arabia: The Ceaseless Quest for Security.* Cambridge, MA: Harvard University Press, 1985.

———, *The United States and Israel.* Cambridge, MA: Harvard University Press, 1963.

Schiff, Ze'ev, and Ya'ari, Ehud, *Israel's Lebanon War.* New York: Simon and Schuster, 1984.

Schmidt, Helmut, "Saving the Western Alliance," in *New York Review of Books,* 31 May 1984.

Schweitzer, Amiral, "Une Stratégie pour la France," in *Défense Nationale* (July 1981).

Shaked, Haim, and Rabinovich, Itamar, eds., *The Middle East and the United States, Perceptions and Policies.* New Brunswick, NJ: Transaction, Inc., 1980.

Sheffer, Edward, *The Oil Import Program of the United States: An Evaluation.* New York: Praeger, 1968.

Shwadran, Benjamin, *The Middle East, Oil and the Great Powers.* New York: Council for Middle Eastern Affairs Press, 1959.

Sick, Gary, *All Fall Down—America's Tragic Encounter with Iran.* New York: Random House, 1985.

Snetsinger, John, *Truman, the Jewish Vote, and the Creation of Israel.* Stanford, CA: Hoover Institution Press, 1974.

Spiegel, Steven, *The Other Arab–Israeli Conflict: Making America's Middle East Policy from Truman to Reagan.* Chicago, IL: University of Chicago Press, 1985.

———, "The Middle East: A Consensus of Error," in *Commentary* (March 1982).

———, ed., *The Middle East and the Western Alliance.* London: George Allen and Unwin, 1982.

Sreedhar, *The Gulf—Scramble for Security.* New Dehli: ABC Publishing House, 1983.

Steinbruner, John, *The Cybernetic Theory of Decision—New Dimensions of Political Analysis.* Princeton, NJ: Princeton University Press, 1974.

Stobaugh, Robert, and Yergin, Daniel, "Energy: An Emergency Telescoped," in *Foreign Affairs,* Annual Review (vol. 58, no. 30), 1980.

Stockholm International Peace Research Institute, *World Armaments and Disarmament, SIPRI Yearbook 1974.* Cambridge, MA: MIT Press, 1974.

Stookey, Robert, *America and the Arab States: An Uneasy Encounter.* New York: John Wiley, 1975.

Strategic Review, "The Salt II Paradox," (Fall 1979).

Thompson, W. Scott, "The Persian Gulf and the Correlation of Forces," in *International Security* (Summer 1982).

Tillman, Seth, *The United States in the Middle East—Interests and Obstacles.* Bloomington, IN: Indiana University Press, 1982.

Treverton, Gregory, "Defense Beyond Europe," in *Survival* (September/October 1983).

———, *Crisis Management and the Superpowers in the Middle East.* Farnborough: Gower for the International Institute for Strategic Studies, 1981.

———, "Global Threats and Trans-Atlantic Allies," in *International Security* (Fall 1980).

Tucker, Robert, "American Power and the Persian Gulf," in *Commentary* (November 1980).

Turner, Stansfield, and Thiboult, George, "Preparing for the Unexpected: The Need for a New Military Strategy," in *Foreign Affairs* (Fall 1982).

———, "Toward a New Defense Strategy," in *New York Times Magazine,* 10 May 1981.

Valenta, Jiri, "From Prague to Kabul, the Soviet Style of Invasion," in *International Security* (Fall 1980).

Van Hollen, Christopher, "Don't Engulf the Gulf," in *Foreign Affairs* (Summer 1980).

Vance, Cyrus, *Hard Choices: Critical Years in America's Foreign Policy.* New York: Simon and Schuster, 1983.

Vernon, Raymond, ed., *The Oil Crisis*. New York: W.W. Norton and Co., 1976.
Waltz, Kenneth, "A Strategy for the Rapid Deployment Force," in *International Security* (Spring 1981).
Wittman, George, "Political and Military Background for France's Intervention Capability," in *A.E.I. Foreign Policy and Defense Review*, vol. 4, no. 1, 1982.
Wohlstetter, Albert, "Half Wars and Half Policies in the Persian Gulf," in W. Scott Thompson, ed., *National Security in the 1980s: From Weakness to Strength*, San Francisco Institute for Contemporary Studies, 1980.
———, "Meeting the Threat in the Persian Gulf," in *Survey* (Spring 1980).
Daniel Yergin, *Shattered Peace: The Origins of the Cold War and the National Security State*. London: Andre Deutsch, 1978.
Yodfat, Aryeh, *The Soviet Union and the Arabian Peninsula—Soviet Policy Towards the Persian Gulf and Arabia*. London: Croom Helm, 1983.
Yorke, Valerie, "The Gulf in the 1980s," Chatham House Papers, no. 6. London: Royal Institute of International Affairs, 1980.
Zagoria, Donald, "Into the Breach: New Soviet Alliances in the Third World," in *Foreign Affairs* (Spring 1979).

VI. Periodicals Frequently Consulted

Congressional Record
Current Policy—U.S. Department of State, Bureau of Public Affairs
Daily Telegraph
Foreign Broadcast Information Service
The Guardian
International Communication Agency—U.S. Department of State
International Herald Tribune
London Times
Le Monde
New York Times
Washington Post
U.S. Department of Defense News Release

Interviews

VII. Washington, D.C.

Robert Hunter, Senior Fellow, The Center for Strategic and International Studies, Georgetown University, 6 August 1985.
Geoff Kemp, Senior Fellow, The Center for Strategic and International Studies, Georgetown University, 6 August 1985.
Lieutenant General William Odom, Director National Security Agency, 6 August 1985.
Paul Wolfowitz, State Department, 5 August 1985.
William Quandt, Senior Fellow, Brookings Institution, 19 September 1983.
David Newsom, former Under Secretary of State for Political Affairs, 19 January 1983.
General P.X. Kelley, former Commander of the Rapid Deployment Joint Task Force, 18 January 1983.
Joshua Epstein, Bureau of Political and Military Affairs, State Department, 17 January 1983.

Hans Binnendijk, Middle East Specialist, House Foreign Affairs Committee, 3 January 1983.
Tom Locher, Staff Professional, Senate Armed Services Committee, 13 January 1983.
Reginald Bartholomew, Director of the Bureau of Political and Military Affairs, State Department, 12 January 1983.
Randy Beers, Southwest Asia Specialist, Office of Policy Analysis, State Department, 12 January 1983.
Thomas McNaugher, Middle East Specialist, Brookings Institution, 12 January 1983.
Richard Halloran, *New York Times* Military Correspondent, 10 January 1983.
Robert Komer, former Under Secretary of Defense for Policy, 10 January 1983.
Harold Saunders, former Assistant Secretary of State for Near Eastern and South Asian Affairs, 10 January 1983.
Frederick Smith, Office of the Secretary of Defense—International Security Affairs, Defense Department 7 January 1983.
Mike Parmentier, Office of Force Planning and Projection, Defense Department, 6 January 1983.
Steve Rosen, former Senior Analyst of Middle Eastern Affairs at Rand Corporation, 5 January 1983.
Frank Church, former Chairman of Senate Foreign Relations Committee, 3 January 1983.

VIII. Brussels—NATO Headquarters

Sir John Graham, British Ambassador to NATO, 15 March 1984.
Mr. Howe, Defense Adviser, British Delegation, 15 March 1984.
General Hansen, Political Adviser, German Delegation, 15 March 1984.
Bernard Bot, Political Adviser, Dutch Delegation, 15 March 1984.
General Roscoe Robinson, U.S. Representative to the Military Committee, 15 March 1984.
Robert Frowick, Political Adviser, U.S. Delegation, 14 March 1984.
Laurence Legere, Defense Adviser, U.S. Delegation, 14 March 1984.
Fredo Dannenbring, Assistant Secretary General for Political Affairs, International Secretariat, 13 March 1984.
Simon Lunn, Head, Plans and Policy Section of Defense Planning Division, International Secretariat, 13 March 1984.
George Olson, Defense Planning Division, International Secretariat, 13 March 1984.
Mr. Cooper, Defense Support Division, International Secretariat, 13 March 1984.

IX. London and Paris

David Bolton, Director Royal United Services Institute, London, 15 May 1984.
John Weston, Defence Specialist, Foreign and Commonwealth Office, London, 15 May 1984.
Sir Clive Rose, Former British Ambassador to NATO, London, 1 May 1984.
General Prestat, Director, Foundation pour les Etudes de Défense Nationale, Paris, 18 March 1984.
Abdullah Bishara, Secretary General of the Gulf Cooperation Council, Discussion at the International Institute for Strategic Studies, London, 11 February 1983.

INDEX